Psychology Revivals

Cognition as Intuitive Statistics

Originally published in 1987, this title is about theory construction in psychology. Where theories come from, as opposed to how they become established, was almost a no-man's land in the history and philosophy of science at the time. The authors argue that in the science of mind, theories are particularly likely to come from tools, and they are especially concerned with the emergence of the metaphor of the mind as an intuitive statistician.

In the first chapter, the authors discuss the rise of the inference revolution, which institutionalized those statistical tools that later became theories of cognitive processes. In each of the four following chapters they treat one major topic of cognitive psychology and show to what degree statistical concepts transformed their understanding of those topics.

Cognition as Intuitive Statistics

Gerd Gigerenzer
and
David J. Murray

LONDON AND NEW YORK

First published in 1987
by Lawrence Erlbaum Associates

This edition first published in 2015 by Psychology Press
27 Church Road, Hove, BN3 2FA

and by Psychology Press
711 Third Avenue, New York, NY 10017

Psychology Press is an imprint of the Taylor & Francis Group, an informa business

© 1987 Lawrence Erlbaum Associates, Inc

The right of Gerd Gigerenzer and David J. Murray to be identified as authors of this work has been asserted by them in accordance with sections 77 and 78 of the Copyright, Designs and Patents Act 1988.

All rights reserved. No part of this book may be reprinted or reproduced or utilised in any form or by any electronic, mechanical, or other means, now known or hereafter invented, including photocopying and recording, or in any information storage or retrieval system, without permission in writing from the publishers.

Publisher's Note
The publisher has gone to great lengths to ensure the quality of this reprint but points out that some imperfections in the original copies may be apparent.

Disclaimer
The publisher has made every effort to trace copyright holders and welcomes correspondence from those they have been unable to contact.

A Library of Congress record exists under ISBN: 0898595703

ISBN: 978-1-138-95022-1 (hbk)
ISBN: 978-1-315-66879-6 (ebk)

COGNITION
as INTUITIVE
STATISTICS

by
Gerd Gigerenzer
Universität Konstanz
West Germany

David J. Murray
Queen's University
Ontario, Canada

LEA LAWRENCE ERLBAUM ASSOCIATES, PUBLISHERS
1987 Hillsdale, New Jersey   London

Printed with the support of the Universität Bielefeld, West Germany.

Copyright © 1987 by Lawrence Erlbaum Associates, Inc.
All rights reserved. No part of this book may be reproduced in
any form, by photostat, microform, retrieval system, or any other
means, without the prior written permission of the publisher.

Lawrence Erlbaum Associates, Inc., Publishers
365 Broadway
Hillsdale, New Jersey 07642

Library of Congress Cataloging in Publication Data

Gigerenzer, Gerd
Cognition as intuitive statistics.

Bibliography: p.
Includes indexes.
1. Cognition. 2. Statistics. 3. Statistical
hypothesis testing. I. Murray, David J. II. Title.
BF311.M73 1987   153.4   86-23937
ISBN 0-89859-570-3

Printed in the United States of America
10 9 8 7 6 5 4 3 2 1

Contents

Acknowledgments   ix

Introduction: Two Revolutions—Cognitive and Probabilistic   xi

1. The Inference Revolution   1

From Tools to Theories: Scientists' Instruments as Metaphors of Mind   1
Metaphors; The Evolution of Metaphors; Statistical Tools as Cognitive Theories

Emergence of Statistical Inference   3
The First Test of a Null Hypothesis; Bayes; Sir Ronald A. Fisher; Jerzy Neyman and Egon S. Pearson

What Did Psychologists Do Before the Inference Revolution?   17

How Statistics Became an Indispensable Instrument: The Inference Revolution   19
The Inference Revolution (1940–1955); The Irrational Revolution; the Permanent Illusion; Consequences and Alternatives; How Could the Inference Revolution Have Happened?

Conclusions   28

vi   CONTENTS

2. Detection and Discrimination: From Thresholds to Statistical Inference   **29**

History: Before the Inference Revolution   29
From Thresholds to Variability in Brain Activity; Why Didn't Thurstone Detect Signal Detection Theory?; Summary

The Emergence of the Statistical Metaphor: Signal Detection Theory   42
The Mind as a Neyman and Pearsonian Statistician; The Conceptual Change; The Receiver Operating Characteristic; Tanner's Conception of the Mind; Beyond Signal Detection Theory: A Metaphor Conquers the Mind

Summary   58

3. Perception: From Unconscious Inference to Hypothesis Testing   **61**

History: Before the Inference Revolution   62
Unconscious Inference; From Unconscious Inference to Intuitive Statistics

The Realist View: Pickup of Information   81
Invariants in the Ambient Light; The Loss of Uncertainty; Information Available and Information Used

The Inductive View: Hypothesis Testing   86
Methods of Science as Metaphor; The Betting Machine Metaphor

The Deductive View: Cognitive Algebra   91
Perception as Cognitive Algebra; The Fisherian Perspective in Hypothesis Construction; The Fisherian Perspective in Hypothesis Testing; The Circle of Hypothesis Construction and Testing

Summary   103

4. Memory: From Association to Decision Making   **106**

History: Before the Inference Revolution   106
The Behaviorist Legacy; Studies of Human Memory: Semon and Bartlett

The Emergence of the Decision Metaphor   113
Research During the 1960s and Early 1970s; The Return of Signal Detection Theory in the 1980s

CONTENTS vii

Other Metaphors 123
Short-Term Memory; Search; Activation Rather Than Search

Conclusions 132

5. Thinking: From Insight to Intuitive Statistics 137

History: Before the Inference Revolution 138
The Fading of Associationism; Insight and Restructuring

Is the Mind a Bayesian? 147
*Conservatism; Base Rate Neglect: The Kahneman and
Tversky Program*

Fundamental Assumptions in the Normative Program 162
*Is There an Isomorphism Between the World and Bayes'
Theorem?; Does Statistics Speak With One Voice?*

The Fisherian Mind: Causal Reasoning 174
*Scientists' Tools = Laws of Causal Reasoning; The
Conceptual Skeleton*

Rationality 179
*Mechanization of Inductive Inference; Elimination of
Subjectivity*

6. Conclusions 182
*From Tools to Theories: In Their Own Image; The Integrative
Perspective; Blind Spots; The Intuitive Statistician
Reconsidered*

References 189

Author Index 205

Subject Index 210

Acknowledgments

This book is about theory construction in psychology. Where theories come from, as opposed to how they become established, is almost a no-man's-land in the history and philosophy of science. We argue that in the science of mind, theories are particularly likely to come from tools, and we are specially concerned with the emergence of the metaphor of the mind as an intuitive statistician.

The idea for the book was conceived when both authors were invited to participate in an interdisciplinary group that studied the "Probabilistic Revolution" in science. About 20 scientists, philosophers and historians of science spent a stimulating year (1982–83) at the Center for Interdisciplinary Research (ZiF) at the University of Bielefeld, West Germany. The organizer of the group and director of the ZiF at the time, Lorenz Krüger, now of the University of Göttingen, deserves our heartfelt appreciation for bringing researchers from different disciplines into a fruitful dialogue and for encouraging the present project throughout its planning. We are grateful to all members of the research group for the superfecundity of their ideas as expressed in countless discussions; their contributions have exerted a strong influence on the form this work has taken. In particular, we wish to thank Wolfgang Prinz, of the University of Bielefeld, who took an active part in the group and in the inception of this book. We are grateful to Kurt Danziger, York University, Wolfgang Hell, University of Konstanz, and William Hockley, University of Toronto, for critically reading portions of the manuscript. A special word of thanks goes to Lorraine Daston, Princeton University, whose advice on conceptual and historical matters and assistance with clarification at all stages of the writing we particularly appreciate.

X ACKNOWLEDGMENTS

The book was written after the year at Bielefeld, and collaborating across the Atlantic Ocean, between Queen's University in Ontario and the University of Konstanz was of course no easy matter. But Queen's University supported a visit by Gerd Gigerenzer to Canada; and a Leave Fellowship from the Social Sciences and Humanities Research Council of Canada, and the ZiF, each supported a visit by David Murray to Germany. We are also grateful to the ZiF for subsidizing the publication of the work. We should both like to thank Günther Fäustle, Thomas Finger, Hilde Manea, and Regina Passauer at the University of Konstanz, and Maureen Freedman at Queen's University for their assistance with the preparation for the manuscript; Maureen Freedman was supported by Operating Grant A8505 from the Natural Sciences and Engineering Research Council of Canada. We are grateful to Helen Tanner and the University of Michigan for permission to reproduce Figs. 2-4, 2-5 and 2-6.

Although the work is a cooperative effort, Gerd Gigerenzer is chiefly responsible for Chapters 1, 3, and 5, and David Murray for Chapters 2 and 4.

Finally, a word of appreciation is due our two universities, the University of Konstanz, and Queen's University at Kingston, for their support and provision of facilities. Both lie at the edge of large and scenic lakes, and one of the most attractive aspects of our endeavour has been the opportunity to appreciate the settings and academic traditions of both.

Introduction
Two Revolutions—Cognitive and Probabilistic

The present book focuses on the intersection between two recent lines of thought. Both have been called "revolutions." The term "cognitive revolution" signifies the transition from understanding humans in terms of overt behavior to understanding them in terms of mental structures and processes. The term "probabilistic revolution" describes the transition from a deterministic understanding of science, in which uncertainty and variability were not permitted, to an understanding of science where probabilistic ideas became indispensable in theorizing. The cognitive revolution is narrower in scope, restricted mainly to psychology, and is a "re-volution" in the original sense of the word. About 1960, psychologists reverted, not always aware that they were doing so, to some of the research goals and programs of the late 19th century, which were concerned with the analysis of mental events. The probabilistic revolution (see Krüger, Daston, & Heidelberger, 1987; Krüger, Gigerenzer, & Morgan, 1987) differs from the cognitive revolution (see Gardner, 1985) in the broadness of its scope and in its genuine novelty. The term "cognitive" denotes the subject matter of a discipline and may include both global conceptions, such as G. A. Kelly's (1955) notion of "man as a scientist" who construes the world in terms of "personal constructs," and localized cognitive events such as the "mental rotation" of images (Shepard & Cooper, 1982). The term "probabilistic," however, refers to a formal calculus linked with the idea of uncertainty. It may thus be interpreted within the context of any discipline and in fact, probabilistic notions have changed the very way in which some disciplines view the world. A frequently cited dramatic example is the abandoning of the "Newtonian world-machine," with God as the master clockmaker who designed a

xii   INTRODUCTION

universe so perfect that it could run indefinitely without need for divine tinkering. In this context, the complacent Victorian physicist was so confident that all fundamental laws of nature had been discovered that he believed there was nothing more to do than to measure the physical constants more and more accurately. Around 1920, this deterministic view was shattered and abandoned by the indeterministic world view of quantum physics.

An equally dramatic example of a "probabilistic revolution" that has changed our thinking about humankind and religion is found in evolutionary biology. The protest against Charles Darwin, which he himself anticipated with fear, was not so much because he promulgated the theory that species had evolved from others, but because he claimed that evolution did *not* unfold according to a predetermined plan. Evolution does not lead toward an "ideal" animal or human; it can go anywhere, without predetermined direction. Darwin illustrated this by the metaphor of the "tree of nature" that has *irregular branches*. An evolution of species that leads finally to God's plan of an ideal species—is predetermined in a theological sense—could have been more easily integrated with the religious beliefs of the time. An evolution, however, that is based on chance processes like mutations or environmental contingencies and whose actual course could not be predicted seemed hard to believe and tolerate.

Let us consider more precisely what we mean by "probabilistic revolution." A common meaning of the term is that, in the history of a discipline, there was a shift from *epistemic* to *ontic* interpretations of probabilistic ideas. By an epistemic interpretation, we mean the notion that probability theory must be incorporated into the discipline because there is error in our measurements or because we are ignorant of some of the variables affecting the data we are collecting; but any randomness observed is not in nature itself. By ontic probabilism, we refer to the notion that chance is an irreducible part of the natural phenomena we are investigating (e.g. spontaneous brain activity).

However, the distinction between an epistemic and ontic interpretation needs amplifying. There is at least one important third position, which we call for convenience the *pragmatic* interpretation. The distinction between epistemic and ontic seems to imply that the scientist is a realist: either he believes that only causes are in reality or that probabilities and chance processes are also real. Not all scientists, however, are concerned with pictures of reality: some are concerned in the first place with empirical prediction and conceptual integrity. It is for these reasons rather than for reasons of ontic realism that some scientists came to consider probabilistic ideas indispensable (Cartwright, 1987). Heisenberg (1927), for instance, stated that physics should only "describe formally the relations of perceptions," and "one might be led to the conjecture that under the perceptible statistical world there is hidden a 'real' world in which the causal law holds. But it seems to us that such speculation, we emphasize explicitly, are fruitless and meaningless" (p. 197).

We shall therefore adopt a definition of "probabilistic revolution" broader than a shift from an epistemic to an ontic view. The term "probabilistic revolution" will be used in the wider sense that probabilistic ideas have become central and indispensable for a science, on the level of either theory construction or method. The transition from an epistemic to an ontic interpretation thus becomes only a special case (Krüger, Gigerenzer, & Morgan, 1987).

In this broad sense, psychology has seen *two* such revolutions, each on a different level, one following the other. The first occurred between 1940 and 1955 at the level of method, not of theory construction, when inferential statistics became widely used and soon institutionalized as the single method of inference from data to hypothesis. These statistical methods were in fact a mixture of those of R. A. Fisher, on one hand, and Jerzy Neyman and Egon S. Pearson on the other, a mixture that none of these statisticians (certainly not Neyman and Pearson) would have approved. We call this first probabilistic revolution in psychology the "inference revolution." The second revolution occurred at the level of theory, when, beginning about 1955, statistical ideas entered cognitive psychology at the level of theory construction. From the intersection of the inference revolution and the rising cognitive revolution a new understanding of the mind emerged: The mind as an "intuitive statistician." It is this second revolution on which the book focuses: It treats the new view of cognitive processes as statistical inference and hypotheses testing. But we claim that the success of the second revolution relies heavily on that of the first and that the new methods of inference have been transplanted to serve as explanations for how many cognitive processes work. And this has brought to cognitive psychology both a unifying perspective and, also, certain blind spots inherent in these institutionalized statistical tools. Cognition as statistical inference—this is the topic of the present book.

In the first chapter, we discuss the rise of the inference revolution, which institutionalized those statistical tools that later became theories of cognitive processes. In each of the following four chapters we treat one major topic of cognitive psychology and show to what degree statistical concepts transformed our understanding of those topics. The topics are (a) detection and discrimination, the classical psychophysical problems; (b) perception, in particular the problem of how properties of objects are judged and classified; (c) memory, the problems of recognition and recall; and (d) thinking, in particular the problems of inductive reasoning and rationality.

1 The Inference Revolution

FROM TOOLS TO THEORIES: SCIENTISTS' INSTRUMENTS AS METAPHORS OF MIND

Metaphors

Metaphors have played their role in the development of all sciences. Charles Darwin, for example, took at least two human activities as metaphors for natural selection, namely, "artificial selection" and "war" (Gruber, 1977). Psychological thinking has been shaped by many a metaphor. Consider the case of memory.

Possibly the oldest metaphors to be found in psychology are those of Plato, who, in the *Theaetetus* likened the impression of a "memory" on the "mind" to the impression of a seal or stylus on a wax tablet. In the *Meno* he also drew the analogy between the mind full of memories and an aviary full of flying birds: Trying to retrieve a memory is like trying to capture a bird in flight—one knows it is there, but it is not easily caught. Through the ages many other metaphors have been introduced for the understanding of memory. St. Augustine likened it to a storehouse, and the word "store" took firm root in the vocabulary of memory theory. More recent metaphors include analogies between memory and houses, gramophones, computer programs, libraries, tape recorders, holograms, and maps (Roediger, 1980).

What is a metaphor? First, it consists of a *subject* and a *modifier* (Beardsley, 1972). In the statement "man is a machine," "man" is the subject and "is a machine" is the modifier. Second, a metaphorical statement differs from a literal one ("man is a vertebrate") by virtue of a certain tension between subject and modifier. The "mind is a statistician" reflects such a tension. Third, in contrast to assertions that are merely odd, metaphorical assertions are intelligible and acceptable, even if somewhat deviant. In poems, another case where deviant discourse is

2   1. THE INFERENCE REVOLUTION

important, strong use is made of metaphorical language, which may result in an effect of beauty, whereas in science it may result in new ways of thinking. Fourth, metaphors are not falsifiable. However, by narrowing the possible flow of connotations and associations with definitions and examples, a metaphor can be transformed into precise and testable statements. This transformation is conventionally called a *model* rather than a metaphor, since it has lost its vagueness, is elaborated in a certain way (there may be other elaborations leading to other models), and offers predictions. We may think of a model as a controlled and elaborated metaphor.

What is the use of a metaphor? Its use is to be found in the construction of theories, rather than in the way they are tested. This means a metaphor may stimulate new ways of looking at the subject matter and create new interpretations of it. A metaphor cannot give us new ideas about how to test theories, but there is a connection between metaphors and theory testing that, as far as we can see, is unique to psychology. This connection is the subject of this book: Statistical tools for testing hypotheses have been considered in a new light as theories of cognitive processes in themselves. Examples are Neyman and Pearson's statistical theory, which has become a theory of object detection, known as *signal detection theory* (see chapter 2), and R. A. Fisher's analysis of variance, which has become a theory of how causal attributions are made (see chapter 5). Both have stimulated immense amounts of research during recent decades.

The Evolution of Metaphors

Metaphors common in psychology have changed over time partly as a result of the invention of new machines such as the telegraph and telephone, which ultimately led to the analogy between a person and a communication system (Attneave, 1959). Since the middle of this century, the "evolution" of metaphors has tended to focus on the *tools* that the behavioural scientist himself uses. Two major tools have been considered as important candidates for analogies with cognitive processes: computers and statistics.

The invention of the computer had, among other effects, the consequence of giving the scientist the opportunity to describe processes in terms of programs, carry out involved calculations, and manipulate lists of data (files). Each of these three aspects has been used as a metaphor of cognitive functioning.

For instance, one metaphor connected cognitive processing with the flow charts useful for depicting the steps in a computer program. Broadbent (1958) produced the first modern flowchart of the organism: He argued that information was received at the sensory receptors in parallel and was then put into short-term memory, where selective attention operated to give certain items a particular degree of "processing." The processed information could either result in an overt response, be put into long-term memory, or be recycled into short-term memory for rehearsal or further cogitation. Moreover, the planning and execution of an act has been compared with the execution of a computer program. Various cognitive processes were reinterpreted as "searching" through lists or files, represented by flow charts containing steps at each of which a decision has to be made. Newell and Simon (1972) have exhaustively examined the question of how far human problem solving can be imitated by devising programs suitable for solving the same kinds of problem by computers.

This book, however, is not concerned with the computer metaphor, but with the second major tool that became a metaphor of mind, namely, statistics.

Statistical Tools as Cognitive Theories

Between 1940 and 1955 statistical theories became indispensable tools for making inferences from data to hypothesis in psychology. The general thesis of this book is that *scientists' tools, which are considered to be indispensable and prestigious, lend themselves to transformation into metaphors of mind*. We call this briefly the *tools-to-theories hypothesis*. In particular, we maintain that statistics and computers exemplify this hypothesis. We restrict the thesis to statistics and cognitive psychology only and are aware of the ambiguity inherent in the term "indispensable." However, in what follows we shall clarify the meaning of this term by showing how statistics became institutionalized in psychology.

EMERGENCE OF STATISTICAL INFERENCE

Statistical inference does not exhaust inference. From time immemorial not only scientists but persons from all walks of life have made inferences daily. Even after the introduction of statistical methods of inference many scientists—for example, physicists—have little or no recourse to them. In this section we discuss the inception of those major theories of statistical inference and hypothesis testing that have provided the armory for the inference revolution in psychology.

Neyman (1976) credits the mathematician and astronomer Pierre Laplace (1749–1827) with the first test of significance. In astronomy, the normal distribution was used as a model for errors of observation. The

4   1. THE INFERENCE REVOLUTION

problem was, what to do with outlying observations, which the normal law makes highly improbable and which seem to be due to extraneous causes. Every experimenter knows this problem of outliers that seem to deviate too much from the others. Probabilistic criteria were developed for the *rejection of outlying observations* (Swijtink, 1987). When the probabilistic ideas of the astronomers were transferred by Adolphe Quetelet into the social sciences, an important shift in interpretation took place. Whereas the astronomers usually inferred from a discrepancy between model and data that the discordant *observations* had to be rejected, social scientists usually concluded instead that the *model* had to be rejected. We shall return to this shift later, in our discussion of Sir Ronald A. Fisher's statistical ideas.

In fact, the first significance test seems to have been published about 100 years before Laplace's in 1710 by John Arbuthnot. The form of Arbuthnot's argument is strikingly similar to modern null hypothesis testing. However, since the content is so foreign to our 20th century concerns, his memoir reveals the pitfalls of this form of statistical inference more clearly than more recent examples.

The First Test of a Null Hypothesis

Arbuthnot held that the external accidents to which males are subject are far more dangerous than those which befall females. In order to repair the resulting loss of males, "provident Nature, by the Disposal of its wise Creator, brings forth more Males than Females and that in almost constant proportion" (p. 188). Arbuthnot favored this hypothesis of an intervening God over the hypothesis of mere chance—in modern terms, the null hypothesis. (He understood mere chance as implying equal chances for both sexes.) His data were 82 years of birth records in London (1629–1710), in which in every year the number of male births exceeded the female births. He calculated the expectation (the concept of probability was not yet fully developed at the time) of this data given the chance hypothesis which is $(1/2)^{82}$. Because this expectation was astronomically small, he concluded "that it is Art, not Chance, that governs" (p. 189).

In a manner similar to that used in modern psychology, he thus rejected a null hypothesis in which he had never believed. Let us bypass the small errors in his argument (first, *any* data would have had the expectation $(1/2)^{82}$, even 41 female-predominant and 41 male-predominant years; second, a chance mechanism with a probability of 18/35 for male births would fit his data well), and turn immediately to his discussion:

> From hence it follows, that Polygamy is contrary to the Laws of Nature and Justice, and to the Propagation of the Human Race; for where Males and

Females are in equal number, if one man takes Twenty Wives, Nineteen Men must live in Celibacy, which is repugnant to the Design of Nature; nor is it probable that Twenty Women will be so well impregnated by one Man as by Twenty. (p. 189).

The inference in this first test of significance (of course, Arbuthnot did not use the term) was from the data to the existence of divine tinkering and in this sense constituted a "proof" of the existence of an active God. The parallel to the modern use (and abuse) is striking. A common practice today—one which, as we shall soon see, is statistically unsound—is to infer from the rejection of a specified null hypothesis the validity of an unspecified alternative hypothesis and to infer from this, as Arbuthnot did, the existence of a causal mechanism responsible for that deviation from "chance." In modern terms, Arbuthnot's chance hypothesis is a point hypothesis, that is, it specifies an exact value, whereas his Wise Creator hypothesis covers all other probability values *except* that single one. This is the first example of *asymmetric* hypothesis testing we know about, and it amply indicates the problems arising when alternative hypotheses are not specified.

The first modern significance test was the chi-square method developed by Karl Pearson (1900). One of the first questions to which Pearson applied his test was whether the inference that an empirical distribution is a normal distribution can be justified. As a result, Pearson's belief in the normal law as a law of nature decreased considerably. In this example, an inference from data to a hypothesis is attempted. However, as the earlier example from astronomers showed, there are other types of inference, such as inference from hypothesis to data.

Let us turn to the origins of psychology's inferential statistics. We consider three widely divergent views about the nature of statistical inference; those of Bayes, Fisher, and Neyman and Pearson. As we show later, what is taught in psychology as "inferential statistics" is in fact none of these theories, but a hybrid of ideas stemming mostly from the latter two views sometimes supplemented by a Bayesian interpretation. We shall describe these ideas only insofar as they have been incorporated into psychology and transformed into metaphors of mind. In contrast to contemporary textbooks, we shall emphasize the *controversial nature* of these statistical theories of inference, and the nonexistence of an agreed upon solution for formal inference outside psychology. This contrasts starkly with the presentation of "inferential statistics" since the early 40s in psychology as *the* uncontroversial and objective technique of inductive inference, one that can be used mechanically.

There are two poles between which ideas about the nature of inductive inference can be located. One considers inference from data to hypothesis as an *informal* cognitive process, based on informed judgment, and

6   1. THE INFERENCE REVOLUTION

therefore strongly *dependent on the content* of the problem and one's specific experience with that content. According to this view, inferences are not independent of the content of the problem. Therefore, it makes little sense to apply the same formal rule of inference to every problem mechanically. This nonformal view, for example, is maintained by physcists and other natural scientists, as opposed to most social scientists. The second view considers inference as a process that can be described by a single *formal* rule, which can be applied *independent of the specific content* investigated. Probability theory has been the single candidate for all such attempts to formalize inductive inference. Since probability theory was conceptualized only around 1660 (Hacking, 1975), the problem of formal inductive inference, or induction, is rather recent, and it seems to be the only major problem in philosophy that is of modern rather than ancient origin.

Bayes

It is not surprising that one of the first attempts to formalize inference came from Laplace. He proposed the following *rule of succession* (see Keynes, 1943, pp. 367–383):

$$p(H|n) = (n + 1)/(n + 2), \tag{1.1}$$

where $p(H|n)$ is the *posterior probability* of the hypothesis H that an event x will happen if the event has been observed n times successively. For instance, if you were 20 years old, you would have observed approximately 7,300 times that the sun rises in the morning. According to the rule of succession, your probability for believing in a sunrise tomorrow should be roughly $(7300 + 1)/(7300 + 2)$, that is it approaches certainty. If something new happens to you and you have no information about the frequency of that event, you should infer that the event will occur again with a probability $p(H|n = 1) = 2/3$. Thus, if you play a lottery (without knowing the chances) for the first time and win the first prize, you should believe that if you play again tomorrow, you will win the first prize again with a probability of $2/3$. Similarly, if you perform a new experiment and obtain result x, then you should expect to find x in a replication with the probability $2/3$.

The rule has been criticized since Laplace's time as making too much out of almost nothing (Keynes, 1943). The criticism exposes a fundamental problem associated with such simple formal rules of inference: the neglect of context and content. (The sun may appear to go on or cease rising, depending whether you are in Paris or in Greenland. The probability that the experimental result will be found again may depend heavily on the specific content being investigated.)

EMERGENCE OF STATISTICAL INFERENCE 7

Nevertheless, not only Laplace but such well-known statisticians as Karl Pearson believed in the *rule of succession* as a valid formula for inferring the future from past experiences (Keynes, 1943, pp. 379–383). The rule had been mathematically derived by Laplace from *Bayes' theorem* (by assuming uniform prior probabilities, see below). Bayes' (1763) theorem, which is better known today than in its own time, can be written as follows:

$$p(H|D) = p(H)p(D|H)/(p|D) \qquad (1.2)$$

The probability $P(H|D)$ is called the *posterior probability,* that is, the probability of an hypothesis H given the data D. It is a function of the *prior probability* $p(H)$, that is the probability of H before the data has been obtained, and the ratio $p(D|H)/(p(D)$, which signifies the impact of the data. The more $p(D|H)$ (the likelihood of the data given the hypothesis H) differs from $p(D)$ (the probability of the data), the greater the impact of the data. Thus, Bayes' theorem states a rule for the revision of a prior probability into a posterior probability in the light of new data. (More technical details are given in chapter 5.)

The Reverend Thomas Bayes himself seemed less enthusiastic about his formula than the psychologists of inductive thinking (e.g. Kahneman, Slovic & Tversky, 1982; Nisbett & Ross, 1980), who equate Bayes' theorem with rational thinking (see chapter 5). Bayes did not even publish the rule, although he must have thought about it for a long time, since it was mentioned for the first time as early as 1749 by David Hartley (1749/ 1970), years before Bayes died in 1760.

Like Laplace's rule of succession, Bayes' theorem offers a formula for the revision of probabilities of hypotheses in the light of new data. The typical interpretation is in terms of subjective degrees of belief, or "subjective probabilities."

It is this subjective element that came under heavy attack by proponents of the so-called *frequency theory* of probability, such as Venn (1888) and von Mises (1957). Specifically, in the case of Bayes' theorem, the frequentists criticized the way in which the Bayesians determined the prior probability. Since in most applications there was no single way to determine the prior probability in terms of previous experience, Bayesians applied the *principle of indifference;* that is, they set the prior probabilities of all hypotheses to be equal. This means that if we have two hypotheses, then the probability $p(H)$ in equation (1.2) is equal to .5. The principle of indifference is subjective because it is a statement about our state of knowledge or ignorance rather than about the world. The frequentists, on the other hand, believed that the only legitimate interpretation of probabilities was in terms of empirical evidence, that is, in terms of observed, relative frequencies of events. Therefore, they were suspicious

8   1. THE INFERENCE REVOLUTION

of Bayes' theorem when the probabilities had to be determined subjectively. This was almost always the case for real applications in contrast to textbook applications such as in the new psychology of inductive thinking.

The abandonment of the concept of prior probability by the frequentists had an important theoretical consequence. One could no longer talk about the *probability of a hypothesis given particular data,* the posterior probability (also called the "inverse probability"), since there was no longer a prior probability available from which it could be calculated. Instead, the frequency interpretation forces one to deal with the *probability of the data given a particular hypothesis,* that is, the likelihood (also called the "direct probability"). In formal terms, the Bayesians focused on $p(H|D)$, the inverse probability, whereas the frequentists focused on $p(D|H)$, the direct probability, because the latter asserted that in reality one could seldom derive the prior probability of a hypothesis from data.

Sir Ronald A. Fisher

Influenced by the criticism of the early frequentists, Fisher rejected *prior* probabilities and refused to commit himself to a definition of probability that was subjective. There was, however, an essential tension in Fisher's writings. On one hand, as a frequentist, he held a lifelong opposition to the very idea of inverse probabilities, that is, to probabilities of hypotheses given data. On the other hand, the notion of inverse probability crept into various parts of his writings, as he himself was willing to admit (Acree, 1978, pp. 119–123). And it was just this element that made his theory attractive to psychologists.

In his writings can be found three major heuristics for indirectly evaluating the probability of hypotheses given data: significance testing, fiducial probability, and likelihood theory. Each of these became a source of controversy and confusion. For instance, von Mises (1957) declared: "I do not understand the many beautiful words used by Fisher and his followers in support of the likelihood theory" (p. 158). And Leonard Savage, urging Fisher to spell out the meaning of the term "fiducial probability," tells us: "I asked Fisher once and he gave me the very candid answer: 'I don't understand yet what fiducial probability does. We shall have to live with it a long time before we know what it's doing for us.' " (Savage, 1963, quoted in Acree, 1978, p. 150)

We shall deal here only with significance testing, the third device for implementing a theory of "inductive inference," as Fisher called it. As is well known, significance testing did not originate with Fisher, but he did consolidate three major conceptions in significance testing. First, recall that the astronomers created a hypothesis that they held to be true (at least, provisionally) and used discrepancies between hypothesis and data to reject *data* (single observations). Fisher, however, used discrepancies to reject what he called the "null hypothesis," not the data. Second, the astronomers' data (which were to be rejected or not) were single observations, whereas in Fisher's theory the data consisted of a sample of observations to be represented by the mean or some other sample statistic. Thus, the astronomers' distribution of single observations became transformed into a *sampling* distribution, the distribution of some sample statistic in an ongoing process of random sampling. The third shift, finally, was from Karl Pearson's (1900) large-sample methods to small-sample methods. In practice, this corresponded to a shift from observational (non-experimental) to experimental data. Large samples were used for the estimation of population parameters, whereas small samples obviously could not be expected to yield reliable estimates. All that one could hope for with the new small sample methods was a simple yes-or-no type of inference concerning the validity of a hypothesis. Thus, along with the shift from large to small samples went a shift from estimation of parameters to a yes-or-no type of inference.

These three shifts led to the Fisherian program of significance testing (see Fig. 1.1), which can be summarized as follows:

1. We set up a single null hypothesis that one or more empirical samples come from a hypothetically infinite population with a known sampling distribution.

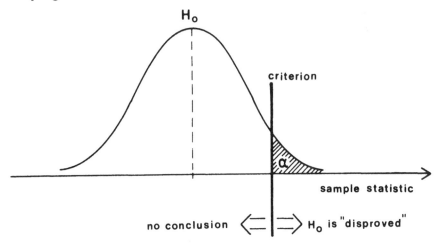

FIGURE 1.1. Illustration of Fisher's theory of null hypothesis testing. The figure shows the theoretical distribution of a sample statistic if H_0, the null hypothesis, is true. If a sample statistic (calculated from an empirical sample) deviates from the mean of the sampling distribution by more than a criterion, then the conclusion is made that H_0 is disproved.

10   1. THE INFERENCE REVOLUTION

2. We infer that the null hypothesis is "disproved" (Fisher's term) if our sample statistic deviates from the mean of the sampling distribution by more than a criterion, which corresponds to alpha, the level of significance. Rejecting the null hypothesis is the only kind of inductive inference we are allowed to draw, since "...the null hypothesis is never proved or established, but is possibly disproved in the course of experimentation" (Fisher, 1935, p. 16).

Fisher suggested using $\alpha = 5\%$ (less frequently, 2% or 1%). This is practically identical to the old criterion of three times the probable error, which covers about 95% of the area under a normal distribution.

The Fisherian program of null hypothesis significance testing has met with severe criticism both on statistical grounds and because it was presented by Fisher as the ideal for scientists in any field. Note that all this program can do is to reject a null hypothesis. *No statistical inference* is possible concerning the validity of an alternative hypothesis, which typically is the research hypothesis. How could psychologists have been persuaded that such a program was exactly what they wanted, namely a technique for inferring the validity of a research hypothesis from the data?

The Persuasion

Fisher's first book, *Statistical Methods for Research Workers* (1925) was almost exclusively concerned with agricultural field experiments on such matters as soil fertility, the weight of pigs, and the effect of manure on potato yields, and he addressed himself to the agricultural researcher. Food shortages in England at the end of World War I had sharpened interest in agricultural research, and Fisher had a position at the Rothamsted Experimental Station, where field experimentation had been conducted since the 1840s. So it was no accident that it was the American agricultural statistician Snedecor (1937) who brought psychology the Fisherian message. Fisher's second book, in 1935, *The Design of Experiments,* is addressed to a wider audience. Let us see how Fisher, in this book, persuaded the experimenters that they could have the frequency cake and eat it too.

On one hand, Fisher as befits a good frequentist, rejects inverse probabilities (probabilities of hypothesis given data). Yet, on the other hand, he promises research workers just what they want, a method of "inductive inference," a formal way of getting from data to hypothesis. Let Fisher speak for himself here:

> I have assumed, as the experimenter always does assume, that it *is* possible to draw valid inferences from the results of experimentation; that it is possible to argue from consequences to causes, from observations to

EMERGENCE OF STATISTICAL INFERENCE   11

hypotheses; as a statistician would say, from a sample to the population from which the sample was drawn, or, as a logician might put it, from the particular to the general. . . . We may at once admit that any inference from the particular to the general must be attended with some degree of uncertainty, but this is not the same as to admit that such inference cannot be absolutely rigorous . . . The mere fact that inductive inferences are uncertain cannot, therefore, be accepted as precluding perfectly rigorous and unequivocal inference. (Fisher, 1935, pp. 3–4).

This passage illustrates the method of persuasion: strong claims such as "absolutely rigorous," "perfectly rigorous," and "unequivocal inference." Although the strong wording seems to have had its effect, these terms carry no meaning for statistical theory—for example, what is an uncertain yet rigorous inference from data to hypotheses?

Fisher (1955), however, continued to suggest throughout his career that he had found the formal solution to the problem of inductive inference: "That such a process of induction existed and was possible to normal minds, has been understood for centuries; it is only with the recent development of statistical science that an analytic account can now be given, about as satisfying and complete, at least, as that given traditionally of the deductive processes." (p. 74).

Let us forget the rhetoric and consider the argument. How can Fisher arrive at a technique of inductive inference from data to hypotheses after having rejected inverse probabilities as in Bayes' theorem? Fisher's logic, spread over many pages in *The Design of Experiments* (1935), can be condensed into the following argument:

1. *Scientific knowledge comes only from inductive inference.* In Fisher's words. "Inductive inference is the only process known to us by which essentially new knowledge comes into the world" (p. 7).

2. *Inductive inference is chiefly disproving null hypotheses.* This is the core message of the book.

3. *Therefore, all scientists must try to disprove null hypotheses.* In Fisher's words, "Every experiment may be said to exist only in order to give the facts a chance of disproving the null hypothesis" (p. 16).

In essence, Fisher's strategy for resolving the essential tension between his frequentist position and his promise of a formal technique for inferences from data to hypotheses is to define inductive inference in an extremely narrow way: *inductive inference is to disprove a null hypothesis.* However, the very meaning of the phrase "to disprove the null hypothesis" remained unclear in the context of statistical theory—as Neyman and Pearson repeatedly pointed out (see next section). A main

12   1. THE INFERENCE REVOLUTION

catch in Fisher's promise is that the scientist's research hypothesis is usually not the null hypothesis. Note that in such situations Sir Karl Popper's (1935/1959) dictum that we should try to falsify our research hypotheses stands in opposition to Sir Ronald Fisher's dictum that we should try to disprove a null hypothesis. Thus the critical question is, does disproving the null hypothesis prove the alternative research hypothesis? Of course not. Null hypothesis testing is not a statistical test of an alternative research hypothesis, if only because no alternative hypothesis is ever defined in a statistically exact way. Fisher himself indicated this (1935, p. 16), though very cautiously and not without ambiguity. Yet he also suggested the opposite, only a few pages earlier: "In relation to the test of significance, we may say that a phenomenon is experimentally demonstrable when we know how to conduct an experiment which will rarely fail to give us a statistically significant result" (p. 14). With only a little wishful thinking, his readers could serenely assume that they were now armed with a valid statistical technique of inductive inference.

Jerzy Neyman and Egon S. Pearson

Jerzy Neyman, a statistician from Warsaw, met Egon S. Pearson, the son of Karl Pearson, at University College in London. In 1928, they published their first joint papers in *Biometrika,* founded and edited by Karl Pearson. Although Neyman (1967b) calls Fisher "a direct descendant of Karl Pearson," a sharp feud raged between Karl Pearson and Fisher. For about a decade, Karl Pearson had declined to publish any more of Fisher's work in *Biometrika,* but when Pearson retired in 1933, Fisher succeeded to his chair of eugenics at University College. As a consequence, the institute was divided into two departments, the department of eugenics under Fisher, and the department of statistics with Egon S. Pearson as its head. Neyman (1967b) asserts that he and Egon S. Pearson did their best to avoid becoming involved in the raging feud. But soon a break occurred between him and Fisher, which gave the controversial issues a bitter and polemical flavour that became acrimoniously personal.

Neyman and Pearson's work on hypotheses testing can be seen as an extension of Fisher's theory into a more consistent and mathematically systematic theory (e.g., Birnbaum, 1977; Hogben, 1957). The theoretical innovation of the Neyman–Pearson theory was the *behavioral* interpretation of tests; that is, a clear distinction was made between the mathematical parts of the theory and the behavioral, or subjective, parts. For instance, the direct probabilities (likelihoods, $p(D|H)$) belonged to the mathematical part; the setting of the decision criterion and the acceptance or rejection of hypotheses, to the behavioral part. This distinction dispelled the confusion between statements aabout data given some hypothesis (direct probabilities) and statements about a hypothesis given some data, the tension inherent in Fisher's program.

The behavioral, or decision, character of the theory is illustrated in Fig. 1.2. In contrast to Fisher's approach, *two* hypotheses, H_0 and H_1, and their sampling distributions, are specified by assumption. This allows for determining two types of errors. The Type I error occurs when H_0 is rejected although H_0 is true. The probability of that error is called α, or the level of significance. The Type II error occurs when H_1 is rejected although it is true. The probability of the latter error is called β. The choice of the decision criterion allows a balance between these two errors, depending on such considerations as the costs of the respective errors, which are heavily content-dependent and lie outside the statistical theory. Depending on whether the empirically obtained sample statistic falls to the left or right of the decision criterion, either H_0 or H_1 will be accepted.

Consider a typical illustration: quality control in industrial manufacturing. A firm produces metal plates that are used in, say, medical instruments. It is important that the diameter of the plates does not exceed an optimal value too much, otherwise this might cause unreliability in the medical instruments. The manufacturer may be interested in the hypothesis H_0, that the diameter is exactly 8 mm, which is considered optimal, and in the hypothesis H_1, that it is exactly 10 mm, which is considered to be definitely bad. Every day a random sample of size n is taken from the production for quality control, that is, to decide whether H_0 or H_1 should

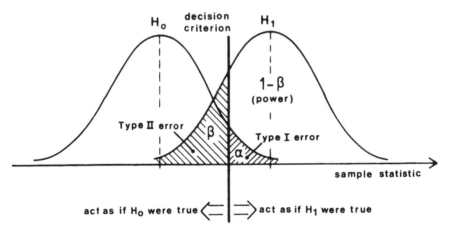

FIGURE 1.2. Illustration of Neyman and Pearson's theory of hypotheses testing. The figure shows the theoretical distributions of a sample statistic if the hypotheses H_0 or H_1, respectively, are true. If the empirically obtained sample statistic falls to the right of a decision criterion—set to balance the costs of both types of error—the decision is made to act as if H_1 were true (and *vice versa*).

14   1. THE INFERENCE REVOLUTION

be accepted. If the mean of the random sample (or a different sample statistic) falls to the right of the criterion in Fig. 1.2, we act as if H_1 were true: we reject H_0 and stop the production; otherwise we accept H_0. There are two kinds of error we may commit. We may decide that H_0 still holds although H_1 is true, and continue production, which may cause damage both to the patients, to whom the instruments are applied, and to the reputation of the firm. Or, we may act as if H_1 were true although H_0 still holds, and stop the production in order to search for a cause. Such a false alarm increases costs and causes a loss in production. Thus, the decision criterion has to be chosen by weighing the possible consequences of each error. This balance of utilities must be based on informed personal judgment; the formal statistical theory does not stipulate how this balance should be achieved. Here is the dividing line between the statistical and subjective, or behavioral, parts of the theory. Once we have agreed on a decision criterion, then the statistical theory tells us exactly the probability of Type I and Type II errors and their relationship to the size n of the sample we choose.

Neyman (1938, p. 56) emphasizes that to reject or accept a hypothesis does not imply that we now *believe* in our hypothesis or that a hypothesis is disproved, as Fisher claims. For instance, we may move the decision criterion in Fig. 1.2 farther to the left because we believe that possible damage to the patients and to the reputation of our firm is a greater cause for concern. Therefore, we anticipate a great number of false alarms. Consequently, if a sample statistic falls to the right of our criterion, we shall *act as if* H_1 were true; we shall stop production and seek the cause of the assumed malfunction. This, however, does not imply that we *believe* in H_1, since we anticipate false alarms. This difference is reflected in Neyman and Pearson's expression that hypothesis testing is "inductive behavior." To act as if a hypothesis were true does not mean to know or even to believe. Therefore, rejecting a hypothesis, including by Fisher's method, gives us no new knowledge about the validity of our hypotheses. All that we know is $p(D|H)$, the probability of the data given a hypothesis.

We shall deal with three major ways in which Neyman and Pearson tried to make Fisher's theory more consistent.

From Asymmetric to Symmetric Hypotheses Testing. Fisher specified only one hypothesis, the null, and left unspecified the alternative hypothesis, typically the research hypothesis in which the experimenter is interested. Therefore, Fisher could not calculate the Type II error, and he never granted it was necessary to do so. Such asymmetric hypothesis testing, however, has obvious shortcomings.

Consider that there is always some difference between the value predicted by a theoretical hypothesis, such as the null hypothesis, and an

EMERGENCE OF STATISTICAL INFERENCE 15

actual empirical value. For a given difference (greater than zero) between theoretical prediction and actual value, one can always increase the sample size to a level where the difference will be significant. Consequently, the null can always be disproved if the sample size n is large enough. Therefore, rejection of the null hypothesis tells us only whether we have included a *sufficiently large number of subjects* into our experiment. This is clearly not what is properly called "new knowledge." To avoid flaws like this, Neyman and Pearson rejected the program of disproving the null and introduced a specified alternative hypothesis. Asymmetric hypothesis testing became transformed into a symmetric competition between two hypotheses. This permitted the determination of both the Type I and Type II errors as a function of the decision criterion, the size of the sample, and the magnitude of the effect, that is, the distance between the means H_0 and H_1 in Fig. 1.2 (assuming equal distributions). In other words, the *power* $(1-\beta)$ of a test—the probability of accepting H_1 if H_1 is true—can be determined during the planning phase of research by choosing an appropriate sample size n. Of course, the level of significance must also be stipulated *before* the experiment; Fisher himself was ambiguous; he even allowed the level of significance to be determined *after* the data had been analyzed (Hogben, 1970, pp. 45-47).

From Nonrandom to Random Sampling. Fisher attempted to build his theory around a specific practical situation, where limited resources (of money or time, as in the agricultural field trial) allow for a single experiment only, and where random sampling from a population was a fiction. In contrast to large-sample statistics, where a population is defined and a random sample can be drawn, Fisher's small sample was not randomly drawn, nor was a population defined. What, then, could be the meaning of a *random sampling distribution* in his theory, if there is no random sample? Fisher's way out was to claim that any sample is a random sample from a "hypothetical infinite population," which is regrettably unknown to us. "The postulate of randomness thus resolves into the question, 'Of what population is this a random sample?' which must frequently be asked by every practical statistician" (Fisher, 1922, p. 313).

But how can the practical statistician find out? What is the population of subjects and conditions, or more generally, of experiments from which the present experiment is a random sample? This idea of an unknown hypothetical infinite population has puzzled many a statistician: "This is, to me at all events, a most baffling conception". (Kendall, 1943, p. 17). In contrast, Neyman and Pearson based their theory on repeated random sampling, which defined the level of significance α as the long-run frequency of Type I errors, and β as the long-run frequency of Type II errors, and the sampling distribution as a distribution of sample statistics

16   1. THE INFERENCE REVOLUTION

in a long-run series of repeated experiments. Therefore, a level of significance does not carry a meaning for a single experiment, but only for situations where the repeated drawing of random samples is a reality, as in the example in quality control.

From Formal Rules to Informed Personal Judgment.   Fisher (1935) presents his theory as if it were the "perfectly rigorous" method of inductive inference. In contrast, Neyman and Pearson have always emphasised two points. First, there is *no single best method* of hypothesis testing. Already, in their first paper, Neyman and Pearson (1928a) presented their approach as one among alternatives, and they continued to emphasize that even if they considered their theory as appropriate for a particular application, the competent reader must always choose for himself. Second, there is no theory of hypothesis testing that can be applied in a purely formal or mechanical way, without informed personal judgment. The process of inference or decision always has two parts that must be carefully distinguished, the statistical part and the subjective part. Even the assumption about the shapes of the sampling distributions represents a subjective commitment, according to Neyman and Pearson. As Pearson (1962) put it: "Of necessity, as it seemed to us, we left in our mathematical model a gap for the exercise of a more intuitive process of personal judgment in such matters—to use our terminology—as the choice of the most likely class of admissible hypotheses, the appropriate significance level, the magnitude of worthwhile effects and the balance of utilities" (pp. 395–396).

Let us summarize. Neyman and Pearson's revision of Fisher's theory, with its conceptual obscurities, into a more consistent theory showed that the theory of hypothesis testing does not provide us, as Fisher pretended, with a single formalized technique of inductive inference. Rather, Neyman and Pearson reconsidered inductive inference as decision making, where statistical theory and personal judgment must be interlocked. At the same time, the conceptual and mathematical revision revealed that the theory is restricted to applications where repeated random sampling from a defined population is a reality, as it is in quality control in manufacturing. Experiments in psychology, however, seldom include repeated random sampling and cost–benefit analysis. Therefore, by making Fisher's theory more consistent, Neyman and Pearson effectively showed that statistical hypothesis testing does not help very much in scientific experiments. It should be noted that Neyman and Pearson's joint papers give no discussion of an application where a scientific conclusion was the primary object of the investigation (Birnbaum, 1977, p. 30). Fisher, however, went on to present his theory as the single instrument of the scientist.

The differences between the two camps became personal as well as conceptual. To give the reader a taste of the tone in which the debate was conducted: Fisher (1955) rejected the decision-theory approach, suggesting that its advocates, such as Neyman and Pearson, are like "Russians who are made familiar with the ideal that research in pure science can and should be geared to technological performance, in the comprehensive organized effort of a five-year plan for the nation" (p. 70). After a talk given by Neyman before the Royal Statistical Society in London, Fisher opened the discussion with the sarcastic remark that Neyman should have chosen a topic "on which he could speak with authority" (Neyman, 1967a, p. 193). Neyman, for his part, stated that Fisher's methods of testing are in a "mathematically specifiable sense worse than useless" (Stegmüller, 1973, p. 2).

The lesson to be learned is that no single solution to the process of inductive inference exists. Frequentist theories, such as Fisher's and Neyman and Pearson's, must refrain from calculating probabilities of hypotheses given data, whereas Bayes' theory, which need not, pays the price that the prior probabilities must be subjectively determined. None of these can formalize the experimenters' inference from data to hypothesis.

WHAT DID PSYCHOLOGISTS DO BEFORE THE INFERENCE REVOLUTION?

How did experimental psychologists draw inferences from their data to their hypotheses before t-tests and analysis of variance became the dominant formal instruments? How did they arrive at their conclusions?

Let us consider the design of the experiment itself before we turn to how conclusions were drawn after an experiment had been completed. Of course, there was the single variable method, where, in the ideal case, all stimuli were held constant except one, which was to be manipulated. A current belief is that the single-variable method was the only type of experiment that existed before Fisher's analysis of variance offered the opportunity of analyzing the multi-factor design. This, however, is an error of hindsight. Lovie (1979) has pointed out that, contrary to this belief, multifactor designs were quite common in English-speaking journals. The same situation prevailed in the German-language literature. For instance, in research on perceptual constancy, the effect of up to three variables on the perception of a fourth variable was investigated (Brunswik, 1934). More important, there even existed different ideas of the nature of experimentation, ranging from "demonstration", for example, of apparent motion in early Gestalt psychology, to Brunswik's (1955a) "representative design" developed in the late 1930s. The strong

18   1. THE INFERENCE REVOLUTION

link between experimental design and statistical analysis, as emphasized by Fisher (1935), was not a matter of concern to the psychologists at that time. However, when in the 1950s analysis of variance became the dominant technique of statistical analysis, Fisher's suggested link became reality: While his multifactor designs became a valuable and important tool in psychological experimentation, they nevertheless led to the repression of ideas about experimentation which deviated from Fisher's.

How did experimental psychologists present the data on which they based their inferences? A typical article in the *Journal of Experimental Psychology* around 1925 reports *single-case data*. There were often fewer than 10 subjects, and, as in Wundt's laboratory, they were frequently staff members, or at least graduate students. Even in a study where 100 students were investigated (Cason & Cason, 1925), individual graphs were drawn for each subject. (The study examined the influence of the sex of the experimenter and the form of the instruction on various measures of performance). After 1930, the use of staff members decreased, and after the inference revolution, reports of single cases became the exception rather than the rule.

The data itself was typically presented in extensive detail, using percentages, sums, ratios, medians, arithmetical means, standard deviations, ranges, correlations, and various idiosyncratic descriptive statistics. The analysis of the data was informal and typically piecemeal. Inferences about the validity of the hypothesis considered were typically based on an evaluation of whether the numbers obtained under the different experimental conditions were "significantly" different. Note that the term "significant" was already widely used in the 1920s and 1930s, although with a broader designation than now. The evaluation of whether differences were "significant" was sometimes done by a simple eyeballing of the numbers, described by such phrases as: "The difference is striking" (Mikesell & Bentley, 1930, p. 20). In the majority of the cases, it was based on an *informal* comparison of mean differences with standard deviations, as in the remark: "In amount of error, therefore, there seems scarcely any significant difference." (Whiting & English, 1925, p. 43). The meanings of "significant" ranged from the vague, everyday meaning of "importance," to designating an absolute size of difference, to designating a difference of "three or more times the probable error".

The use of probable errors to evaluate the significance of mean differences goes back to the treatise of Jules Gavarret (1840). A probable error is that deviation from the mean of a normal distribution that corresponds to the point dividing the area between mean and tail into two equal halves. Similarly, "critical ratios," the ratio of the difference between the means to the standard deviation of the differences, were often calculated as a more formal guide to the evaluation of these differences. Both the probable error and the critical ratio provided formal criteria for comparing differences between the means with some measure of dispersion.

The overall picture is an extensive, piecemeal, and above all nonstandardized presentation of descriptive statistics, and a comparatively flexible and negotiable attitude toward the issue of inference from data to hypothesis. The reader is informed extensively about details of the experiment, apparatus and results for the numerous individuals, and independent and dependent variables investigated. After the piecemeal discussion of the various aspects of the data, any inference to the hypothesis is sometimes made informally, sometimes made using probable errors or critical ratios. The separate processes of description and inference are often not distinguished at all. There are cases where the concluding section contains no inferences to hypotheses, but simply repeats the descriptive results; there are cases where generalizations to hypotheses are made without discussion of how the author arrived at them, and there are ambiguous expressions in which description and inference are not even distinguished. The topic of inductive inference was incidental, rather than central, for experiments in psychology before about 1940.

HOW STATISTICS BECAME AN INDISPENSABLE INSTRUMENT: THE INFERENCE REVOLUTION

What we call the inference revolution happened between about 1940 and 1955 in psychology. For the first time, this revolution made certain statistical ideas, known as "inferential statistics," an indispensable instrument for the psychologist.

In what sense was the event a revolution? The picture of scientific change as a revolution is itself a metaphor that became standard when the concept of revolution in politics became common. I.B. Cohen (1987) has traced the history of the metaphor and pointed to the French revolution of 1789 and Lavoisier's revolution in chemistry as prime examples in each area. The most prominent attempt to elaborate the metaphorical use of the term into a precise structure is Thomas Kuhn's *Structure of Scientific Revolutions* (1970). Although Kuhn's structure does not deal with psychological theories, it has become one of the books most frequently cited by psychologists, topped in the Science Citation Index only by best sellers such as textbooks on "inferential statistics." Part of the book's popularity may be attributed to its ambiguities. From monitoring conversations, in particular among the book's enthusiasts, Kuhn himself (1977) conlcuded: "I have sometimes found it hard to believe that all parties to

20   1. THE INFERENCE REVOLUTION

the discussion had been engaged with the same volume. Part of the reason for its success is, I regretfully conclude, that it can be too nearly all things to all people." (p. 293).

The two recent volumes on *The Probabilistic Revolution* (Krüger, Daston, & Heidelberger, 1987; Krüger, Gigerenzer, & Morgan, 1987) show clearly that this event in science is not of the Kuhnian type. For instance, whereas Kuhnian revolutions are discipline-specific, the probabilistic revolution is clearly an interdisciplinary event (Hacking, 1987). The inference revolution is also an interdisciplinary event, although a much less extensive one. There was none in physics, and it has most affected psychology and adjacent disciplines, such as psychiatry, education and sociology. There are, however, more impressive differences. Recall, for instance, the basic sequence of Kuhnian revolutions, a normal science, a crisis, a revolution, and a new normal science. As we have shown, however, no "normal science" of inference existed before 1940. There was neither a single, agreed upon school concerning inference from data to hypothesis, nor a "number of competing schools, each claiming competence for the same subject matter but approaching it in quite different ways" (Kuhn, 1977, p. 295). In fact, there was general tolerance, and the issue itself was not considered a very important one. Linked to this, no "crisis" of inference existed in psychology. If one wants to look for something like a "crisis," it must be sought outside of psychology, in the competing attempts to statisticians and philosophers to find a single, formal solution to the inference problem or to prove that there is none. No single, formal solution has ever been accepted. This "crisis" of inductive inference still exists both in philosophy and in statistics (see e.g. Hacking, 1965; Stegmüller, 1973), although many psychologists who use inferential statistics seem to be ignorant of these controversies. In short, despite tentative claims to the contrary (e.g. Rucci & Tweney, 1980), the inference revolution was not a Kuhnian revolution. Rather, the inference revolution institutionalized a certain kind of statistics for making inference from data to hypotheses, thus unifying psychology at the methodological level.

The Inference Revolution (1940–1955)

Researchers started to use methods of null hypothesis testing, such as the *t* test and Fisher's analysis of variance, as a supplement to numerous descriptive statistics as well as to critical ratios. Rucci and Tweney (1980) found 17 psychological articles using analysis of variance before 1940, starting with 1934, roughly half of them from parapsychology (which had a long statistical tradition) and from education. As early as 1942, Maurice Kendall commented on the conquest by the statisticians in new fields of

HOW STATISTICS BECAME AN INDISPENSABLE INSTRUMENT   21

application—the result, indeed, of a century long struggle—as follows: "Beginning as a small sect concerned only with political economy, they have already overrun every branch of science with a rapidity of conquest rivalled only by Attila, Mohammed, and the Colorado beetle." (p. 69).

As mentioned earlier, psychology received its "inferential statistics" from agriculture, by way of Snedecor's *Statistical Methods* (1937). This book, carrying the Fisherian message, became the most frequently cited book in 1961 according to the *Science Citation Index* (Kempthorne, 1972).

The situation, however, soon became complicated when, particularly after World War II, the position of Neyman and Pearson became known. It became complicated because the early textbook writers had started to present Fisher's method of null hypothesis testing just as Fisher and many psychologists wanted it to be, that is, as the single instrument for inductive inference. But how were psychologists to cope with the fundamental disagreement between the two camps, with the subtlety of the issues, and with the personal, polemical, and bitter tone of the controversy? There were only a few texts, such as Anderson and Bancroft (1952), that presented both Fisher's and Neyman and Pearson's theories. The great mass of textbooks, however, tried to fuse the writings of the two antagonists into a single, hybrid theory, of which neither Fisher nor, certainly, Neyman and Pearson would have approved. For instance, Fisher's idea of disproving the null hypothesis was retained, and Neyman and Pearson's concept of Type II error was also taught, although the latter had no meaning in the context of null hypothesis testing, nor could it be determined. The unsolved tension between the two camps was transformed into the hybrid theory and, from there, into research.

Acree (1978) wrote:

> The Neyman-Pearson theory serves very much as the superego of psychological research. It is the rationale given, if still anonymously, by the most sophisticated and respected textbooks in the field, which teach the doctrine of random sampling, specifying significance levels and sample sizes in advance to achieve the desired power and avoiding probability statements about particular intervals or outcomes. But it is the Fisherian ego which gets things done in the real world of the laboratory, and then is left with vague anxiety and guilt about having violated the rules. (p. 398)

Of course, the attempt to assimilate Neyman and Pearson's theory into the Fisherian program of disproving the null meant doing the impossible, and thus the textbook-hybrid was an ongoing source of confusion and errors. Nevertheless, the hybrid was still presented as the only truth, as the single solution to inductive inference, as Fisher had presented his theory. And a growing majority of psychologists seemed to want to

22   1. THE INFERENCE REVOLUTION

perceive it in exactly this way, as a cookbooklike mechanical prescription of "what to do." The hybrid soon revolutionized American research practice. By 1952, the percentage of articles using the t-test and analysis of variance had increased to 30% and 20%, respectively, in six American journals (Rucci & Tweney, 1980, p. 171). As early as 1955 and 1956, significance testing of null hypotheses had skyrocketed to 81.5% in four leading journals (Sterling, 1959). The history of that revolution in psychology between 1940 and 1955 has been traced in detail by Acree (1978), Edgington (1974), Lovie (1979), and Rucci and Tweney (1980).

The Irrational Revolution

There is no question but that the inference revolution unified psychology by prescribing a common method, in the absence of a common theoretical perspective. But the question remains, how could psychologists have convinced themselves that the hybrid statistical theory is the single valid instrument for inferences from data to hypotheses? As we argued earlier, this is an illusion, and we shall explain here how this illusion could be created and maintained.

(1) *Neglect of controversies and controversial issues.* Many of the readers of this book may have been surprised by the previous sections, because in the textbooks from which they learned statistics, there was absolutely no mention of a controversy between Fisher and Neyman and Pearson and consequently no mention of the controversial issues. Usually even the names of the originators are not mentioned at all, and, if they are, as in the exceptional case of Hays' (1963) otehwise excellent text, the only reference suggests a story of cumulative progress: "The general history of hypothesis testing first took form under the hand of Sir Ronald Fisher in the nineteen-twenties, but it was carried to a high state of development in the work of J. Neyman and E.S. Pearson, beginning about 1928" (p. 287).

(2) *Neglect of alternative approaches.* As we have already mentioned, the textbooks do not present alternative approaches such as Neyman and Pearson's theory, Bayes' theory, or others (e.g. Cohen, 1980; Shafer, 1976). They teach a mixture of ideas from Neyman and Pearson and Fisher, sometimes supplemented by a Bayesian interpretation, which we call the "hybrid theory." The practice of presenting a single approach as the only truth is otherwise unusual in psychology, where textbooks typically present one alternative view after another, say, on the nature of perceptual illusions or of reactive depression. Even on the level of methods, alternatives are otherwise tolerated; for example, the issue of measurement is a bundle of alternative approaches, and controversies are well known (see Gigerenzer, 1981). Inferential statistics, however, gener-

HOW STATISTICS BECAME AN INDISPENSABLE INSTRUMENT   23

ated both the strongest consensus about methodology and consequent neglect of alternatives.

The neglect of controversies and of alternative approaches in the psychological texts should not be seen as a conspiracy of silence. Rather, it should be viewed as the result of a meeting between statisticians eager to sell their product and researchers equally eager to buy. Both parties to the transaction acted in good faith, but both labored under an illusion: In reality there existed no single, simple statistical answer to the problem of inductive inference, however much researchers longed for one.

(3) *Anonymous presentation of the hybrid.* Deviating from common scientific practice, the textbooks do not indicate who the authors of the ideas are. For instance, the idea of disproving the null is not referred to as Fisher's idea, nor is the concept of power or Type II error referred to Neyman and Pearson. The latter are not even mentioned at all in 22 out of 26 textbooks on statistics we looked through. Of course, an anonymous presentation facilitates the neglect of controversies and alternatives and thereby fosters the illusion of a single, true method of inference.

(4) *Institutionalization of the hybrid.* Along with the textbooks, the hybrid theory entered the university curricula and affected the publishing policies of the major journals (see Acree, 1978; Bakan, 1966; Rucci & Tweney, 1980). The quality of research became measured by the level of significance. For instance, editors of journals (e.g. Melton, 1962) as well as of the APA Publication Manual (1974) use the term "negative" results synonymously with "not rejecting the null" and "positive" results for "rejecting the null". Melton (1962, pp. 553f) after editing the *Journal of Experimental Psychology* for 12 years, stated that "negative" results submitted for publication were usually rejected, that there was a "strong reluctance" to accept results that were significant at only the .05 level, whereas those which were significant at the .01 level deserved a place in the journal.

Even Fisher (1933, p. 46) himself, and of course Gosset, who invented the *t*-test in 1908, had warned of such a ritualistic use. In Gosset's words, "obviously the important thing . . . is to have a low real error, not to have a 'significant' result at a particular station. The latter seems to me to be nearly valueless in itself" (quoted in Pearson, 1939, p. 247).

(5) *Confusion.* The attempts to present both the Fisherian Ego and the Neyman and Pearsonian Superego as a consistent and anonymous hybrid theory was a hopeless task for the textbook writers. As a necessary consequence, the textbooks became filled with conceptual confusion, ambiguity, and errors, as has been described in detail by Bakan (1966), Bredenkamp (1972), Carver (1978), Hogben (1957), and Wilson (1961).

For instance, as we mentioned, according to Melton's (1962) editorial, the quality of research has been measured by the level of significance.

24   1. THE INFERENCE REVOLUTION

Why? In the editorial, Melton states that the level of significance reflects the degree of confidence that the result is *repeatable* and that it specifies the *magnitude* of the effect (p. 553f). However, both assertions are incorrect; there is nothing magical about the level of significance that justifies such wishful thinking (Bredenkamp, 1972). The magnitude of effect is given directly by the data; there is no need to test a null hypothesis (or, calculate an F-value) in order to find the magnitude. In contrast, significance *per se* tells us nothing about the magnitude; whether or not a given magnitude of effect is significant depends on the number of subjects used. But how could Melton be to blame, inasmuch as statistical textbooks themselves put forward the same errors? For example, Nunally (1975) teaches us that a statistical significance at the .05 level "means that the investigator can be confident with odds of 95 out of 100 that the observed difference will hold up in future investigations" (p. 195). Of course, this, again, cannot be inferred, and we refer the misinformed reader to Bakan (1966) and Lykken (1968), where this "replicability illusion" is discussed.

The Permanent Illusion

Since the 1960s it has been repeatedly pointed out that what we call the hybrid theory cannot provide answers to those questions in which the experimenter is interested (Bakan, 1966; Hogben, 1957; Lykken, 1968; Rozeboom, 1960; Schwartz & Dalgleish, 1982). Nevertheless, these clarifications have had almost no effect on research practice. Writers and consumers of null hypothesis testing still believe that the anonymous "statistics" tells us exactly what we want to know. However, null hypothesis testing tells us only $p(D|H_0)$, that is, the probability of the data given the null hypothesis. We cannot even calculate $p(D|H_1)$, as we can in Neyman and Pearson's theory. Both likelihoods are probabilities of *data* (given a hypothesis); from none of these can we derive the probability of a *hypothesis* (given data), such as $p(H_0|D)$ and $p(H_1|D)$. (Any elementary text on probability theory makes clear that from the probability of A given B only, one cannot calculate the probability of B given A.)

Nevertheless, even in psychology textbooks it is claimed that the level of significance specifies the probability of the hypothesis. For instance, in the statistical appendix of Miller and Buckhout's (1973) otherwise excellent introduction to psychology, the author (F. L. Brown) "explains" the logic of testing statistical hypotheses using an ESP experiment, in which a subject tries to read the mind of the experimenter. He guesses 69 out of 100 coin tosses correctly. The likelihood that the subject does this well or better if the null hypothesis (the probability of a correct guess is .5) is true is about 1 in 10,000. From this, the student is taught that the "probability that the null hypothesis could be correct" is "about 1 in 10,000", and that the "probability that the null hypothesis is incorrect" is "about 9,999 in 10, 000" (p. 523). Here the likelihood $p(D|H_0)$ is erroneously equated with $p(H_0|D)$, the Bayesian posterior probability. This is what we mean by the "Bayesian interpretation" of "significance levels." Of course, such errors are necessary to maintain the illusion that null hypothesis testing can tell us what we want to know, that is, give us information about the validity of hypotheses.

It might be asked how such illusions and errors could have persisted since they were introduced in the early years of the inference revolution. We believe that such illusions were *necessary* to maintain the dream of mechanized inductive inference. Emptied of all illusions, we would understand that what we really have with the hybrid is simply $p(D|H_0)$. Psychologists seem not to wish to be cured of these illusions, for the consequence would be the abandonment of the indispensable instrument and hence the abandonment of the unification of psychological methodology institutionalized by the inference revolution.

Consequences and Alternatives

What are the alternatives to the hybrid theory? There is no gain from simply replacing the hybrid theory by another statistical theory that is also considered as the sole general-purpose technique of inference. The general alternative view is to realize how little the hybrid theory (as well as others) overlaps with the problems we are dealing with, or, in different words, how few of the important questions it can answer. The scientist's attention may then shift from the obsessive idea that significance testing is the most important step toward new knowledge as suggested by Fisher, to other fundamental issues, which have been pushed into the background. Here are some examples:

1. *The measurement problem.* Since the inference revolution, the question of whether and how psychological phenomena can be represented by numbers (the measurement problem) has received much less attention than the statistical question of how to transform given numbers into new numbers (e.g., calculation of variances and F-values), although measurement logically and temporally precedes the calculation of statistics. Tukey (1962), for instance, believes that the attention paid to statistics diverts attention away from the data generation process. The interesting point is that this asymmetry on the level of method was later transported to the level of theory, when the mind became interpreted as a

26   1. THE INFERENCE REVOLUTION

statistician. With the new metaphor, for instance, thinking came to be considered as statistical calculation, and information or "data" search processes were neglected (see chapter 5).

2. *To analyze the meaning of "error variability" and minimize the "real" error* should be the basic issue in research, as Gosset, the inventor of the *t*-test pointed out (Pearson, 1939). However, a theoretical analysis of the nature of different variabilities such as inter- and intraindividual variability is a rare event (Gigerenzer, 1983a; see also chapter 3), and minimizing is often not even attempted; the "error" variability is inserted into the formula and automatically accounted for by the statistical technique.

3. *The size of an effect* was considered a result of secondary importance after the inference revolution and is sometimes not even reported in experimental articles.

4. *Replication of experimental results* has repeatedly been reported to be a rare event (Bredenkamp, 1972; Sterling, 1959). The belief in the single experiment may have been reinforced by Fisher's claim (as opposed to that of Neyman and Pearson) that the level of significance carries a meaning with respect to a single experiment, suggesting that the null hypothesis can be disproved in one experiment.

5. *Theory construction.* The inverse relation between the attention paid to significance tests and that paid to theory construction has been pointed out by Gigerenzer (1987a) and Lovie (1979). It is obviously present in the kind of inductive research where one waits for what turns out to be significant and then presents *post hoc* explanations. It is interesting to note that many of those psychologists who were both influential theoreticians and involved in experimental work rejected significance testing. You won't catch Jean Piaget or Wolfgang Köhler calculating a *t* or *F*-value, and such different eminent figures as Sir Frederick Bartlett, S. S. Stevens, and B. F. Skinner all explicitly rejected statistical inference. They preferred to trust their own informed judgment.

These are examples of issues sometimes pushed into the background by the fascination with mechanized inference methods.

Numerous alternatives to the hybrid theory exist, such as the use of informed judgment reflecting the particular situation instead of a mechanized method of inference. As we have mentioned, physicists operate this way. Alternatives have long been known (e.g. Bakan, 1966; Hogben, 1957) but have had little impact. We shall present only one example.

6. *Planning of research.* Cohen (1962) analyzed the 1960 volume of the *Journal of Abnormal and Social Psychology* and found that the power of most of the studies published was ridiculously low. This means that experiments were planned without realizing that the power, the probabil-

HOW STATISTICS BECAME AN INDISPENSABLE INSTRUMENT   27

ity of finding an effect, *if there was one,* was small. The concept "power" is a blind spot in the hybrid theory, and as a result time and money can be wasted. One alternative is *planning of research* as suggested by Neyman and Pearson. First, we specify the minimal desired size of effect as the alternative hypothesis (H_1 in Fig. 1.2); second, we specify the level of significance; and third, we specify the power we want. We can then calculate from these the number of subjects we need to achieve the desired power (see Cohen, 1962).

How Could the Inference Revolution Have Happened?

It is remarkable that despite two decades of counterrevolutionary attacks, the mystifying doctrine of null hypothesis testing is still today the Bible from which our future research generation is taught.

Meehl (1978) put it strongly: "I suggest to you that Sir Ronald has befuddled us, mesmerized us, and led us down the primrose path. I believe that the almost universal reliance on merely refuting the null hypothesis . . . is . . . one of the worst things that ever happened in the history of psychology." (p. 817).

The interesting question is, how could such an event ever happen? This question has seldom been posed. However, Danziger (1987) points to the early applications in education and to the needs of educational administrators for an "objective" technique to justify their practical decisions, such as whether or not to establish a new curriculum. Significance testing in the context of group comparisons seemed to give them exactly what they needed, a simple yes-or-no answer, and an aura of "objectivity" to defend their decisions. Danziger believes that statistical methods were successful not because they were appropriate for the traditional problems of psychology, but because experimenters became interested in supplying statistically valid information that would be useful to a general science of social control. Earlier educational applications provided the most successful model for such a science. The link between socially useful science and laboratory work had been much closer in America than, for example, in Germany. Accordingly, one finds that American psychology took the lead in introducing statistical thinking into the laboratory, whereas the German experimentalists of the time did not consider such procedures to be relevant to their concerns. Gigerenzer (1987a) points to two traditional ideals in experimental psychology, objectivity and determinism, arguing that inferential statistics allowed for an application of probability theory that promised objectivity in inductive inference without threatening determinism. The dream of the scientist who arrives at new knowledge by a completely mechanized process seemed to have become real.

CONCLUSIONS

We have argued that there is in cognitive psychology a marked preference for explanatory metaphors that derive from the scientists' own tools. The more prestigious and well entrenched the tools are, the more pronounced the preference, as in the case of statistics and computers. We are concerned with the metaphor of the mind as an intuitive statistician that emerged from the intersection of the inference and cognitive revolutions.

This chapter has described how inferential statistics entered psychology and in what form. Prior to 1940, the issue of inductive inference was peripheral both to psychological method and to psychological theory. Between 1940 and 1955, statistical methods were institutionalized in psychology; we have called this the "inference revolution." These methods were in a fact a hybrid of theories that professional statisticians regarded as distinct and even incompatible: Fisher's theory of null hypothesis testing, supplemented by concepts from Neyman and Pearson and sometimes by Bayesian interpretations. Unaware of the controversies within statistics proper, and driven by the hope of mechanizing inductive inference, most psychologists systematically misunderstood and exaggerated the power of these methods. But this did not prevent the hybrid statistics from becoming the methodological orthodoxy throughout psychology, governing both the design and publication of research.

With the advent of the cognitive approach in the 1960s, these statistical methods supplied theories with a new conceptual vocabulary—likelihoods, prior probabilities, sampling processes, decision criteria, and so forth. The statistical tools that had unified psychology at a methodological level now promised a unifying theoretical perspective as well. However, the blind spots and illusions that flawed the hybrid statistics were often carried over into the theories they inspired. In the following chapters, we examine how statistical metaphors transformed our understanding of cognitive processes—creating new research questions and even new data, but also repeating some of the confusions in the tools that suggested the metaphor of the mind as intuitive statistician.

2 Detection and Discrimination: From Thresholds to Statistical Inference

In this chapter, we deal with an elementary cognitive process: detecting an object, or discriminating between two objects (detecting a difference). Examples are detecting whether there is a signal on the radar screen or only noise, whether two coins have different weights, whether sugar has been added to wine, and whether the cab involved in a hit-and-run accident at night is blue or green. Such detection processes have long been explained using a metaphor derived from Herbart (1816): It is considered that detection of an object or stimulus occurs only if the effect the stimulus has on the nervous system exceeds a certain *threshold* value. Detection of the stimulus against a background can occur only if the excitation exceeds the "absolute threshold," and detection of a difference between two stimuli occurs if the excitation from one exceeds that of another by an amount greater than a "differential threshold." After the inference revolution, however, the concept of *fixed thresholds* was largely abandoned in favor of the idea that object detection is *inductive inference* as defined by statistical hypothesis testing. Although the notion of a "threshold" was from the beginning linked to probability theory, it was only after the inference revolution that probability theory became an essential part of our understanding of the process of object detection itself. The picture of the cognitive process shifted from a passive response based on fixed thresholds to that of an active "intuitive statistician."

HISTORY: BEFORE THE INFERENCE REVOLUTION

From the attempt by Fechner (1860) to prove the essential unity of mind and matter, the experimental psychology of the 19th and early 20th century inherited two main questions: the measurement of thresholds and

30   2. DETECTION AND DISCRIMINATION

the formulation of the equation relating sensation intensity to stimulus intensity. In Fechner's view, the measurement of differential thresholds (or just noticeable differences) was a necessary step toward a scale of sensation intensity; he defined the intensity of sensation as the number of just noticeable differences (j.n.d.s), from the absolute threshold to the sensation being measured. This shows that the absolute and differential thresholds were considered to be *fixed,* otherwise they could not have been considered as an appropriate yardstick for sensation intensity. The concept of a fixed threshold was the principal explanation for whether or not we perceive a stimulus (absolute threshold) and whether or not we perceive a difference between two stimuli (differential threshold). Probability theory was linked with the measurement of thresholds and construction of scales of sensation from Fechner to Thurstone, although in different ways.

In this section we argue that understanding of the role of probability in object detection slowly developed toward key ideas of what was later called signal detection theory. However, the developmental process was prematurely halted in the 1930s and 1940s for two reasons. The first is that although key concepts of signal detection theory such as the ideas of random noise and overlapping normal distribution of subjective values were already developed in the late 1920s, nobody thought of interpreting such concepts in terms of *cognitive inference* or *hypotheses testing*. The second reason is the influence of Stanley S. Stevens (1957), who rejected Fechner's concern with differential thresholds as yardsticks, Thurstone's concern with variability and probabilistic models (Thurstone, 1927a, b, c, d) and, finally inferential statistics.

From Thresholds to Variability in Brain Activity

Fixed Thresholds

The classical formula for object detection is given by Weber's law:

$$\Delta I/I = k \tag{2.1}$$

where ΔI is the j.n.d., I is the stimulus intensity (both are measured in physical units), and k is a constant. Thus, Weber's law states: The just noticeable difference is a constant fraction of the stimulus intensity. But the operational meaning of the term "j.n.d." is as yet undefined. To avoid this ambiguity, the following statement of the law is the more appropriate one: The stimulus difference ΔI, which is correctly detected in a specified proportion of repetitions (in between 0 and 100%), is a constant fraction of the stimulus intensity. For instance, if 12 coins in your hand have been judged heavier than 10 coins (eyes closed, same coins) in 75% of the trials,

HISTORY: BEFORE THE INFERENCE REVOLUTION 31

Weber's law predicts that the same percentage of correct detections occurs when 30 coins are compared with 25 coins.

Typically, the classical textbooks on psychophysics, such as Titchene (1905), Brown and Thomson (1921), Woodworth (1938), and Guilford (1936, 1954) give the impression that the task of psychophysics is to measure these thresholds and that such measurements are subject to so many sources of "error" or variability that statistical calculations must be applied to the data in order to estimate the "true value" of the threshold. In all of these texts, for example, the measurement of the differential threshold from data collected by the method of right and wrong cases is discussed exhaustively. The following is an example of such an early use of probability theory as a device for estimating the "true value" of the threshold.

Two stimuli are given, one a standard that remains constant, the other a comparison stimulus that differs from the standard by a small amount. In one experiment, reported by Brown and Thomson (1921, p.59), for example, the standard was a weight of 100 gms. The subject had to judge whether the comparison weight was "greater" than the standard. Each measure was based on 450 trials. Table 2.1 shows the raw number of judgments of "greater" for each weight as well as these numbers expressed as a proportion P.

TABLE 2.1

Comparison weights:	84	88	92	96	100	104	108
Judgments of "greater":	1	9	40	100	186	403	423
Proportion P	.0022	.0200	.0889	.2222	.4133	.8956	.9400

It can be seen that P rises slowly at first, then climbs steeply, then slows down when the comparison weight can be clearly distinguished as heavier than the standard weight. On a graph, if P is plotted as a function of the comparison weight, the curve is S-shaped, or ogival, which is the shape of the cumulative normal distribution. The differential threshold, like the absolute threshold, has been derived from such data by a variety of methods, including graphical estimation of the midpoint of the curve, that is, the point below which 50% of measures would fall (i.e. an estimate of the median of the curve). Other methods include a way devised by Spearman (1908) of estimating the arithmetic mean of the curve; and a procedure that involves finding the parameters of the normal distribution that best fit the observed data. This last procedure is laborious and involves estimating h, where $h = 1/\sqrt{2}\,\sigma$ and σ is the standard deviation of the normal curve, and then using one of several possible methods to derive a best-fitting curve with a particular single value of h as its

32   2. DETECTION AND DISCRIMINATION

parameter. The median of this curve was treated as the differential threshold. The parameter h, which is now replaced by the standard deviation, is a measure of the "sharpness" or "lack of variability" in the normal distribution: the more sharply peaked the bell of the curve, the greater h is. The methodological details are spelled out in several sources, including Titchener (1905, pp. 275-318), Brown and Thomson (1921, pp. 64-76), Guilford (1936, pp. 166-214), and Woodworth (1938, pp. 400-419). The measurement of thresholds supplied the experimenters with many a problem to be solved, such as whether subjects should be permitted 'equal' or 'doubtful' judgments, as opposed to being restricted to only two categories of judgments, 'heavier' and 'lighter.'

It was by this onerous route, rather than by Karl Pearson's statistics, that many psychology students in the first half of the 20th century were introduced to the normal distribution (and, incidentally, learned to dread psychophysics). And, in contrast to the Galton-Pearson program, the students learned that the probability distribution reflects measurement error only, since its use is to estimate the single "true value" of the threshold. It would be incorrect, however, to say that this "taming of measurement error" was the only intersection between cognitive theory and probabilistic thinking in the 19th century. Fechner is probably the figure with the broadest grasp of probabilistic thinking, and the example he offers may illuminate the most penetrating intrusion of probability into the experimental psychology of that time.

Fechner's Probabilistic Ideas

Besides the foregoing use of probability theory to estimate the "true value" of a threshold, which was due to G.E. Müller rather than to Fechner, Fechner himself used probabilistic ideas in the following contexts: (a) philosophical indeterminism, (b) data description, (c) statistical inference, and (d) Weber's law.

Philosophical Indeterminism. In 1849 Fechner proclaimed his indeterminism, based on his theory of psychophysical parallelism (see Heidelberger, 1987). Like the mind, which is not completely determined but possesses a certain degree of "free will," nature also is not completely determined. A steady stream of novelty pours into the world, and this amount of indeterminateness, like free will, "truly depends on freedom," not on "our ignorance of the conditions." Nevertheless, the causal law pertains—like circumstances have like consequences. A novel element may have a novel consequence, but it has always the same one. Heidelberger (1987) considers Fechner to be the first universal indeterminist, anticipating C.S. Peirce's indeterminism (Peirce, 1931/1958), and

HISTORY: BEFORE THE INFERENCE REVOLUTION   33

considers Fechner's *Kollektivmasslehre*, which was begun in 1850 and published posthumously in 1897, as the mathematical formulation of his indeterminism.

Data Description.   A main issue in the *Kollektivmasslehre* is how to choose a measure of central tendency depending on the shape of the probability distribution. For asymmetric distributions, for instance, Fechner argued in favor of the mode; this contrasts with the widespread current use of the median for such distributions.

Statistical Inference.   In the same book, Fechner developed a statistical test for the independence of measures in a series of numbers, such as the amount of rainfall on successive days.

Weber's Law.   This law is important for what later became known as Fechner's law,

$$S = k \log I \tag{2.2}$$

since the latter can be derived from the former, assuming that each differential threshold (although increasing with I) corresponds to exactly one unit of sensation S.[1] It is noteworthy that Fechner tested the validity of Weber's law by analyzing the *variability* in judgments rather than mean tendencies. He predicted that the variability should remain constant for all stimulus intensities, if Weber's law holds, and concluded that the actual increase of variability was so small relative to the increase of the stimulus level itself that the prediction seemed to be supported (Fechner, 1860/1966, pp. 85-93).

These examples show the broad range of probabilistic ideas in Fech-

---

[1]Fechner (1860) derived his law by relating S, the strength of a sensation, to I, the intensity of a stimulus, as follows. He assumed that if a sensation strength S was to be perceived as just noticeably different by being incremented by ΔS, this increment would be a constant multiple k of the Weber fraction: $\Delta S = k(\Delta I/I)$. This is known as the "fundamental formula." Rearranging terms gives: $\Delta S/\Delta I = k(1/I)$.

Assuming that ΔS and ΔI become so small that they can be written as differentials dS and dI, then solving the equation gives: $S = k \log_e I + c$, where c is the constant of integration. That is, sensation strength is a function of the logarithm of stimulus intensity.

Fechner (1877) showed that a change in the fundamental formula yields the following solution. Instead of assuming that it is ΔS that varies with the Weber fraction, assume instead that the *relative* difference in sensation strength $\Delta S/S$ varies with the Weber fraction. Let ΔS and ΔI become dS and dI as before, and we have: $dS/S = k(dI/I)$. Then solving the equation gives: $\log_e S + \log_e c' = k \log_e I + \log_e c''$, where $\log_e c'$ and $\log_e c''$ are constants of integration. Taking antilogs, $c'S = c''I^k$ or $S = (c''/c')I^k$. That is, sensation strength is now a power function of stimulus intensity. Plateau had formulated this law earlier, but later retracted it.

34   2. DETECTION AND DISCRIMINATION

ner's thought. But despite his philosophical indeterminism, he did not use probability theory as a model of cognitive processes such as detection and discrimination, and, even more important for our topic, he did not consider the tools of statistical inference as a metaphor of the mind. Rather, his psychophysical program was based on the idea of fixed thresholds, and these gave him a measure of sensation and his logarithmic law.

Variability in Brain Activity

An essentially new look at the processes of detection and discrimination arose around the turn of the century. The new idea was to explain detection and discrimination in terms of fluctuating brain activity rather than thresholds, by inner processes rather than by stimulus differences measured on a physical scale.

Historically, the founder of this view was Solomons (1900), but early students of sensory physiology at the time of Fechner had already speculated that a stimulus has its effect only if it is added to a resting level of activity in the brain. Helmholtz (1856/1962) proposed that in absolute threshold experiments with light intensities, one should consider the intensity of the stimulus as being added to the light sensations generated internally, which could be represented by a number I_0, the intensity of a corresponding stimulus.

Similarly, Delboeuf (1873) believed that the activation from a stimulus of intensity I was added to a "quantity" I_0 necessary for sensibility that was inherent in the sense organ, and he produced a fundamental formula identical with that of Helmholtz. But he went on to develop it more simply than did Helmholtz. Delboeuf's variant of Fechner's Law was:

$$S = \log \left[(I_0 + I)/I_0 \right] \tag{2.3}$$

He argued that his own data on the differential discrimination of shades of grey supported equation (2.3) rather than Plateau's. Plateau (1872), who postulated a power function rather than a logarithmic function, felt this was sufficient grounds for him to admit that his power law was probably wrong. Fechner (1877) seized on this retraction as an excuse to champion his own logarithmic law, much to the later chagrin of Stevens (1957), who claimed Plateau had been right all along.

All these early attempts to introduce an internal variable (such as I_0) in addition to the external variable (I) have in common the idea that the internal variable is considered as a stable value just like the external variable. It was Solomons (1900) who first postulated that the source of 'internal' stimulation might fluctuate randomly rather than remain stable. The essential claim was that the concept of threshold is not needed, but

HISTORY: BEFORE THE INFERENCE REVOLUTION   35

can be completely replaced by the concept of "variability in brain activity." The empirical facts were obtained in experiments on sudden pressure change. Solomons found that a physically constant pressure is perceived not as constant, but as constantly changing. Such facts were not new, but his explanation was. He explained this fluctuation not by measurement error, but by "the well-known fact of variability of brain activity," caused by "a variety of bodily and mental conditions which are constantly changing" (p. 235). A few pages later Solomons admits that the term "well-known" is perhaps an exaggeration, but he insists that the concept of "variability of sensation" or "brain activity" or "irritability" (Solomons had many terms) comes very near to ranking as a simple fact of observation rather than as speculation. What was previously considered as a threshold is simply the range of brain variability. Therefore, two stimuli must differ by more than the range of this variability for their difference to be detected. The understanding of what it means to detect a difference thus changed from surmounting a fixed threshold to surmounting the range of brain variability.

Except for the mathematics, Solomons presents explicitly the relation between stimulus difference and relative frequency of detections, which became the basis of Thorndike's (1910, 1919) scaling methods and for which Thurstone (1927 a, b, c, d) later became famous: If "there is a very slight difference between the stimuli the judgment will be correct as often as incorrect. As this difference increases, however, the proportion of correct judgments will increase; . . . For any given difference between the stimuli there will be a corresponding percentage of correct judgments, the percentage depending upon the extent and distribution of the variations" (Solomons, 1900, p. 235). Thurstone had only to define these distributions as normal distributions and derive his "law of comparative judgment"— although we do not know whether he knew Solomons' work, since he did not mention it.

Solomons did not attempt to make this relationship precise by introducing probability theory but, without referring to fixed thresholds, went on to show that the notion of brain variability offers a new explanation of Weber's law. He derives Weber's law by the following argument. First, the range of variability is defined in terms of a percentage q (of the stimulus intensity I). Second, the percentage q is assumed to be independent of I, and constant. Therefore, the range of variability qI increases linearly with I, which is in perfect analogy to Weber's law, which holds that ΔI increases linearly with I.

Of course, Solomons' new explanation did nothing but rephrase Weber's law in terms of brain variability. The important point is, however, the emergence of a new perspective, making variability rather than fixed thresholds the basis for explaining object detection. "But once grant this

36   2. DETECTION AND DISCRIMINATION

variability and nothing more is necessary; all the phenomena connected with thresholds follow easily from this" (Solomons, 1900, p. 240).

Thresholds Replaced by Probability Distributions

Solomons had introduced fluctuations in brain activity as an alternative to thresholds in order to understand the process of stimulus detection. Louis Leon Thurstone (1887–1955) went one step further: He rejected the concept of a just noticeable difference and focused entirely on fluctuations, or, in his terms, on the variability of *discriminal* or *perceptual processes*. In his own words: "Every one who works at all seriously in psychophysics knows that just noticeable differences have never been found, and that it is necessary to specify quite arbitrarily a stipulated frequency of discrimination in order to put any sense in the j.n.d." (Thurstone, 1927c, pp. 421–422). The main difference between Thurstone and the previous proponents of threshold measurement can be condensed as follows. For threshold measurement, an arbitrary relative frequency such as 75% was agreed upon, and the corresponding physical distance between two stimuli was empirically determined and interpreted as the differential threshold or just noticeable difference. In contrast, Thurstone empirically determined the relative frequencies with which one stimulus was judged greater than another. From these relative frequencies, considered as estimates of the probabilities p_{ab} that stimulus A is judged greater than B, he derived the desired distances $(a\text{-}b)$ of the stimuli on a psychological continuum as follows.

He assumed that repeated presentations of the same physical stimulus result in a normal distribution of subjective values, which he called "discriminal processes." The mean of such a normal distribution is defined as the subjective stimulus value sought for. Figure 2.1 shows two such distributions, corresponding to two physical stimuli, A and B, which vary on a single dimension, for example, stimulus frequency (Hz.). The question is, how to derive the subjective values a and b, the means of the respective distributions? Thurstone suggests presenting pairs of stimuli, such as A and B, repeatedly to a subject. The subject indicates which one in a pair is the greater (louder, brighter, etc.). In the example in Fig. 2.1, the subject says in the frst trial "$A>B$" (because $a_1>b_1$), and "$B>A$" in the second trial ($b_2>a_2$). It is evident that the probability p_{ab} of judgments "$A>B$" is a function of the distance $(a\text{-}b)$. For instance, if $(a\text{-}b) = 0$, then $p_{ab} = p_{ba} = .5$, and if $(b\text{-}a)>0$ (as in Fig. 2.1), then $p_{ab}<.5$.

Assuming equal variances in all distributions and independence of the subjective values elicited in a particular trial, the exact function is:

$$p_{ab} = N\,(a\text{-}b) \qquad (2.4)$$

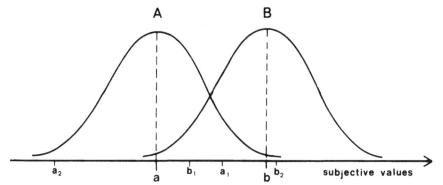

FIGURE 2.1. Illustration of Thurstone's law of comparative judgment. A and B are physical stimuli; a_1 and b_1 are examples of subjective (or discriminal) values on a psychological continuum corresponding to A and B on trial 1, a_2 and b_2 are examples for subjective values evoked at trial 2. The mean of all values a_1 and $a_2, \ldots,$ in repeated presentations of A is defined as the subjective value a of the stimulus A.

where N is the cumulative normal distribution function. Equation (2.4) is known as the "law of comparative judgment" and is called Case V thereof (because of the above assumption concerning variances and independence).

The important point is that the metaphors of "statistical inference" or "decision" are nonexistent in Thurstone's writings. Although there is a decision rule involved in his model, he apparently did not deem it worth mentioning (except in Thurstone, 1927a, p. 381). The decision rule involved is: Judge that stimulus as the larger which has the greater discriminal value on the psychological continuum. Thurstone spent much time discussing all other assumptions and the relationship of his law to Fechner's and Weber's, but there is virtually no discussion of the decision rule. Consequently, the idea that rules of inference or decision might be experimentally manipulated (as in signal detection theory), instead of being fixed, was still unthinkable. Thurstone and many of his followers, who generalized his theory to absolute identification and category judgments, failed to see this (Luce, 1977a). Only after the inference revolution was it realized that models such as Thurstone's could be interpreted in terms of statistical decision making.

Finally, it might be interesting to ask about the nature of Thurstone's discriminal variability and Solomons' fluctuations in brain activity, or irritability. Solomons' interpretation seems to be epistemic, attributing fluctuations to insufficient knowledge. He stated that if "we know more about the factors which make up irritability, . . . the law of chance will no longer hold . . . , and we have a constant error" (Solomons, 1900, p. 238). He even believed that by rhythmical accent we might gain control over

38   2. DETECTION AND DISCRIMINATION

irritability and make the brain vary synchronously. What did Thurstone think about the nature of his discriminal distributions? Thurstone (1927a) states at the outset that he is not now interested in the nature of "the process by which an organism differentiates between two stimuli" (p. 368) (he never became so) and that he will not even make an assumption about whether his discriminal processes are psychological or physiological. Thurstone's interpretation may be seen as pragmatic, rather than epistemic or ontic, and centered on application. For instance, he soon left psychophysical theory and applied his law to the measurement of attitudes and values; he was prepared to reconsider anything as "discriminal error," from intraindividual to interindividual variability (Gigerenzer, 1983a).

Against Probability

Stanley S. Stevens (1906–1973), who has been called "without question the most powerful voice in psychophysics since G. T. Fechner" (Galanter, 1974, p. 1) established new, "direct" methods of scaling sensations, notably the method of magnitude estimation. He simply asked subjects directly to report numbers in proportion to the subjective sensation arising from signals and then averaged these numbers over subjects. The resulting value was considered the psychological magnitude of the signal. Such psychological magnitudes, or "internal scalable magnitudes" have been discussed from a historical perspective by Murray (1987). Using these methods, Stevens found that in general the function relating physical magnitude to psychological magnitude was not logarithmic, as Fechner had suggested, but instead followed Plateau's power function. He also distinguished between two kinds of sensory continuum; a "prothetic" kind, in which such variables as brightness, loudness, or other measures of "how much" were subsumed; and a "metathetic" kind, in which such variables as hue, pitch, or other measures of "what kind" and "when" were included. Scales on the two kinds of dimension differed in a number of ways (Stevens, 1957, pp. 154–161).

Stevens argued (a) that a psychological magnitude scale that did not reflect a power transformation of the stimulus magnitude scale was probably erroneous, and (b) that measures of the subjective size of the "just noticeable difference" behaved differently for prothetic than for metathetic continua. For metathetic continua, the subjective size of the j.n.d. at different points on the metathetic scale could remain relatively constant; but on a prothetic continuum, such as weight, the subjective size of the j.n.d. at a low level of intensity would be smaller than the subjective size of a j.n.d. at a high level of intensity. That is, any measure of the subjective size of a j.n.d., *including a discriminal dispersion,* would

HISTORY: BEFORE THE INFERENCE REVOLUTION   **39**

increase systematically with stimulus magnitude—an intensity 100 j.n.d.s above threshold would psychologically appear to be *more* than twice as intense as an intensity of 50 j.n.d.s above threshold. So the first objection to Thurstone's argument was that the assumptions of Case V of the "law of comparative judgment," equal dispersions in particular, were unwarranted. Stevens claimed that the 14 scales he had derived from magnitude estimation could not have been derived from any method of paired comparisons, because in his view "equally often noticed differences" did not imply equal sense-distances. Hence, Thurstone's Case V and related methods were not strictly applicable to the study of prothetic continua. It should be noted that Stevens (1966) claimed that had Thurstone conceived of a case VI in which σ increased proportionally with intensity, he might have arrived at a power function relating sensation magnitude to intensity.

Stevens dominated psychophysics from the late 1930s to about 1960. Under his influence, Thurstone's probabilistic law was largely forgotten, both as a theory of how one stimulus is detected as greater than another and as a yardstick for measurement. However, it was not only in this case that Stevens reacted against probabilistic ideas. For instance, in the first chapter of his *Handbook of Experimental Psychology*, entitled "Mathematics, Measurement and Psychophysics" (Stevens, 1951), he included a separate section headed "Probability" (pp. 44–47). This section seems to serve only one purpose, namely, to warn the reader of all the confusion that may result from the application of probability theory to *anything*. Psychophysics is not dealt with here; moreover, all connections between psychophysics and probability are carefully avoided. Rather, the reader is repeatedly informed that "nobody has the slightest notion what [probability] means" (a quotation from Bertrand Russell), and that we must separate probability theory from the nature of empirical events. For instance, the following story about the Casino of Monte Carlo is meant to destroy the idea that probability theory gives us a picture of reality, albeit only of roulette wheels. "We are told that an English engineer patiently tabulated thousands of winning numbers for a particular wheel, and then alarmed the management by running up a long series of wins. In desperation the Casino spoiled his game by interchanging the parts from one wheel to another. This interchange is still a daily precaution" (p. 45). Stevens' warnings center on the idea that a probabilistic model can be neither proved nor disproved with certainty: ". . . for no *finite* set of data can we ever be quite sure either that the model fits or that it does not" (p. 47). He is deeply suspicious of probabilistic models on the grounds that they can never be definitively proven: he admits that this is a problem for all scientific theories, but singles out probabilistic models as especially

40   2. DETECTION AND DISCRIMINATION

treacherous. Needless to say, he also rejected inferential statistics as a methodological instrument.

Stevens antiprobabilistic attitude may have been influenced by that of his teacher, Edwin G. Boring. Boring believed in determinism (e.g. Boring, 1963) and wrote the history of psychology around the deterministic forces of *Zeitgeister* and *Ortsgeister,* as opposed to the uncalculable and arbitrary influences of "Great Men." For instance, he managed not even to mention Thurstone's probabilistic law (Thurstone, 1927a, b, c, d) in his major accounts of the history of experimental psychology (Boring 1942, 1957) and of the history of measurement in psychology (Boring, 1961). Boring's *Zeitgeist* identified progress with Stevens.

Why Didn't Thurstone Detect Signal Detection Theory?

It may seem as if Thurstone had all the elements of signal detection theory: two overlapping normal distributions of "discriminal values" as the internal representation of two signals, the likelihoods of the discriminal values, and even a decision rule, albeit hardly mentioned. So it appeared to later writers like R. Duncan Luce (1977a), who puzzled over why Thurstone and his followers did not take the next step and introduce the tradeoff of errors and with that the idea of a variable decision criterion. The tradeoff of errors, in Neyman and Pearson's theory, is the balance of Type I and Type II error and leads to the receiver operator characteristic (ROC) in signal detection theory (see "The Emergence of the Statistical Metaphor," this chapter). But Thurstone did not take this step. Luce wonders whether Thurstone was at least aware of this:

> Was Thurstone aware of the ROC tradeoff? He neither discussed it explicitly nor emphasized its importance. But he did write: 'The writer has found experimentally that the normal probability curve was not applicable for certain stimuli. In most of the experiments the distributions are reasonably close to normal,' (Thurstone, 1927a, p. 373). How did he draw these conclusions? He did not say. Is it possible that he generated ROC data and plotted it in z-scores, as we do today? I find it difficult to understand the quote otherwise; but I also find it remarkable that he failed to write about it. (Luce, 1977a, p. 464)

But these are questions that can only be posed with the benefit of hindsight, after a new metaphor has reorganized old elements and given them a different pattern of emphasis. It seems hard for Luce to believe that Thurstone did not think about cognitive processes in terms of the error tradeoffs that a statistician considers when making inferences involving two hypotheses. Luce even stretches the metaphor of a "decision" rule so far as to reconsider Stevens' direct scaling methods as

HISTORY: BEFORE THE INFERENCE REVOLUTION   **41**

invoking "the following simple decision rule: respond with a number proportional to the value of the internal representation of the signal" (Luce, 1977a, p. 464).

The decision rule that was simply incidental for Thurstone became paramount for signal detection theorists in the wake of the inference revolution. Thurstone may well have given this element of his theory short shrift because of the then subjective connotations of "decision," suggesting a homunculus within the brain that actually does the deciding. Although Thurstone abandoned the fixed threshold approach, he still sought an account of object recognition as an automatic process, and the common understanding of "decision" at that time would not have been compatible with such a process. However, after the inference revolution had made the role of statistical inference and decision central among psychologists, it became possible to rearrange the elements of Thurstone's theory in a way undreamt of by Thurstone himself, with the new focus being on the element of statistical decision. Luce's recasting of Steven's direct scaling method in terms of a "decision" rule illustrates how greatly the domain of the decision metaphor has expanded, to the point where it is hard to understand how earlier theories did not use the concept.

Summary

The question whether or not an object, or a difference between two, can be detected was answered in the 19th century by pointing to the existence of fixed thresholds. These were measured in physical units, and their relationship to stimulus intensity was expressed by Weber's law. The measurements showed, however, considerable variability rather than a stable value for the size of a threshold. As a consequence, thresholds had to be defined by specifying arbitrarily a certain relative frequency of detections (often 75%).

Probably provoked by the existence of this variability, a second explanatory concept was introduced as early as the 19th century: the idea that object detection is a function of an internal level of brain activity. The assumption that such brain activity might fluctuate gave rise to the view, first, that brain variability might be an alternative explanation to thresholds, and later, with Thurstone, that "discriminal" variability is the better concept. Thurstone's probabilistic theory had a structure similar to signal detection theory but was not given any interpretation in terms of the metaphor of the "intuitive statistician". Even the "decision rule," to use the post-inference revolution term, although present in Thurstone's law, is hardly mentioned by Thurstone himself. The metaphorical use of conscious processes like statistical inference and decision for unconscious processes was not the practice at the time, and thus Thurstone

42   2. DETECTION AND DISCRIMINATION

could hardly see the possible extension of his theory, which seems so obvious with hindsight. Thus, both the "fixed threshold" explanation and the "discriminal variability" explanation viewed the detection process as a passive response of the organism either to external stimulus differences or internal variabilities; the active metaphors of "inference", "selection of a decision criterion" and "analyses of utilities" were still invisible. The final blow to Thurstone's idea was delivered by Stevens, whose antiprobabilistic attitude dominated the field for decades.

THE EMERGENCE OF THE STATISTICAL METAPHOR: SIGNAL DETECTION THEORY

In the mid-1950s, the Neyman and Pearson theory of statistical hypotheses testing was reconsidered as a theory of detection and discrimination. The new look was called a theory of signal detectability (TSD), or, more briefly, signal detection theory (Tanner & Swets, 1954). The theory originated in the context of engineering problems concerned with the performance of ideal sensing devices in such tasks as detecting a signal on a radar screen; this engineering context has left its traces in terms such as "signal" and "noise." Tanner and his coworkers brought this analogy between statistical hypothesis testing and ideal sensing devices into psychology and changed it into an analogy between statistical hypotheses testing and the way the mind works: "It is our thesis that this conception of the detection process may apply to the human observer as well." (Swets, Tanner & Birdsall, 1964, p. 6). Or, again: "His task is, in fact, the task of testing a statistical hypothesis" (Tanner & Swets, 1954, p. 403)

The Mind as a Neyman and Pearsonian Statistician

Figure 2.2 shows the isomorphism between the Neyman and Pearson theory and signal detection theory. Neyman and Pearson distinguished two hypotheses, H_0 and H_1, and the two corresponding distributions of some sample statistic, such as the mean. Recall that for Neyman and Pearson an inference from data to hypotheses involved *decision making* (see chapter 1). The experimenter sets a decision criterion on the basis of knowledge that lies outside statistical theory, such as the respective costs of Type I and Type II errors. If a sample statistic falls to the right of the criterion, the experimenter acts as if H_1 were true (H_0 is rejected) and vice versa.

This theory of hypothesis testing is reinterpreted in a straightforward way as a theory of how the mind detects a weak "signal" against a background of "noise." The distribution of a sample statistic given H_0 is

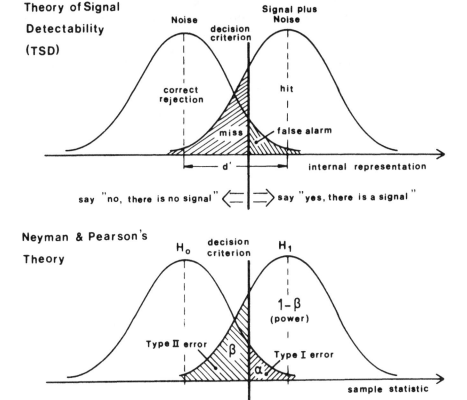

FIGURE 2.2. The isomorphism between the Neyman and Pearson theory of statistical hypotheses testing and signal detection theory.

reconsidered as a distribution of internal representations given noise only, in the absence of a signal. Similarly, the sampling distribution given H_1 is reconsidered as a distribution of internal representations given a signal plus noise. Like Thurstone, Swets, Tanner and Birdsall (1964) assert that there is no need to clarify the nature of the internal representation, but they suggest that it might be helpful to think about it as "some measure of neural activity, perhaps as the number of impulses arriving at a given point in the cortex within a given time" (p. 7). Thus far, the model is formally equivalent to Thurstone's: there are two overlapping distributions, and there is the assumption that these distributions are normal, which allows for determining the likelihood of the internal representations given either noise or signal plus noise.

The Gestalt switch comes with the metaphorical language of statistical

44 2. DETECTION AND DISCRIMINATION

hypotheses testing: The mind makes inferences from data to hypotheses, as the scientist does. Therefore, "noise" and "signal plus noise" are now seen as hypotheses rather than as mere "stimuli," and the internal representation is seen as the *data* or *observation*. Since inference from data to hypotheses involves a decision criterion, the mind uses a decision criterion, too. As in Neyman and Pearson's theory, the selection of such a criterion is dependent on the relative costs of the possible errors and on knowledge about the prior probabilities of "noise" and "signal plus noise." If an internal representation falls to the left side of the criterion, that is, if it is smaller than the criterion value, then the human observer says "No, there is no signal," just as the experimenter rejects H_1 and acts as if H_0 were true. If the internal representation exceeds the criterion, the observer says "Yes, there is a signal."

To complete the analogy: The Type I error, whose probability is alpha, is now called *false alarm*, which means wrongly rejecting the noise hypothesis. The Type II error, whose probability is beta, is now called *miss*, which means wrongly rejecting the signal plus noise hypothesis. The power of the test—the probability that H_1 is accepted if it is true—is called the *hit* rate, that is, the probability that a signal is detected if there is one. The proper rejection of H_1 is called *correct rejection* of the signal plus noise hypothesis. Finally, the difference between the means of the two distributions is called d', which measures the strength of the signal. (Tanner and Swets (1954) used the symbol d' rather than d for the difference because Peterson and Birdsall (1953) had already used d to denote the square of d'). Note that the false alarm rate is assumed to vary with the hit rate (d' constant), just as the probability of a Type I error varies with the power.

In further analogy to Neyman and Pearson, who spoke of "optimal tests," signal detection theory considers the observer who behaves according to the theory as an "optimal observer." "Optimal" means that the probabilities of Type I and Type II errors (false alarms and misses) are minimized (on this, see Green & Swets, 1966, pp. 23–25). For instance, an observer would be nonoptimal if he sometimes said "Yes, there is a signal" and sometimes "No, there is no signal" if the internal representation exceeded the criterion.

What happens if the response of the visual or acoustic system (the internal representation) is not unidimensional, as in Fig. 2.2, but has many dimensions? This case can easily be incorporated into signal theory by using the language of *likelihood ratios*. In the unidimensional case, there exists a likelihood ratio for each internal representation or "data" x, which is the ratio of the probability density $f(x|N)$ that x occurs under noise (N) alone, to the probability density $f(x|SN)$ that x occurs under signal plus noise (SN). In Fig. 2.2, the first probability density, or likelihood, is the value of the ordinate of the noise distribution at point x,

THE EMERGENCE OF THE STATISTICAL METAPHOR   45

the second is the value of the ordinate of the signal plus noise distribution at the same point. The criterion can be expressed as a likelihood ratio too: in the example in Fig. 2.2 $f(x|N)$ is smaller than $f(x|SN)$, which means that the criterion corresponds to a likelihood ratio smaller than one. The process of object detection can now be rephrased as follows: The mind transforms an internal representation into a likelihood ratio and compares this with a second likelihood ratio, which corresponds to the decision criterion. Now, if the response of the sensory system has more than one dimension, we can represent this m-dimensional internal representation as a point x in m-dimensional space and use the same terminology. Since for each m-dimensional point x there exists a likelihood ratio $f(x|N)/f(x|SN)$, we can generalize easily to the multidimensional case if we consider the data as a likelihood ratio, the criterion as a likelihood ratio, and the decision axis as a likelihood ratio axis. Thus, the assumption of a unidimensional decision axis can be maintained independently of the dimensionality of the internal representations (Swets, Tanner & Birdsall, 1964).

In summary, the cognitive process of detecting a signal against a background of noise, formerly explained by the existence of a fixed threshold, is now seen as a "decision" between two normal distributions. One distribution, with a mean equal to zero, is associated with noise alone; the other, with a mean equal to d', is associated with signal plus noise. The mind makes the decision like a Neyman and Pearson statistician.[2]

The Conceptual Change

The mind's new look as a Neyman and Pearson statistician changed the understanding of the nature of the detection process and generated new questions and new data. It is interesting that the new metaphor was not the consequence of new data (facts such as variability had been known since Fechner), but rather the other way around.

There is more than sensory information involved in detection. This is what Swets, Tanner and Birdsall (1964) call the "main thrust" of their conception: "This separation of the factors that influence the observer's attitudes from those that influence his sensitivity is the major contribution of the psychophysical application of statistical decision theory" (p. 52). The independence of d', the measure of signal strength, from the decision criterion allows us to separate the measure of sensitivity (d') from nonsensory factors ("attitudes"), which are integrated into the decision criterion. Note that this distinction has its counterpart in Neyman and

---

[2]The analogy can also be drawn with respect to the extension of Neyman and Pearson's theory by Wald (1950); Swets, Tanner and Birdsall (1964, p. 3) themselves mention this.

46 2. DETECTION AND DISCRIMINATION

Pearson's distinction between the mathematical and the subjective part of their theory: Choosing a criterion depends on subjective, extramathematical considerations, to be distinguished from the formal part of the theory.

Although internal influences on object detection had been discussed earlier, the metaphor of decision opened the door to a broad range of "internal influences," such as cost–benefit analysis of false alarms and hits (which in turn depend on memory), or, more generally, attitudes toward making certain errors under specific circumstances. Thus, the study of object detection became linked with the study of a range of other cognitive processes. Seen from the new point of view, psychological theories before the inference revolution had confounded sensory and nonsensory factors in the "threshold" explanation.

A new question emerges: How to manipulate the decision criterion? With the new perspective, a major new question arose: What are the experimentally separable variables that cause changes in the decision criterion? For instance, experiments on visual and acoustic signal detection (see: Green & Swets 1966; Swets 1964) showed that humans can adjust their "threshold" (old concept) or "criterion" (new concept) in response to the experimenter's verbal instructions concerning the relative costs of misses and false alarms as well as to real monetary payoffs. Such experiments revealed the limits of the fixed threshold explanation.

New data emerges: Two Types of Error. Recall that in threshold measurements such as Fechner's method of right and wrong cases, a threshold was defined as that physical value corresponding to a fixed percentage of correct "greater" judgments. The data generated in the language of signal detection theory was the hit rate (the percentage of right cases, which determines the percentage of wrong cases, or the misses, since both sum up to 100%). Similarly, Thurstone generated data showing how frequently a stimulus a is judged greater than a stimulus b. This gave him the probabilities p_{ab}, which correspond again to percentage of hits. As far as we can see, the idea of generating both hits and false alarms as data or, equivalently, both types of errors, misses and false alarms, did not exist before the inference revolution. The consideration of these two types of errors, however, was the very subject of Neyman and Pearson's theory. And it became the new data of signal detection theory, generating new facts and hypotheses.

The Receiver Operating Characteristic

According to the distinction between sensory and nonsensory factors, the two major uses of signal detection theory are to measure the observer's sensitivity d', and to measure the decision criterion, as well as to identify

THE EMERGENCE OF THE STATISTICAL METAPHOR   47

the variables that influence the setting and change of the criterion. How can this be done? An outline of the procedure follows:

The experimental data is the hit rate and the false alarm rate of an observer, obtained in repeated presentation of either noise or signal plus noise and under various experimental conditions designed to influence the criterion and d'. If for simplicity we assume normal distributions with equal variances as in Fig. 2.2, then the theory predicts that the proportion of hits and false alarms depends only on the setting of the decision criterion and the sensitivity d'. For instance, if the decision criterion in Fig. 2.2 is moved to the left in order to decrease the number of misses (with d' constant), then the hit rate and the false alarm rate increase in a proportion that can be read off from Fig. 2.2. If we keep the criterion value constant but increase d' by introducing a stronger signal, this moves the "signal plus noise" distribution to the right, and increases the hit rate but not the false alarm rate.

Figure 2.3 illustrates these quantitative relationships between hit rate,

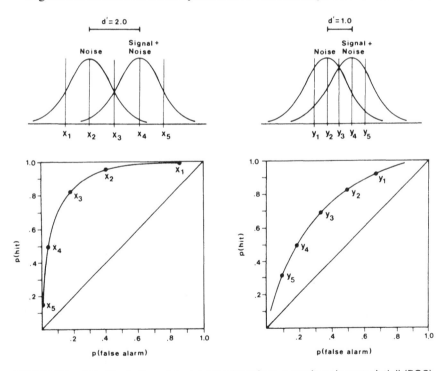

FIGURE 2.3. This illustration shows how a "receiver operating characteristic" (ROC) curve follows from a series of criterion settings. The ROC curve on the left follows if $d' = 2$, and that on the right if $d' = 1$ (assuming normal distributions with equal variances). A d' of 1 signifies that the distance between the means of the two distributions is one standard deviation of the noise distribution.

48   2. DETECTION AND DISCRIMINATION

false alarm rate, sensitivity d', and decision criterion. The probability of a hit is plotted against the probability of a false alarm, for each value of d' and each value of the criterion. (Note that d' is measured in units of the standard deviation of the noise distribution.) Each combination of a d' and a criterion value determines a point in the plot. If the decision criterion is moved from the far left to the far right, a sequence of points on a curve results; this curve is called the "receiver operating characteristic," or the ROC curve. In other words, an ROC curve is the family of all points corresponding to different locations of the criterion for a fixed d'. Different ROC curves, however, result from manipulating d' rather than the criterion: The smaller d' is, the closer the ROC curve is to the diagonal, as shown in Fig. 2.3. The diagonal itself is predicted if both distributions in Fig. 2.3 completely overlap, that is, if $d' = 0$. We can thus deduce hit and false alarm rates, or, ROC curves, from theoretical assumptions. In the experiment, we must go in the opposite direction: empirical ROC curves are used to estimate both d' and the criterion value. The value of d' can be calculated after the hit rate and false alarm rate are transformed into z-scores (for technical details, see Green & Swets, 1966, & McNicol, 1972), and in chapter 5 we give an example in which d' is calculated.[3]

Again, the empirical use of signal detection theory is closely related to the use of Neyman and Pearson's theory. As referred to in chapter 1, the latter specifies the relationship between the power desired (hit rate), the

---

[3]Strictly speaking, the term d' is limited to describing the distance between the means of two normal distributions, with equal variances, in units of the standard deviation of the noise distribution. An ROC curve based on z-scores should have a slope of one if the equal variance assumption holds. If the variance of the signal distribution is greater than that of the noise distribution, the slope of the ROC curve will be less than one. The variance of the signal is given by the reciprocal of the slope. It is common in this case to call the distance between the means "d_e" and to measure it as being twice the z-score associated with the point at which the negative diagonal intersects the ROC curve. In their pioneer paper, Tanner and Swets (1954) suggested that the equal variance assumption might not always hold, and Green and Swets (1966) suggest that it might be necessary for the signal variance to vary with the mean if their particular model of the observer as a detector of energies was to be consistent with Weber's Law. But experimental demonstrations that signal variance is a function of d_e are hard to find. Markowitz and Swets (1967) obtained relevant data from an absolute detection experiment in which the ROC curves were derived from confidence ratings. The slopes of the ROC curves decreased with signal contrast.

Measures of sensitivity other than d_e have also been studied. Tolhurst, Movshon, and Dean (1983) recorded impulses from single cells in the visual cortex of anesthetized cats and monkeys. They found that as signal contrast increased, so did the number of impulses recorded from the cells in question; at the same time, the variance of these responses also increased, and a plot of log variance against log mean number of impulses was linear. Note, however, that if magnitude estimations are made of stimuli varying in intensity, the coefficient of variation of the responses (the ratio of the standard deviation to the mean) can *decrease* with stimulus intensity (see Baird, Green, & Luce, 1980, Fig. 5).

level of significance (false alarm rate), the magnitude of effect (d'), and the number of subjects needed to achieve the desired power. (The number of subjects influences the variance of the distributions—the greater the number, the smaller the variance; for simplicity, we have not dealt with different variances in TSD). In both theories, the *same* mathematical relationship between these elements is used to estimate one or two of them given the others: The ROC curve is analogous to the function relating power, level of significance, effect size, and number of subjects. The difference is that in the Neyman and Pearson theory the decision criterion and the magnitude of effects is decided on subjectively by the experimenter, whereas these are experimentally searched for in signal detection theory. This difference illustrates the metaphorical use of the term "decision" in signal detection theory: Whereas for Neyman and Pearson the decision criterion is determined by a conscious act of informed judgment, the meaning of the decision criterion in signal detection is not linked with "consciousness," and the location of the criterion is not assumed to be accessible by introspection.

A final parallel is noteworthy. Recall that Neyman and Pearson's theory, in contrast to Fisher's, emphasizes a subjective element in addition to the mathematics: the experimenter decides upon a criterion on the basis of his subjective, but informed judgment. This personal element is mirrored by TSD studies, which analyze the *single* observer, his or her shifts in criterion and his or her sensitivity. The subjectivity of the experimenter becomes the subjectivity of the observer. With this, the 19th century practice of obtaining many responses from a few observers replaced Stevens' practice of obtaining a few responses from many observers. This change was a direct result of the subjective element in the new metaphor.

TANNER'S CONCEPTION OF THE MIND

In the early days of signal detection theory, a popular question was how the human observer compared with the optimal observer. The emphasis of Green and Swets' 1966 text was that the human might be an ideal detector of energies, at least in the case of audition. At about the same time, psychophysicists were beginning to consider how tasks as elementary as absolute threshold tasks or increment detection tasks might be influenced by memory. This question was also dealt with, at the very start of psychophysical inquiry, by Weber (1846/1978), who presented one after the other two lines slightly differing in length and asked subjects if the lines looked different. He found that accuracy decreased as the interval between the two lines became longer, a result that was confirmed by

2. DETECTION AND DISCRIMINATION

Hegelmaier (1852) in what might be considered one of the earliest experimental studies of memory. Tanner (1965) started with the same question of how the human observer might be influenced by memory in making judgments about auditory stimuli and was led by this inquiry to put forward an elaborate model, presented in stages of increasing complexity, in which the observer was treated as a tester of hypotheses about auditory data. It was assumed that the setting of the criterion could be influenced by memory as follows.

The model starts with an assertion of the fundamental cognitive process, as shown in Fig. 2.4. The sensory input is transduced into a form that will allow the brain to make estimates of the likelihood that a given experience arose from a signal event in the external world rather than from a noise event. In order for the brain to do this, a likelihood ratio must be computed and a criterion established that will allow the observer to respond. The criterion will be set by the observer's knowledge of the probabilities of signals and by the utilities, that is, by the costs of making "false alarms" and the payoffs of making the correct "yes" responses. The likelihood ratio computer operates on the information provided by the distribution computer, which in turn operates on the information provided about the physical properties of the noise and the signal-plus-noise.

This model does not yet deal with memory. But in any typical detection task the subject must take account of events in previous trials. If we refer

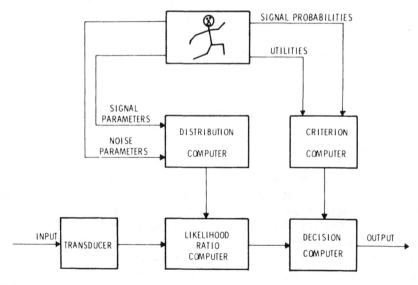

FIGURE 2.4. Tanner's representation of signal detection theory as a flow chart. From Tanner, 1965, p. 15. Reprinted by permission.

TANNER'S CONCEPTION OF THE MIND 51

to the problem of the ideal observer, an observer with imperfect memory will bring uncertainty into the interpretation of the data he is presented with. Tanner suggested that in a signal detection task concerning a tone, the observer in a yes–no detection task needs to have memories of at least five characteristics of the signal—amplitude, frequency, phase, starting time, and duration. With the signal superimposed on a segment of sinewave that matched the signal in frequency, phase, starting time and duration (a "pedestal"), memory for amplitude alone can be examined in the detection task. By varying the time between successive signal trials, it was possible to show how the efficiency of performance reached a peak at an interval of about 1 second and then declined over the course of the next 10 seconds.

Tanner believed, moreover, that much of our processing of sensory information is acquired. For example he found three "tone-deaf" individuals who, after intensive practice, acquired the ability to discriminate differences in frequencies of tones. Over the years a person acquires a way of coding those features of the environment which are "important to his well-being," and this led Tanner to an analysis of the code in which information from the transducer is weighted with respect to its significance, with insignificant information being discarded, and the distribution of the significant events are fed into a "decomposer" that separates out the factors in the distributions. These are then placed in "code storage" where they are used in the generation of hypotheses about events in the environment. In particular they will influence the "memory" component needed for the detection of signal events. This process is shown in Fig. 2.5.

Tanner carried out experiments on the development of a code for use in a detection task unlikely to have been encountered before in the observer's experience: an extremely brief auditory signal (one 10-millisecond pulse) was placed at one of four positions in time on a carrier tone lasting 100 milliseconds. The subject's task was to identify at which point the pulse occurred. At first d' was near zero, but it increased to about two after 20 days of extensive practice. The final version of the model, shown in Fig. 2.6, incorporated the effects of learning on the functions of the decomposer and on the decision computer. Tanner (1965) wrote:

> The block diagram is expanded to include the past experience storage and the storage of immediate prior knowledge. The . . . arrows, connected by dotted lines through some of the blocks, constitute an attempt to trace the processes through which the hypotheses to be tested are established. The "little man," in a manner which is not treated here, searches the storage for currently interesting hypotheses.
>
> When he has made his selection, he hands them to the block "immediate prior state of knowledge," which questions the code storage to determine

52   2. DETECTION AND DISCRIMINATION

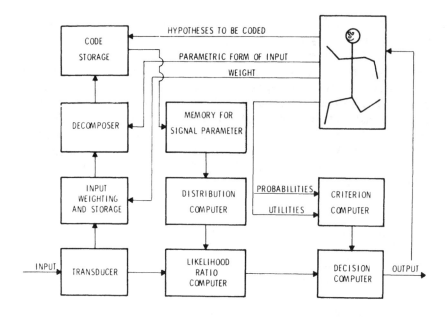

FIGURE 2.5. Tanner's elaboration of signal detection theory to include a memory for signal parameters. From Tanner, 1965, p. 36. Reprinted by permission.

how each of the hypotheses would be coded at the input. The coded form is then sent to the memory for signal parameters, and from there to the distribution computer and to immediate prior knowledge. The decision computer selects one of these hypotheses in its coded form, and the output is a description of the hypothesis accepted. (p. 45)

This model illustrates clearly the kind of conception of the mind that resulted from the metaphor of the mind as a Neyman and Pearson statistician. Tanner himself recognized the connection to the Neyman–Pearson theory of hypothesis testing and noted that an ideal observer has "often been called a Neyman–Pearson detector" (Tanner, 1965, p. 66). There are many competing flow-charts proposing cognitive structures in the human processing system (see chapter 4), but Tanner's is the most complete we have found in which individual structures can be calculators as well as stores. Tanner's belief that sensory processing is acquired rather than innate is receiving some support from contemporary research on the plasticity of the nervous system. For example, Neville (1985) has reported evidence of activity in the visual areas of the brains of deaf persons that is not found in hearing persons, and Greenough (1985) has reported increased development of dendritic fields in the brains of animals exposed to enriched environments.

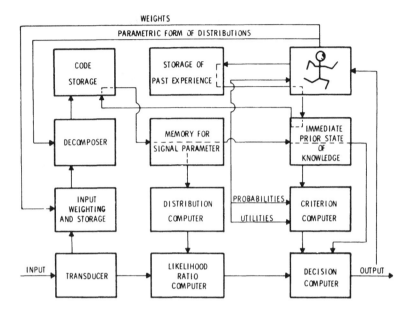

FIGURE 2.6. Tanner's full extension of signal detection theory. The extension includes both memory for computing the likelihoods and a store of long term past experience that influences the setting of the criterion. From Tanner, 1965, p. 44. Reprinted by permission.

Tanner believed that a model of this form could be derived from a system of education that encouraged the development of an appropriate code storage, the development of a store of hypotheses about the environment, and the establishment of a scale of values permitting decisions about society to be made.

BEYOND SIGNAL DETECTION THEORY: A METAPHOR CONQUERS THE MIND

Beginning with signal detection theory, the explanation of cognitive processes in terms of statistical inference was soon extended to other processes besides the detection of weak signals and the discrimination between two signals, and the resulting theories transcended the assumptions of TSD (e.g. Luce 1977a; Luce & Green 1972, 1974; McGill 1963, 1967; Swets, 1986). What remained invariant in these new developments was the portrayal of the mind, or brain, or central nervous system—whatever name was used—as a statistician who makes inferences from data to hypotheses. This new look provided new questions and gave new emphasis to old questions. We shall focus on three of these, and illustrate

54 2. DETECTION AND DISCRIMINATION

them with the neural timing theory of R. Duncan Luce and David M. Green.

What is the Internal Language of the Nervous System?

Luce and Green (1972) assume that a sense organ such as the ear is a *transducer,* as in Tanner's theory (see Fig. 2.4–2.6). A transducer transforms sensory signals, such as the intensity of an incoming fixed-frequency signal, into the internal language of the nervous system. This internal language is the "data" upon which a "decision" is based. Since the mind is portrayed as a statistician, the data must be numbers. But numbers of what?

As we have seen, Thurstone did not care about the nature of the internal language, and in TSD the internal representation was identified with likelihood ratios. Luce and Green put forward the following more elaborate theory. A transducer transforms the intensity of a signal into sequences of "neural" pulses in parallel nerve fibers. For instance, in the human ear, there exist about 30,000 such peripheral fibers. Only a subset of these fibers is activated by each signal. The question is, how does the central nervous system (CNS) infer the intensity of a signal from the activated fibers? Does it try to identify the signal by identifying the active subset of fibers, as postulated in so-called place theories? Luce and Green consider the pulse train in the individual fiber rather than the localization of a subset of fibers as the data basis. In fact, Rose, Brugge, Anderson and Hind (1967) have shown that both intensity and frequency information are encoded in the pulse train on a single fiber. But what are the numbers? Two major answers have been proposed. First, *counting models* (e.g. McGill, 1967; Siebert, 1970) assume that the data is the number of pulses counted in a fixed period of time. Second, *timing models,* such as that of Luce and Green (1972), assume that the data is the time required to complete a fixed count, in other words, the *interarrival time,* which is the time between successive pulses. The number of successive interarrival times "measured" by the CNS may depend on the times available; Luce and Green assume that when signals are both faint and brief or the observer is under strong time pressure, only a single interarrival time is measured for each fiber. The difference between counting and timing can be illustrated by the example of estimating the heart rate. Either the number of beats within, say, 60 seconds is counted, or the time between two successive beats is measured. The first estimate is more stable, less sensitive to brief flucuations, but more time consuming. The interesting point is that the two types of data lead to different predictions for ROC curves. From such experiments, Luce (1977) concluded that well-trained observers switch from timing to counting. Timing seems to be the natural

BEYOND SIGNAL DETECTION THEORY   55

process whereas brief signals of fixed duration, such as occur in typical psychophysical experiments, appear to cause a shift to counting.

Of course, the question of whether the CNS uses counting or timing or is "bilingual" has not been settled. The point we wish to make here is that the metaphor of the mind as a statistician has set the fundamental assumptions: The internal representation of a signal is numerical and is a random variable, suitable for subsequent statistical analysis by the mind, just as in TSD.

What is the Shape of the Distribution?

Whereas in TSD the distribution of "observations," or internal representations, was usually assumed to be normal, Poisson distributions have become increasingly popular in both counting models (e.g. McGill, 1963, 1967) and timing models (e.g. Luce and Green, 1972). In most cases, however, the choice is made because a distribution is mathematically tractable, not for experimental and theoretical reasons. A notable exception is Luce (1977a), who deduces different distributions from different assumptions about how the central nervous system (CNS) functions. In Luce's theory, the CSN is seen as a statistician who draws random samples, estimates parameters, aggregates data, and uses a decision criterion (see Fig. 2.7). After the transducer has transformed the intensity of a signal into neural pulse trains, the CSN draws a random sample of all activated fibers. The size of the sample is assumed to depend on whether or not the signal activates fibers to which the CNS is "attending." From each fiber in this sample, the CNS estimates the pulse rate by either counting or timing, for instance, by measuring the interarrival time between two successive pulses. These numbers are then aggregated into a single internal representation of the signal intensity. The question is, how does the CNS aggregate the numbers? From the answer to this question one can deduce the shape of the distribution of the resulting aggregated estimates. These aggregated estimates correspond to the internal representations or "observations" in TSD, and to Thurstone's "discriminal values."

If the CNS *averages* the values from the individual fibers, and if these are of comparable magnitude, then it follows from the Central Limit Theorem that the resulting estimates is approximately normally distributed. If the CNS, however, takes the most extreme "observation," the *maximum*, then the resulting distribution is not normal, but rather is approximately a double exponential distribution. Both kinds of aggregation can be seen as physiologically meaningful under different conditions and have been discussed in the context of choice behavior (McFadden,

56 2. DETECTION AND DISCRIMINATION

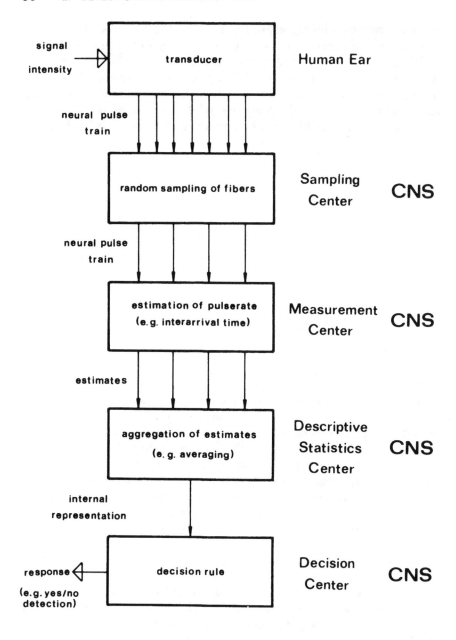

FIGURE 2.7. Representation of Luce's (1977) view of the central nervous system (CNS) as a statistician.

1974; Yellott, 1977). Since the shape of the distributions influences the hit and false alarm rates, as can be seen from Fig. 2.2, different distributions lead to different predicted ROC curves.[4] From such experiments, Luce (1977a) concludes that for auditory intensity Thurstone's choice of the normal distribution was correct, although not well justified at that time. Of course, the basic problem with such studies is to infer from observed differences in ROC curves whether a change in the shape of the distribution, in the variance, in the criterion, in d', or in some or all of these can be considered as the explanation for the differences.

The Nature of the Decision Process

These sketches of the theories of Luce (1977a) and Luce and Green (1972) illustrate the development following the early years of signal detection theory: Specific assumptions have been questioned, changed, and added (e.g. Massaro, 1969; Parducci & Sandusky, 1970; Thomas & Legge, 1970), but the new perspective of cognitive processes as statistical calculations has endured and indeed been consolidated. The new language was now considered indispensable for understanding detection, discrimination, and other processes, just as the techniques of inferential statistics were considered indispensable for the experimenter's inference from data to hypotheses.

We have already shown that the new perspective generated new questions. The new terminology is more than merely a change in language, as is demonstrated by the expression that the brain "decides" (between two hypotheses). For instance, in Luce and Green's theory, the "decision process" is assumed *to take time*. The experimentally obtained reaction time is assumed to be composed of a "decision time," in addition to the time that nervous activity and muscle activity need (Luce & Green, 1972):

> The third major component of the theory is the sum of all times taken to complete the response excluding the time absorbed by the decision process.

---

[4]Laming (1985) has attempted to specify the distributions underlying visual sensory analysis. He suggested that a visual stimulus was a Poisson distribution whose density varied with its luminance. At the level of retinal receptors, it was postulated that excitatory and inhibitory interactions took place, and that noise was added, so that the input to the retinal ganglion cells was a sample of Gaussian noise. Green and Swets (1966, ch. 6) had shown that the energy in such a distribution was distributed as chi-square, and Laming argued that from such a distribution one could predict ROC curves for both differential detection and increment detection tasks. These ROC curves differed between the tasks, being symmetric for the former, where a same–different judgment is made on two stimuli presented separately from each other, and asymmetric for the latter, where the subject must detect an increment added to the stimulus. Egan (1975) describes the shapes of ROC curves predicted by different kinds of distribution of noise and signal.

58   2. DETECTION AND DISCRIMINATION

> This includes, at least, the times (a) needed to transduce the energy into pulses, (b) required for a pulse to travel from the transducer to wherever decisions are made, (c) taken in travel from there to the locus of the response, and (d) needed for the muscles to act. . . . The sum of all these nondecision times we call the residual latency. (p. 19)

The "decision mechanisms of the brain" (p. 19) are put side by side with afferent and efferent neural pulse trains and muscle actions: they all absorb time and are, in this sense, all equally "real." The unconscious "decision" of the brain is assumed to take time just as a conscious decision takes time.

SUMMARY

In this chapter we traced the transformation of the scientific understanding of a fundamental perceptual process: how an object or a difference between two objects is detected. The traditional explanation posited the existence of fixed thresholds, although by the turn of the century this view had been challenged by the concept of "brain variability", a challenge that culminated in Thurstone's theory.

The Birth of a Metaphor

The major shift occurred around 1955, with signal detection theory (TSD). The nature of the detection process was reinterpreted as a statistical inference from data to hypotheses, and the mind as a statistician of the Neyman and Pearson school. We have shown that the metaphor of "inference" and "decision" were not parts of psychological theories before the inference revolution, despite a formal theory similar to TSD (Thurstone's). Only after the inference revolution, when inferential statistics finally was considered an indispensable instrument and had to some extent mechanized inductive reasoning and decision, did it become possible to reconsider the instruments as a theory of how the mind works. We see this transition as an instance of our *tools-to-theories hypothesis,* which says that successful instruments such as statistics are prone to become metaphors of the mind. Besides the temporal sequence, our thesis is supported by the isomorphism between the Neyman and Pearson theory and signal detection theory, and by the interesting fact that Thurstone's similar formal theory had existed since 1927 yet neither Thurstone nor his followers were able to make the small step (small, that is, with hindsight) toward signal detection theory. The new theory of object decision was not developed by a step-by-step process from older theories, but by the sudden emergence of a metaphor from a quite different field.

Our thesis emphasizes that the birth of the new metaphor *was not motivated by new facts*, which lead to the rejection of an old theory and shaped the new theory. Variability in detection and discrimination might be considered such a fact, but we have shown that this had been known since Fechner. Rather, it was the birth of the metaphor that *gave rise to new facts*. Our thesis also points out that theory development was *discontinuous*. Thurstone's theory was not developed in the direction of TSD; it was only the emergence of a new metaphor that suddenly changed theory construction. Only with hindsight can we see the formal parallel and the short "distance" between the 1927 theory of Thurstone and the post-inference revolution theory of signal detectability.

The Conceptual Shift

The effect of a new metaphor went far beyond a simple change in language; it generated new questions, a new kind of experiment, new data, new answers to old questions, and a new conception of the mind.

New Questions. The new analogy between detection processes and the Neyman and Pearson theory separated nonsensory processes (the decision criterion) from sensory processes (the sensitivity d'). The subjective part in Neyman and Pearson's theory became the subjective, nonsensory process in TSD, depending on the attitudes and cost–benefit considerations of the observer. Thus, besides the measurement of sensitivity, a new question emerged: How could the decision criterion be manipulated? This, in turn, gave rise to a new kind of experiment, for instance, combining detection tasks with monetary payoffs.

New Data. The emphasis in Neyman and Pearson's theory on the analysis of both kinds of errors, Type I and Type II (as opposed to Fisher's theory), was transplanted into TSD. The new data generated were the corresponding types of detection errors, false alarms and misses. In contrast, the data generated before the inference revolution included only one kind of error, numbers of "correct" or "not correct" responses, as in the method of average error in psychophysics or in recall tasks in memory research.

Revision of the Threshold Concept. The assumption of a single, fixed threshold was rejected or at least had to be revised: First, the threshold concept is a confusion of two independent processes: sensory (d') and nonsensory processes (criterion) (Swets, 1964). Second, there exist no fixed thresholds because of the intervention of nonsensory processes that can be manipulated experimentally. Third, there exist no fixed thresholds in the sense that detection processes are subject to changes imposed by

60   2. DETECTION AND DISCRIMINATION

learning. This is not to say that all theorists in the TSD tradition completely abandoned the notion of a threshold. It is still believed that levels of intensity exist that never evoke a response; for these levels d' is always zero (Gescheider, Wright, Weber, & Barton, 1971). Such an "energy threshold" (Krantz, 1969) is, however, no longer considered as a sufficient explanation for object detection, and supplementary kinds of "threshold" have also been postulated.[5]

Learning to Detect. The shift to a learning perspective was hinted at in our discussion of Tanner's conception of the mind. He assumes that the processing of sensory information is plastic and flexible and that even such elementary processes as the detection of a signal could be subject to changes imposed by learning. This shift from a static model of a passive recipient with fixed thresholds to a dynamic model of an active percipient with constantly changing criteria for responding allows for a Darwinian view of the mind as continuously adapting to a changing environment. Such a view was common to the late Victorian associationists, among them Bain, Spencer, and Romanes, and was elaborated by William James (1890/1950). The postinference revolution version differs from the Victorian version by the addition of hypotheses testing techniques as filtering devices, which allow certain responses to take precedence over others. The older view, which persisted throughout the period of behaviorism, was that response competition determined which response would finally "win out" in a conflict situation.

Cognition as Intuitive Statistics. After the inference revolution, cognitive processes came to be understood as statistics. In the case of detection and discrimination, the mind was now pictured as a statistician of the Neyman and Pearson school. The processes of "inference," "decision," and "hypotheses testing" were freed from their conscious connections and seen as unconscious mechanisms of the brain. Thus, uncertainty, in the sense of uncertain inferences and decisions, became an essential feature of cognitive processes, and computation of distributions and likelihoods, random sampling and power analysis became the mind's way of coping with this uncertainty.

---

[5]If a stimulus is strong enough to exceed the energy threshold and cause activity in the nervous system, it still might not be strong enough to elicit detection responses consistently: perhaps there is a threshold inside the observer such that a signal has to exceed yet another level before being reliably detected. There was a sophisticated discussion of such 'observer thresholds' in the 1960s, with Luce (1963) and Krantz (1969) showing that the actual data obtained in absolute detection tasks could be almost as well fitted by ROC curves derived from observer thresholds theory as by ROC curves derived from the signal detection model shown in Fig. 2.3.

3 Perception: From Unconscious Inference to Hypothesis Testing

In the preceding chapter we showed the impact of the statistical metaphor on the scientific explanation of the nature of the detection process. The present chapter addresses a more complex cognitive process, the process by which our perceptual system finds out "What is there?" rather than "Is there anything (different)?", the latter being the detection (discrimination) problem. Thus, the present question is, how does the perceptual system classify an object or estimate properties of the object such as its position and size, after having detected it? Classifying and estimating properties of objects, which we summarize under the heading "perception," may result in a nominal classification—the object is a face—or in an ordinal or quantitative estimate of one or more of its properties—the object is behind the tree, or it is about 150 cm long.

In this context the inference metaphor is nothing new. Roughly 100 years before the inference revolution, the inference metaphor had already been introduced to explain the mechanism of object perception, in the guise of Hermann von Helmholtz's notion (1856–66/1962) of "unconscious inferences." Neo-Helmholtzians such as R. L. Gregory (1980) complain that Helmholtz's lead was not followed for a century or more. Instead the focus was on physiological theories and on Gestalt theory, which Gregory calls the "Dark Age." However, it is only partly true that unconscious inferences were neglected for almost an entire century. Between 1930 and 1950, Egon Brunswik transformed the meaning of Helmholtz' unconscious inferences into unconscious multiple regression statistics. Brunswik's conception, however, was rejected by the community of experimental psychologists at the time. Brunswik's "intuitive

62   3. PERCEPTION

statistician" was in part rejected because his contemporaries could not yet understand the link between the perceptual system and a statistician. This first model of the "intuitive statistician" had no future, armed as it was only with old-fashioned tools, namely, Karl Pearson's correlational statistics. It did not have the new hypotheses testing statistics of the rising inference revolution. Given the failure of Brunswik's challenging view, Gregory is right in claiming that the inference metaphor did not reenter perceptual theory until the 1960s. Brunswik's case is of interest not only because he coined the present-day term "intuitive statistician," but also because it is an excellent example of how difficult it was to grasp the power of the analogy between the mind and a statistician before the inference revolution. In this sense, Brunswik's case is as instructive as Thurstone's case (see chapter 2), and we shall therefore devote special attention to it. Thurstone and Brunswik are both important for our *tools-to-theories hypothesis,* for both show that the analogy between the mind and the statistician was either not seen before the inference revolution, or, if it was, as in Brunswik's unique case, it was not understood and was rejected by his contemporaries. Not until the inference revolution had run its course could psychologists see the mind as an intuitive statistician, one that reasoned as the psychologists themselves now did.

Therefore we shall concentrate in this first, historical, section on Helmholtz's unconscious inferences and Brunswik's transformation of them, and exclude other theories that do not use the inference metaphor. Using three case studies, we shall try to represent the situation after the inference revolution and the cognitive revolution, when perception reentered American psychology as a major topic. We have selected one major contemporary representative for each of the three classical views of perception and knowledge: The naive realistic view ("We see what is there"), the inductive view ("We infer what is there"), and the deductive view ("We compute what is there"). The three case studies are James J. Gibson's view of perception as direct pickup of information, R. L. Gregory's view of perception as hypotheses testing, and Norman H. Anderson's view of perception as cognitive algebra. In these three case studies, we argue that the inference revolution not only gave the inductive view a new conceptual language, but also strongly influenced the deductive view. The naive realistic view, however, still resisted the metaphor.

HISTORY: BEFORE THE INFERENCE REVOLUTION

Unconscious Inference

I can recall when I was a boy going past the garrison chapel in Potsdam, where some people were standing in the belfry. I mistook them for dolls and

HISTORY: BEFORE THE INFERENCE REVOLUTION 63

asked my mother to reach up and get them for me, which I thought she could do. The circumstances were impressed on my memory, because it was by this mistake that I learned to understand the law of foreshortening in perspective. (von Helmholtz, 1866, p. 283)

Thus Hermann von Helmholtz (1821-1894) described his boyhood interpretation of distance cues in Vol. III of his *Physiological Optics*. It was to him a very good example of the fact that one must *learn* to interpret sense data in an adaptive fashion. The sweep of his great work on vision results from not only its penetrating analysis of the physics and physiology of vision but also from his belief that psychology is relevant to the proper understanding of visual experience. Above all, Helmholtz was an empiricist. In contrast to his colleague Hering, who offered an "intuitionist" or "nativist" account of many phenomena, Helmholtz believed that the raw data of sensation were perpetually subject to judgments based on experience. It was only by experience that Helmholtz learned that distance makes large objects look smaller, and the main thrust of Vol. III of his work, which is largely about the perception of space as mediated by the two eyes, is that we bring to bear on the data presented by the eyes judgments that allow us to make inferences about the external world.

The term "unconscious inference" is a probabilistic syllogism, that is, a syllogism with a major premise that is not absolutely certain. Consider the following example:

Major premise: A stimulation of those nervous mechanisms whose terminals lie on the right-hand sides of the retinas of the two eyes is *nearly always* associated with a luminous object on my left.
Minor premise: The stimulation on the right side is present.
Conclusion: There is a luminous object located on my left.

The major premise is an inductive generalization from experience, such as that previously we have had to lift the hand toward the left to hide the light, or that we have had to move to the left to reach the object. The generalization has a degree of uncertainty, as indicated by the "nearly always," which is the source of illusions; for instance, the stimulation of the retina can also occur by mechanical pressure. A remarkable instance where a major premise suddenly becomes incorrect is the case of a person whose leg has been amputated. Although the major premise ("A stimulation of certain nerves is associated with that toe") no longer pertains, nevertheless long after the operation the patient might feel pain in specific toes, even though the toes are no longer there. This example of the "phantom limb" illustrates both that unconscious inferences or conclusions can explain illusions and also the impossibility of correcting the illusion in spite of our knowledge to the contrary.

64   3. PERCEPTION

These "inferences" posed something of a problem to Helmholtz. He was a great admirer of John Stuart Mill (1846) whose *Logic* he often quoted, and he believed that the conscious process one uses in making inductive inferences about the world had a parallel at a different cognitive level, where words were not required. In the first version of the *Optics* (1856–1866/1962) he called these unverbalized inductions "unconscious inferences" *(unbewusste Schlüsse);* later he was attacked because his critics thought that, by definition, an "inference" had to be the result of a conscious, verbal process. Moreover, Schopenhauer had used the words quite differently in a way from which Helmholtz wished to disassociate himself (see Schopenhauer, 1918/1966, pp. 135–136). Nevertheless, at the end of his life, in his Founder's Day address at the University of Berlin, Helmholtz (1879/1968) decided to stay with his original term because he believed that when we make an unconscious inference about what we perceive, it has the same spontaneity and impressiveness as a raw sensation itself, and furthermore is not open to introspective analysis.

Unconscious inferences were invoked by Helmholtz mainly to account for phenomena of depth and space perception. The rapid judgment of distance from the usual cues of perspective, shadowing, and overlapping, was for Helmholtz, as it had been for Berkeley, the result of an apperception or direct apprehension, with little conscious cognitive effort. More strikingly, many phenomena of binocular fusion and binocular rivalry, which at first might have been thought to be due to a built-in brain mechanism, were shown to be subject to change as a result of selective attention or the introduction of new characteristics such as contours. Helmholtz even parried Hering's (1868/1977) insistence that the two eyes worked by an innate linkage and argued that instead it is only as a result of experience that we normally perceive a fused and integrated world free from double images or fuzziness. Helmholtz also explained Lotze's (1852) "local signs" as being due to the incorporation of unconscious inference: if a sensation that results from a particular retinal point being stimulated is always associated with the presence of an object in a particular region of space, say, to the left, then by induction the observer learns that objects on the left stimulate that retinal point. Common visual illusions, such as the Müller-Lyer or Zöllner illusions, were ascribed to inferences being made on the basis of evidence that was usually reliable, but in these cases was unreliable because of the presence of countervailing tendencies in the pictures, such as "contrast" or "confluence." That unconscious inference does not always lead to a correct induction about the world was stressed by Helmholtz in his Founder's Day lecture (1879/1968):

> An expectation corresponds to the result of an *inductive conclusion* (Induktionsschluss). This expectation may deceive when it is based on an insuffi-

cient number of cases. Animals can also draw similar inductive conclusions, and as a matter of fact many more incorrect ones than is common with humans, as one can observe often enough by their behavior, e.g. when they shy back from some object which looks similar to another one on which they have burned themselves on an earlier occasion. (p. 255)

Helmholtz at this time admitted that in the early stages of an experience with inductions about sensations, one might be more aware of their occurrence than at later stages.

In summary, Helmholtz used inductive reasoning to explain perception. Neural processes go some of the way toward explaining perceptions and illusions, but they must be supplemented by "unconscious inferences" based on past experience. These "unconscious inferences" can be understood as a probabilistic syllogism in which the major premise is a generalization learned by experience, the minor premise is the neural stimulation, and the conclusion is the unconscious inference, or the percept. For many of his contemporaries, however, the notion of "unconscious inferences" seemed to be selfcontradictory.

From Unconscious Inference to Intuitive Statistics

In Helmholtz's empiricist associationism, what had been thought of as a conscious activity, inference, was introduced as a metaphor of perception. Of all the proponents of empiricist associationism, Egon Brunswik (1903-1955) followed the implications of the inference metaphor furthest and developed two original and radical research programs. These failed to attract a following at the time, although they anticipated major trends currently in vogue. Brunswik, whose system was described by Boring (1942) as a "modern equivalent" of the doctrine of unconscious inferences, was the first to draw explicitly the analogy between the perceptual system and a statistician. He transformed the meaning of unconscious inferences from probabilistic syllogisms to the calculation of correlations and multiple regressions. And this is the original meaning of the now popular metaphor of the mind as an "intuitive statistician," a phrase coined by Brunswik.

In this section we discuss the birth of that metaphor. We shall argue that the metaphor, as spelled out during Brunswik's second career, at Berkeley, was *not* a necessary consequence of the data that he obtained during his first career at Vienna. Rather, it was the new metaphor that generated new facts and questions, as in the case of signal detection theory. We shall show this by analyzing the facts and explanations of the Vienna Brunswik.

66 3. PERCEPTION

The Program of the Vienna Brunswik: Multidimensional Psychophysics

In his two academic careers, the first in Vienna and the second beginning in 1937 in Berkeley, Brunswik pursued two different research programs. The first, and less well known, was his *multidimensional psychophysics*, the better known and second program was his *probabilistic functionalism*. Both programs were original and revolutionary at the time, but neither became established. The Vienna program of multidimensional psychophysics ended prematurely with Brunswik's emigration to Berkeley in 1937 and Hitler's occupation of Austria in 1938, which forced Karl Bühler (his doctoral supervisor and head of the institute) and others into emigration and destroyed the impact of the approach of the Vienna Psychological Institute. Once in the United States, Brunswik gave up the Vienna program in favor of his probabilistic functionalism, which he understood as an attempt to reconcile "European academic with Anglo-American statistical tradition" (Brunswik, 1956, p. 58).

Facts

What are the facts generated by the program of multidimensional psychophysics? Let us consider one typical experiment that Brunswik conducted during a stay as a visiting professor at the University of Ankara, Turkey. The stimuli were coins varying in area, value, and number. For instance, the subject was shown a standard group of 2½-piaster coins (40 pieces, arranged in such a way that is it impossible to count them at first glance), and was asked to select a group of 25-piaster coins (which were larger) that matched the first group with respect to the joint area (or value, or number) of the coins. Results showed that perceived area increased with the value of the coins, for example, subjects would select a number of 25-piaster coins that was too small to match the standard group with respect to area. Similar results were obtained for judgments of value and number. None of these—area, value, or number—could be perceived independently of the others (Brunswik 1934, pp. 147ff.) The general conclusion was: The judgment of one property depends on other properties of the same object; even the perception of physical variables is strongly context dependent. In Brunswik's terms, what we see are *perceptual compromises*.

It is obvious that such findings and the concept of perceptual compromises disproved the fundamental assumption inherent in the one-dimensional psychophysics associated with Fechner and the Wundtian structuralist program, that is, the assumption that one can study one variable such as perceived size or loudness in isolation, holding all other variables constant, and generalize to other situations where these variables are not

HISTORY: BEFORE THE INFERENCE REVOLUTION 67

held constant (or held constant at different levels). In other words, the structuralist's assumption holds that subjective values for one property of an object exist *independently* from the variation of other properties in that same object. This fundamental assumption can be stated in a precise way. We consider for simplicity only two variables, A and B, with A being the *target* variable to be judged (such as area) and B being one *context* variable present (such as the value). Let $f(A_i)$ be the subjective values of A_i (where f may be called the psychophysical function if the A_i can be measured in physical units). Thus, the assumption (which is in contradiction with Brunswik's findings) can be written as follows:

$$f(A_i) = f(A_i|B_j) \text{ for all } A_i \epsilon A \text{ and } B_j \epsilon B$$

(context independence assumption), where $f(A_i|B_j)$ is the subjective value for A_i in the presence of the context variable B_j. The assumption states that the subjective values for A_i are independent of the variation of the context B_j. The generalization of the assumption to more than one context variable is straightforward. Of course, Brunswik did not claim that every context variable influences the perception of the target, and to the same extent. In consequence, the goal of his program is to find out where context dependencies exist, and what their quantitative effect is.

Fighting the context independence principle did not mean fighting a straw man. On the contrary, Brunswik even fought the future of psychophysics, although of course he could not know this. The future was to be dominated up to the 1960s by Stanley S. Stevens' one-dimensional approach. For instance, Stevens' (1957) program of determining the psychophysical functions f in the equation $a = f(A)$ is an instance of the context independence principle. And, as we shall see, still a dogma in cognitive psychology today is the assumption that subjective values such as subjective length (Anderson, 1981) and subjective probabilities (Kahneman, Slovic & Tversky, 1982) exist independently from the context variables present (in the task, or in the instruction).

Explanations

The program of multidimensional psychophysics therefore involved varying many properties of an object and studying the *dependence* of the perception of one of them on the variation of the others. To "perceive" a property meant to make a perceptual compromise. What is the explanatory principle offered for this phenomenon, which today we call the "context dependence" of perception? It must be noted that Brunswik himself was not much interested in speculating about the mechanisms. His commitment to Vienna Circle philosophy made him focus on what is physically measurable—on the *degree* of perceptual compromise rather

68   3. PERCEPTION

than on the nature of the mediation process. From time to time he went so far as to suggest (for instance, to Otto Neurath, a leading member of the Vienna Circle), that the term "psychology" be replaced by "behavioristics" (Wellek, 1956, p. 155) and that psychologists refrain completely from speculating about anything that goes on within the organism, a view similar to B. F. Skinner's psychology of the "empty organism" (Brunswik, 1937, p. 238). In other places, however, he accepted the study of mediation but consistently rejected the introspective approach. The latter explains why he did not distinguish between perception and judgment: to reduce the introspection involved in judgments to a minimum, subjects were asked only for simple judgments of *equality*. Here, the difference between perception and judgment may be considered minimal.[1]

In the following we shall try to make explicit two explanatory principles often only implicit in Brunswik's writings. It will be revealed that the facts can be and actually were explained by a principle that does *not* use the key ideas of cue uncertainty and inductive inference—the basis of the metaphor of the "intuitive statistician." In this sense, the "intuitive statistician" view of perception is not a *necessary* consequence of the facts. On the other hand, Brunswik also used another explanatory principle, which does rely on cue uncertainty and inductive inference. We shall show that these two explanatory principles give contradictory predictions. As far as we can see, Brunswik himself never realized this; his arguments jump back and forth between two fundamentally different principles.

Cue Learning

The latter explanatory principle, which relies on inference, is essentially in the empiricist tradition of Helmholtz's "unconscious inferences." We call this principle "cue learning." It is based on the fundamental distinction between the *proximal* and the *distal* stimulus. For instance, in size perception, the distal stimulus is the actual size of an object (measured in physical units), whereas the retinal image (measured by the visual angle) would be an example of a proximal stimulus. This distinction is *essential* for the metaphor of perception as inference: If there were no

---

[1]During his second career, in Berkeley, however, Brunswik did not hesitate to ask the subject directly for numbers (estimates of size, IQ, etc.). What the Vienna Brunswik might have rejected as "numerical introspection" became the essential data base for the Berkeley Brunswik—otherwise he could not have calculated the correlations (functional validities and cue utilization coefficients) that characterized the functioning of the "intuitive statistician." However, Brunswik was not criticized for this, because, since at least the time Stevens had introduced his "direct scaling" methods, asking the subject for numbers had been considered as an established measurement technique in experimental psychology.

difference between the information available (the proximal stimuli) and the world to be perceived (the distal stimuli), there would be no need for inference. Hence, as we shall soon see, Gibson does not make this distinction and consequently does not use the metaphor of inductive inference. With him, perception is certain.

Let us consider the cue learning principle more closely, using the phenomenon of size constancy. This phenomenon can be observed all the time: You approach an object such as a chair, or an object such as a person approaches you, and the size of the object is perceived to be relatively constant although the retinal image increases according to the laws of optics. The question "Why is perceived size (shape, brightness, color, etc.) relatively constant?" is the so-called constancy problem. One classical answer is given in Bühler's (1913) *duplicity principle*. This states that the perceptual system uses two kinds of information or proximal cues: the retinal image and some distance cues. Distance cues are, for example, the convergence of eye axes during fixation, clarity of the object, perspective, vertical position, and overlapping of objects. A mountain, for instance, tends to be seen as nearer when it is clear than when we can see only its unclear outline. Since at least the Renaissance, painters have been aware of these distance cues and have used them to create the illusion of space on a two-dimensional surface. It is assumed that use of these cues is acquired by learning. We may summarize this explanatory principle as follows:

Cue Learning Principle. By experience we learn that some stimuli are associated in time or space with other stimuli. Proximal stimuli that have been previously associated with some distal stimulus are automatically used by the perceptual system as probabilistic cues for the distal stimulus. To perceive means to infer the proximal from the distal.

How could the "cue learning" explanation be applied to the results of the coin experiment, that is, to the perceptual compromise between area and value? The explanation would be the following (note again that this is not Brunswik's, since he is occupied with measurement rather than explanation). First, there exists in the environment of the subjects a relation between the visual proximal stimulus—indicating the value of a coin—and the tactual proximal stimulus—indicating its size or area. In fact, in most Western countries the area of a coin increases with its value, although in Canada, West Germany, and the United States there are exceptions, such as the dime, which make this association imperfect. Second, this association is learned, and "value" thereby becomes a cue for "area" and vice versa. Third, when the subject is instructed in the experiment to judge the joint area of a group of coins, the perceptual system automatically draws an inference from the values of the coins to their area. The prediction is that the area of the more valuable coins will be overestimated, which is the actual result obtained.

Perceptual Compromises by In-Between-Objects

The second explanatory principle, which Brunswik calls *in-between-objects* ("Zwischengegenstände") is not distinguished in his writings from the cue learning principle. The principle does not involve the concepts of cue uncertainty and perceptual inferences. The following example from an experiment on the perception of area and shape (Brunswik, 1934) illustrates this second principle and will be used subsequently to demonstrate that we are dealing in fact with two different explanatory principles.

The subject was shown a standard rectangle (see Fig. 3.1) and instructed to adjust the height of a comparison rectangle with fixed width so that the *area* of the two rectangles appeared equal. The same standard rectangle was used for a second task, which was to adjust the height of the comparison stimulus so that the *shape* of both rectangles appeared equal. The solid lines in Fig. 3.1 show the physically correct solution; the dotted lines show the average judgments of 12 subjects. The height is adjusted too high when area is matched and too low when shape is matched. Similar results had been reported earlier by Bühler (1913) and Peters (1933). With this experiment we can state more precisely the principle of

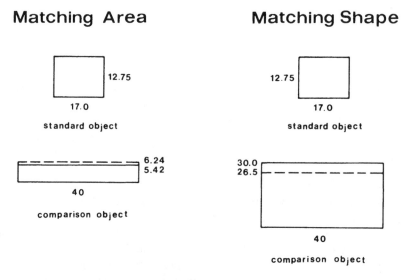

FIGURE 3.1. Perception of area and shape. The height of the comparison object (with a fixed width of 40 mm) has to be adjusted so that the areas (shapes) of the comparison and the standard object match. Solid lines represent the correct solution, dotted lines represent the actual judgments (after Brunswik, 1934, p. 121).

HISTORY: BEFORE THE INFERENCE REVOLUTION

perceptual compromise. In the case of rectangles, there exist *two* distal variables we might judge, area, and shape (and there may be even more, such as height and width). Brunswik calls these "poles of intention"; we call the judged variable the *target pole* and the other variable(s) the *context pole*(s). When the subject is instructed to match the area of two objects, his or her perceptual system actually matches area *and* shape, although the latter to a lesser degree. As Fig. 3.1 shows, the deviation in area judgment from the correct response is in the direction that alters the shape of the comparison stimulus toward that of the standard. The same "compromise" can be shown for shape perception as well. The deviation in matching the shape is in the direction that makes the area of the comparison stimulus more similar to that of the standard. That is, both poles are automatically "attended" to, although with different weights depending on the instruction. What is seen as equal is actually a compromise between a conscious effort to match the target pole and a residual automatic effort to match the context pole. This mixing is illustrated in Fig. 3.2, where the quantitative measures of Fig. 3.1 are used. The

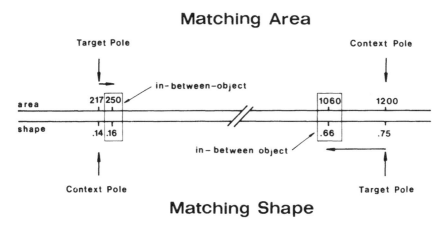

FIGURE 3.2. Illustration of the perceptual compromise principle (using the experiment of Fig. 3.1). Each rectangle varies along two dimensions, area (in cm, shown on the upper horizontal line) and shape (height/width, shown on the lower horizontal line). Since the width of the comparison object is fixed, area and shape covary for all possible comparison rectangles; thus, to each area shown on the upper line there corresponds a shape, shown directly beneath it on the lower line. For matching area, the target pole is the area of the standard (12.75 × 17.0 = 217), but the context pole is the shape of the standard (12.75/17.0 = .75). If the subjects could match area independently of the context (shape), they should have produced the rectangle on the left (area, 217 cm²; shape, .14). If the subjects could match the shape independently of the context (area), they should have produced the rectangle on the right (area, 1200; shape, .75). In each case, however, they produced a perceptual compromise, an in-between object lying in between the target and the context poles.

72 3. PERCEPTION

direction and degree of perceptual compromise is indicated by the horizontal arrows. The arrows always point to the context pole, which means that the in-between-objects lie in between the two poles. We are now able to state the perceptual compromise principle in more abstract terms for the simple case of a two variable situation with one target variable A and one context variable B.

In-Between-Object or Compromise Principle: The principle applies to a situation where a standard object (A_0,B_0) is presented and an object has to be selected from a set of objects (A_i,B_j) so that A_0 appears equal to A_i. The situation is nontrivial in the sense that there exists no duplicate (A_0,B_0) in the comparison set, that is, the attributes A and B cannot be independently manipulated; but there is a correct solution (A_0,B_c), with $B_0 \neq B_c$. Let us call the object selected (A_s,B_s); which means $f(A_s|B_s) = f(A_0|B_0)$, i.e. the subjective values f with respect to A are the same. The principle asserts:

$$(1)\ f(A_s|B_s) = f(A_0|B_0) \neq f(A_0|B_c);$$

the latter inequality implies that the *context independence principle* does not hold, and

(2) $B_0 < B_s < B_c$ (or $B_0 > B_s > B_c$), which means that an (incorrect) object (A_s,B_s) is chosen so that B_s is closer to B_0 than B_c would be. Thus, B_s lies *in between* B_0 and B_c, which reduces the difference of the objects on the context dimension.

That A and B cannot be independently manipulated is illustrated in Figs. 3.1 and 3.2, where area and shape covary because the width of the comparison object is held constant. Another example is the coin experiment, where there is a monotonic relationship between value and area: both cannot be manipulated independently. The in-between-object principle, as it is stated in the foregoing, is our formulation not Brunswik's, and we cannot be sure if it is not too strong an explication of what is implicit in his writings. Nonetheless, the principle in the present version is falsifiable and is, of course, applicable beyond psychophysics, for instance, to social perception.

The Conflict Between the Two Principles

As mentioned earlier, Brunswik treated the two principles as if they were alternatives: Perceptual compromises by in-between-objects appear to be an instance of the learning of uncertain cues and perceptual inferences. Brunswik (1956) seems to echo this even in his last book: "It may even be that perceptual compromise is but one of the manifestations of the uncertainty of the ecology and of the resultant basically statistical nature of perceptual functioning" (p. 80).

HISTORY: BEFORE THE INFERENCE REVOLUTION   **73**

Using the area of rectangles as an example, we shall demonstrate that the two principles in fact give different predictions. In Fig. 3.3a we show the result from Fig. 3.1, whereas in Fig. 3.3b we have introduced a new comparison object with a fixed width that is *smaller* than that of the standard stimulus. What is the prediction of the cue learning principle? Here we must assume that the subjects have learned from experience that shape is a cue for area. But does a more elongated shape indicate a large area or a small area? From the result in Fig. 3.1 we are forced to conclude the latter: The subjects adjusted the height beyond the true value required, suggesting they underestimated the area of the elongated shape. Therefore, we must conclude that an *elongated* shape indicates *small* area (here we exclude from consideration more complicated relationships between shape and area such as U-shaped functions). This gives us the prediction for the new situation in Fig. 3.3.b: The new comparison object with the short base is also an elongated object, and therefore its area will be underestimated with the result that the height it is given to match the standard in area will be too great.

The in-between-object principle, however, gives a prediction in the opposite direction: The deviation from the correct solution (solid line) goes in that direction that makes the two shapes more similar.

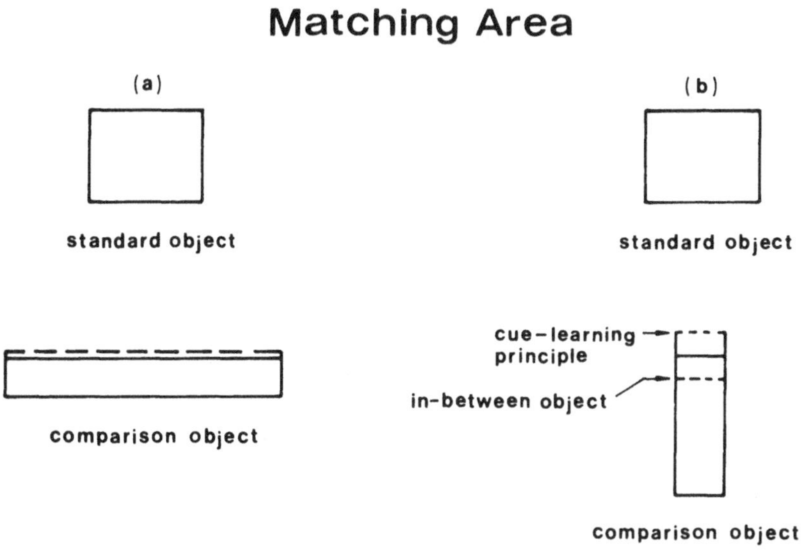

Matching Area

FIGURE 3.3   Diverging predictions for area judgments from the cue-learning and the perceptual compromise principle: (a) results from Fig. 3.1 for comparison, (b) predictions for a new comparison object. Solid lines are again physically correct answers, dotted lines in (b) are predicted directions of deviation.

74   3. PERCEPTION

Note that a 90° rotation of the standard object does *not* change the predictions of either principle, either in situation (a) or (b).

We see, then, that we are dealing with two different principles that explain the way objects are perceived. Both oppose the classical (and modern) context independence principle, but they lead to contradictory predictions.

Our point is that since Brunswik did not distinguish between the two principles, the in-between-object principle (which does not involve cue uncertainty and perceptual inference) would have been sufficient to account for the context dependence found in his program of multidimensional psychophysics. He could have developed his Vienna program, where he dealt with the simultaneous dependence of up to four(!) variables, into a kind of cognitive algebra. This would have portrayed a perception as the calculation of all matches with respect to all poles (target and context) and the calculation of the final in-between-object by a weighted sum of these matches. But it was the cue learning and perceptual inference principle that Brunswik elaborated in Berkeley. We therefore conclude that it was not the facts—his evidence for context-dependence—that forced Brunswik to adopt the metaphor of the "intuitive statistician."

The Perceptual System as an Intuitive Statistician

It was with the metaphor of the perceptual system as an "intuitive statistician" that Brunswik wanted to reconcile the European academic with the American statistical tradition. It is curious that his strong concern with probability and uncertainty developed only after he had left Europe for the United States (after 1937). One influence besides the suggested adaptation to the American emphasis on statistics (at the time, mainly correlational statistics) was the emerging probabilistic world picture of physics, as put forward in Werner Heisenberg's uncertainty principle and Max Born's ontic probabilism (Cartwright, 1987). The devil of uncertainty entered Brunswik's thoughts from the new physics by way of the Vienna Circle, whose members were strongly interested in the philosophical implications of indeterminism. However, American experimental psychologists did not seem to welcome such an emphasis on uncertainty in psychological theory; they already had had enough of it in practice and looked forward to the certainty of Newtonian physics (Gigerenzer, 1987b).

After his emigration to Berkeley in 1937, Brunswik transformed Helmholtz's notion of unconscious inferences into the metaphor of the perceptual system as an "intuitive statistician." As Brunswik (1950, p. 24) sees it, there are three lines of progress in his system as compared with

Helmholtz's notion of unconscious inference. These three lines represent his commitment (a) to the views of Karl Bühler, the head of the Vienna Institute; (b) to the methodological position of the Vienna Circle, of which he was a member; and (c) to a Darwinian view of perception, which reflected the biological orientation of German-language psychology before World War II. First, Brunswik held that perceptual inference is different from rational inference, whereas Helmholtz believed that the two are alike except that one is conscious and the other has become gradually unconscious. Following Bühler rather than Helmholtz, Brunswik considered perception and thinking as fairly independent functions, perception being more primitive and quick and acting like a "stupid animal" despite the superior knowledge of the intellect. (Here, it seems to us, Brunswik is not so far from Helmholtz as he claims.) Second, Brunswik pointed to the introspective implications of Helmholtz's idea that the perceptual inference, now automatic, had been previously conscious. Instead, following the dogma of "intersubjectivity" of the Vienna Circle, he rejected any reference to introspection. All aspects of perception, even unconscious inference, have to be operationally defined and measured. Third, Brunswik's emphasis was on the *function* of perception (and reasoning) as an adaptation to the environment. Adaptation is the only purpose of perception, and to measure the degree of adaptation became the central purpose of Brunswik's psychology.

The important steps toward the metaphor of the intuitive statistician are: (a) the idea that the nature of perceptual processing is *vicarious functioning,* and (b) the analogy between vicarious functioning and *multiple regression.* The concept of vicarious functioning is a straightforward extension of the cue learning principle: Any perceptual cue is only an uncertain index of the distal stimulus. As a consequence, in order to survive, the perceptual system does not rely on a single cue but rather improves the perceptual bet by combining many cues. The concept of vicarious functioning denotes the ability to analyze many cues simultaneously and to *substitute* any missing cue by others, finding alternative pathways to the distal stimulus. Consider for instance the perception of distance and motion of objects, which was as critical for the survival of our ancestors as it is today in an environment of cars and traffic. On a clear day, many cues for distance and relative motion are available. However, in situations like driving at night and in rain, some of the cues, such as converging lines and boundary lines of overlapping objects, may no longer be available. These may be substituted for by new cues, such as the change in the intensity and size of lights from approaching cars. Brunswik considers vicarious functioning as the most fundamental principle of a science of perception and behavior and points to various examples. For instance, the same goal can be reached by quite different

76   3. PERCEPTION

behaviors, as emphasized in Clark Hull's (1943) habit-family hierarchy, and the same underlying conflicts and drives may express themselves through alternative manifestations of symptoms, as emphasized in the psychoanalytic writings of Frenkel-Brunswik (1942).

But how does vicarious functioning work? How are the cues selected, substituted, weighted, and combined if we perceive an object having a certain size or judge a person as having a certain intelligence? Brunswik (1950, p. 24) assumes that the perceptual system is an intuitive statistician that calculates *correlations* and *multiple regressions*. Thus the act of perception can be decomposed into the following steps:

1. *Cue Learning.* As in Helmholtz's theory and as stated in the cue learning principle, the association between a cue and a distal variable is learned through experience. This association is uncertain in nature: "The natural cues used by the perceptual system are, *without exception,* ambiguous in character" (Brunswik, 1939a, p. 175, italics ours).

2. *Cue Sampling.* About this Brunswik is not explicit, but he implies that the perceptual system identifies a subset of cues that were previously associated with the distal variable in the ever changing sample of cues available in the natural environment.

3. *Cue Weighting and Combining.* The final percept is estimated by weighting these cues and summing them up in the same way as a criterion is estimated by multiple regression. The resulting estimate is the percept. The weights might correspond to the learned strength of association between cue and distal stimulus.

The first "intuitive statistician" is thus a statistician of the correlational school of Karl Pearson, and his conceptual apparatus mirrors the statistical tools known in the late 1930s, when Brunswik developed these ideas. It should be added that from reading Brunswik's work we must infer that he had no sophisticated knowledge about statistics—statistics was not considered as important in German-speaking countries as in the Anglo-American World—and it took him some time to find his metaphor (see Gigerenzer, 1987b). Nevertheless, beginning about 1940, Brunswik even ceased to measure perceptual constancies by the "Brunswik-Ratio" (Brunswik, 1933) and relied exclusively on correlation coefficients.

The New Program: Probabilistic Functionalism

The new metaphor of perception generated new questions, new data, and a new idea of experiment. The radical conclusion Brunswik drew is that vicarious functioning can be studied only in the natural environment, where unrestricted, free-floating cues are available. The classical experiment, in which one or a few variables (cues) are isolated and all others are controlled, can tell us only what the perceptual system might do in such an extremely restricted environment, but not how it proceeds if vicarious functioning is given full rein, unhindered by the principles of isolation and control. Perception is seen as adaptation to the natural environment through vicarious functioning. Here again, the pre-World War II affiliation of German-language psychology with biology comes through: psychology's neighbour is biology, not physics. And, the rejection of the classical experiment reflects the focus of the Galton–Pearson program (Pearson, 1920) on the correlational analysis of *many* "environmental" variables rather than the experimental analysis of a few systematically controlled variables.

New Questions. Brunswik's (1955a) second research program, which he called "probabilistic functionalism," centers on three questions (see Fig. 3.4). The first question is, what is the *functional validity* of individuals with respect to a distal variable? This is the question of how well the perceptual system estimates distal stimuli, and it is answered by calculating the correlation between what Brunswik called "perceptual responses" (e.g. judgments of size, distance, or IQ) and the actual measures of the distal variable (physical size, distance, result of an IQ test). Brunswik considered this correlation as a measure of the degree of adaptation to the environment, and this first question is identical with the old question about the degree of perceptual constancy.

The remaining two questions are new. Recall that perception means that the intuitive statistician uses correlational statistics to infer his or her world from uncertain cues. Figure 3.4 shows the simple case of one distal variable that must be inferred from six proximal cues. For instance, the distal variable could be the size of an object, and the proximal cues could be the size of the retinal image (visual angle), convergence of eye axes, horizontal position of the object, number of in-between objects, and so on. Then the second question is, what are the *ecological validities* of the proximal cues with respect to the distal variable? A high ecological validity means that the cue is a good indicator of the distal variable in many situations. Thus, the second aim of the program is to measure the ecological validities, which is done by the correlation of the proximal cue with the distal variable. Note that these ecological validities are independent of any characteristics of the observer, and the idea of studying the relationships between potential cues and distal variables (what Brunswik called the "texture of the environment") without reference to observers seem not to have occurred before in psychology. Apart from a few empirical studies, however, this question remained largely unanswered as a consequence of the rejection of Brunswik's program.

3. PERCEPTION

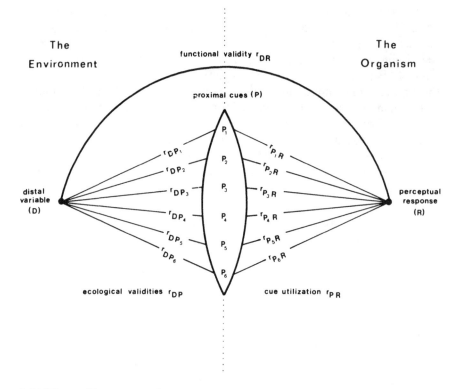

FIGURE 3.4. The perceptual system as an intuitive statistician, according to Brunswik. The perceptual system estimates a distal variable (D) from uncertain proximal cues (P_1, P_2, . . .). The diagram shows six, for example. The ecological validities r_{DP} are the correlations between the distal variable and each proximal cue, the cue utilization values r_{PR} are the correlations between the perceptual response (R) and each proximal cue, and the functional validity r_{DR} is the correlation between the values of the distal variable and the perceptual response.

The third question is, what cues are "used" by the perceptual system to estimate the distal variable? The measure of the degree to which a cue is used is defined as the correlation between cue and perceptual response. For instance, if the distal variable is the IQ (as in Brunswik, 1939b, 1945), cues like "bodily weight" and "wearing of spectacles" show ecological validities of only about r = .10. Nevertheless, the *cue utilization coefficients* may be around r = .50, which indicates that the individual "trusts" unreliable cues. Consequently, as reported by Brunswik, the functional validities for the judgment of IQ were close to zero.

New Data. At the core of Brunswik's program was the Darwinian view that perception means adaptation to a natural environment. This brought a new kind of data into the center of his program: measuring the texture of

HISTORY: BEFORE THE INFERENCE REVOLUTION   **79**

a natural environment. "Texture" means the relationships between environmental variables such as the vertical position of objects, the size of objects, overlapping of objects, shadows, and contour lines. Since Fechner, *isolated* physical variables had been measured in the laboratory and plotted against psychological variables to determine, for example, psychophysical functions. However the new focus was on relationships between physical variables, in order to determine the structure or texture of a particular environment. The new kind of data provided the ecological validities and revealed potential cues in an environment.

For instance, Gestalt psychologists stress that certain Gestalt factors such as "proximity" explain why certain elements are perceived as belonging to the same figural unit. An example is a series of parallel lines of which those that are close together are seen as belonging to the same object. For orthodox Gestalt theory, such organizing factors rest on innate dynamic processes in the brain field, whereas a Helmholtzian would claim that individuals have learned that the proximity of lines indicates boundary contours of a single object (e.g., a tree trunk). To test the cue learning explanation, Brunswik and Kamiya (1953) measured the proximity of lines in pictures from *Life* magazine, determined whether these lines belonged to the same object, and found ecological validities up to $r = .37$. They concluded that the perceptual organization effect of proximity, as well as other Gestalt factors such as "closedness," may be due to learning the texture of natural environments rather than to an autochthonous Gestalt dynamics in the brain field.

Brunswik, however, made only a few attempts to collect data about the texture of natural environments; and photographs from magazines are of course a very peculiar environment. But, as we shall see, in Gibson's theory the texture of the environment became the central issue, although without correlational statistics and uncertainty.

New Idea of Experiment. The new look of the perceptual system as a statistician of the Karl Pearson school led Brunswik to reject the classical idea of experiment based on the principles of isolation and control. Just as the Galton–Pearson program focused on the achievement of individuals when confronted with many stimuli (such as questions in an IQ test), Brunswik studied the achievement of the perceptual system in the *natural environment*. Here he followed Darwin even further than did the followers of Galton and Pearson who made a compromise between Darwin's natural environment and Galton's ideal of quantification as exemplified by standard methods of intelligence testing. Brunswik's new idea of experiment, which he called *representative design,* was the following: First, the experimenter accompanies the subject in the subject's natural environment rather than the subject visiting the experimenter in the laboratory.

80   3. PERCEPTION

Second, at random intervals, the experimenter asks the subject to estimate a distal variable (such as size) of objects on which the subject is focusing at the moment, and measures potential cues as well as the distal variable. With this, all three questions concerning the ecological validities, the cue utilization, and the functional validities can be answered.

The Rejection of the Intuitive Statistician

Brunswik's probabilistic functionalism anticipated major trends and issues of current concern: the question of generalizability from laboratory experiments (e.g. Flanagan & Dipboye, 1980; Gigerenzer, 1984a), the emphasis on random sampling of stimuli in addition to the sampling of subjects (e.g. Hammond & Wascoe, 1980), the analysis of cue utilization and integration (e.g. Brehmer, 1979; Gigerenzer, 1983b), the study of the texture of the environment (e.g. Gibson, 1979), and the metaphor of the mind as an intuitive statistician (e.g. Nisbett & Ross, 1980; Peterson & Beach, 1967). Nonetheless, in his own time, Brunswik's program was rejected. The reasons for the rejection have been discussed in detail elsewhere (Gigerenzer, 1987b). Here we shall summarize some major facts and suggested reasons. First, the 1941 and 1953 discussions of probabilistic functionalism by major figures in experimental psychology (published respectively in the Psychological Review, 1943, 255–310, and 1955, 193–242; see also Brunswik, 1955b) show that many of the discussants in fact were unable to understand Brunswik's new metaphor. For instance, Clark Hull (1943b) and Ernest Hilgard (1955) drew analogies to the indeterminism of quantum physics and the statistical laws of thermodynamics, which have nothing to do with Brunswik's metaphor, and rejected Brunswik's program. Before the cognitive revolution and the inference revolution had arrived, the suggested link between the mind and a statistician was hard to understand. Second, correlational statistics was not considered the appropriate instrument for experimental psychology: it was the tool of the second discipline of psychology, the Galton–Pearson program. To quote Hilgard (1955) discussing Brunswik: "Correlation is an instrument of the devil" (p. 228). The first intuitive statistician knew the wrong statistics. To Brunswik's embarrassment, when the inference revolution did arrive, the new statistics became tied to experiments in restricted and controlled environments rather than to the free-floating stream of information in natural environments. Fisher's analysis of variance linked statistics with the old principles of isolation and control.

Let us summarize. At the beginning of the book we claimed that the metaphor of cognition as intuitive statistics emerged from the intersection of the inference revolution and the cognitive revolution. According to our tools-to-theories hypothesis, cognitive processes were equated with statistical inference only after statistical inference came to be viewed as an indispensable instrument for the experimental psychologist. Brunswik's intuitive statistician would have been the counterexample had it been successful. With Brunswik, the link between cognition and statistics was clearly drawn before the inference revolution. But his intuitive statistician used instruments that at the time were not considered indispensable by experimental psychologists, although they were essential for the competing discipline, the Galton–Pearson program. Thus, this first attempt at a link was rejected by the experimental community. Brunswik's case, like Thurstone's (chapter 2), is a revealing test case, which supports rather than contradicts our thesis. Thurstone and his followers had the formal structure of signal detection theory but did not see the link between the mind and a statistician. In the unique case of Brunswik, who explicitly drew the link between correlational statistics and the mind, this link was rejected by his contemporaries.

We shall now turn to theory construction after the inference revolution, which is heterogeneous with respect to the link between perception and statistical inference. We shall deal first with Gibson's "naive realism," where no cognitive processes are postulated, and consequently no link between such processes and statistical inference is made.

THE REALIST VIEW: PICKUP OF INFORMATION

Today we find neurophysiologists, biochemists, ophthalmologists, and computer programmers working on the traditional problems of visual perception. The main questions posed still seem to be those of the mid-19th century, when Helmholtz published his *Physiological Optics* (1856–1866/1962). How should we explain perceptual constancies and illusions? How do we perceive space, form, and color? The answers reflect the three old competing approaches to knowledge, which were long linked to perception: the inductive view, the deductive view, and the "naive" realistic view. We shall consider a major representative from each tradition and begin with the realist view of James J. Gibson (1904–1979) and his case against inference.

As we mentioned earlier, Helmholtz's idea of "unconscious inferences" was challenged by the nativistic thinking of his younger colleague and consistent opponent, Ewald Hering (1834–1918). According to Hering (cited in Rock, 1977), the relevant proximal cue is not the local retinal image of an object but rather the relation of that local image to the neighboring images. For instance, we perceive an object as having a constant "brightness" under changing illumination because the luminance ratios of the object to its neighboring objects remain constant. The argument is, if we take ratios, or relationships, as proximal cues rather

82   3. PERCEPTION

than the traditional "simple" cues such as the intensity of light (reflected by a single object) on the eye, there is no need to introduce "unconscious inferences" from past experience. Which explanation is correct? It is probably safe to say that neither can do justice to all phenomena and that the majority of researchers today believe that perceived brightness (achromatic color) is determined by Hering's luminance ratios, whereas perceived size is determined by Helmholtz's unconscious "taking account" of learned distance cues.

The major contemporary opponent of the inference metaphor, and proponent of a "higher order stimulus theory" *sensu* Hering, is James J. Gibson (1950, 1966, 1979). Gibson's (1979) claim, in essence, is that all information necessary for constancy is already in the ambient light: "So when I assert that perception of the environment is direct, I mean that it is not mediated by *retinal* pictures, *neural* pictures, or *mental* pictures. *Direct perception* is the activity of getting information from the ambient array of light. I call this a process of *information pickup* that involves the exploratory activity of looking around, getting around, and looking at things" (p. 147).

Invariants in the Ambient Light

Gibson's view, like Brunswik's cannot be understood without considering its emphasis on the function rather than on the process of perception. Both men studied perception in its relationship to the natural environment rather than under laboratory conditions, where the flow of information is restricted. Just as there were two Brunswiks, there were also two Gibsons. Gibson (1959) still defined perception in the traditional, psychophysical way as the mapping of stimuli into percepts. Soon he abandoned that view and reconsidered perception "as an experiencing of things in the environment in terms of what actions they afford" (Shaw & Todd, 1980, p. 400). Over the years, possibly influenced by Brunswik, he became increasingly interested in the relationship between perception and the natural environment. Gibson realized that a changing optic array (in Brunswik's terms, changing retinal images), gives much more information about the environment than a stationary array. Therefore, it is advantageous for an animal to move around (Gibson, Kaplan, Reynolds, & Wheeler, 1969). Note here that a central problem for the Helmholtzian tradition, the changing retinal images, is reinterpreted by Gibson (1979) as the central advantage of perception. "So we must perceive in order to move, but we must also move in order to perceive" (p. 223). Here is a first distinction between the two ecological approaches to perception: Brunswik's "intuitive statistician" is a stationary perceiver, whereas Gibson's being explores its environment actively.

THE REALIST VIEW: PICKUP OF INFORMATION   83

A second distinction appears in the answer to the question of whether the proximal information is certain or uncertain. Recall that according to Brunswik all proximal information is in principle uncertain, and the task of the "intuitive statistician" is to infer the world from these unreliable cues. For Gibson, however, the ambient light contains sufficient information for object constancies. For instance, the light surrounding the freely moving observer contains flow patterns that are produced by motion parallax. Motion parallax means that when an observer moves, as in a train, nearer objects are more displaced in his field of view, or disappear faster, than objects that are farther away. The claim is that under normal viewing conditions certain features in the flow pattern are perfectly correlated with the observer's direction and speed of movement and with the layout of sizes, planes, and surfaces in the environment. This means that although the invariant object undergoes a continuous transformation, there are corresponding invariants in the light (in Brunswik's terms, in the retinal image), such as "texture gradients," that specify the spatial layout of the objects completely. For Gibson, "perceiving" means that these invariants are "picked up" directly. Consequently, the Gibsonian research program is the search for these "higher-order invariants." For instance, there are attempts to specify mathematically the Gibsonian invariants from hypothesized or known neurophysiological brain processes (e.g. Blavais, 1975; Hoffman, 1966). For Gibson, these supposed invariants provide certainty to the observer.

The Loss of Uncertainty

Both Gibson and Brunswik concerned themselves with Berkeley's claim that we cannot know the world with certainty, and the two men took diametrically opposed views on this issue. In Brunswik's terms, Gibson claims that (a) there exists a one-to-one relationship between the distal variables and the invariants in the retinal image (the proximal cues) and (b) there exists another one-to-one relationship between proximal cues and the percept. These two one-to-one relationships make perception certain and veridical. The Gibsonian research program is concerned with the first one-to-one relationship, the search for higher-order invariants; the second is simply referred to by the term "information pickup."

By introducing the ideas of "higher order stimulus invariants" and "direct information pickup," Gibson eliminates uncertainty and thereby the inference metaphor from perceptual theory. Statistical ideas retreat to their original field of application, the handling of errors in measurement. Inferencelike processes may operate only in situations where the information available is either ambiguous or reduced to a minimum, such as in the traditional perceptual laboratory. This leads Gibson, like Brunswik, to

84   3. PERCEPTION

reject the traditional "peep-hole" experiment as a proper means of studying perception. "The laboratory *must* be like life!" (Gibson, 1979, p. 3). It is a curious fact that Brunswik came earlier to the same conclusion for the quite contrary reason that only the natural, unrestricted flow of information allows us to study how the organism comes to terms with an environment that presents itself through cues that are in principle uncertain.

What does it mean to say that information is "picked up"? This remains undefined in the sense that no mechanism is offered that explains a one-to-one mapping of information into the percept. We know more about what "immediate pickup" does *not* mean. It does not mean inferences such as Helmholtz's "unconscious inferences." And it rules out other cognitive processes such as unconscious combining of information as in "cognitive algebra" (see "The Deductive View," this chapter) and unconscious computing, as in the cognitive science approach to vision (see Pylyshyn, 1984; Ullman, 1980). Thus, the "pickup" is negatively defined as something that requires no processing of any sort. Besides this, what does it mean to say that perception is "immediate" or "direct"? If it means that the "immediate pickup" of gradients of motion parallax and other higher order stimuli is innate, the issue turns into an empirical question. What do we know about this? On one hand, it has been demonstrated, following Spalding (1872), that young chicks and other animals who have had no opportunity to learn the association between visual and nonvisual cues can nevertheless react properly to distance and depth on the basis of visual cues alone (for an overview, see Rosinsky, 1977). This rules out any explanation that considers the perception of objects in space *completely* based on inferences from nonvisual sources and on (lengthy) learning processes. On the other hand, we know that the *familiar size* of an object (such as the average size of an adult or a child) can have an effect on its apparent distance and can even overcome depth information from other distance cues (Ittelson, 1962; Wallach, 1976). Since familiar size can become a depth cue only by learning, this and similar results rule out an explanation that rests exclusively on an innate "pickup" of information. We may conclude from such results (Haber, 1979; Hochberg, 1979; Rock, 1980, 1983) that both an extreme cue learning view and a nativistic "pickup" view would overstate the respective positions.

Information Available and Information Used

The stimulating challenge in Gibson's "direct" view is that the Helmholtzians have worked with a simplistic conception of the retinal stimulus. Consider size constancy again. The relevant information is not simply the

THE REALIST VIEW: PICKUP OF INFORMATION   85

retinal size of the object in question; it is all the information over the entire retinal surface, which corresponds to Gibson's texture gradient (i.e., the ratios, contours, overlaps, etc.). However, the claim that these higher order stimuli can specify the distal objects completely seems to be widely overstated, given the abundant literature on perceptual illusions, such as Wertheimer's (1912) phi phenomenon as an example of illusory motion, and errors in perceived size such as the moon illusion and the Müller–Lyer illusion. Nevertheless, in his search for invariants, Gibson even went so far to attempt the impossible, namely to specify three dimensions completely in two.

But even if complete information about the external world were available in the invariants, does this imply that perception would be veridical, as Gibson's theory implies? Of course not, if one accepts the distinction between having information and using it. Another comparison between Brunswik and Gibson helps make the point. Using Brunswik's terminology, Gibson claims that if Brunswik had really examined the richness of stimulation reaching the eye, he would have found that both the ecological validities (the correlation between proximal and distal stimuli) and the functional validities (the correlation between percept and distal stimuli) are perfect. For Brunswik, however, the ecological and the functional validities are not necessarily coupled in a one-to-one fashion: Functional validities (e.g. object constancies) may be considerably lower than ecological validities. In other words, the perceptual system may not be able to *use* all the information available or may not "know" (either by learning or heredity) how to weight and combine the pieces of information. For instance, the gradients that carry the supposed invariants may be too small to be detected in the small span of the fovea and may be unresolvable in the peripheral areas (Hochberg, 1979, pp. 129ff.). Even if there were complete information about the world on the retina or in the ambient light, this would not imply that perception is "direct" or "veridical," since having information available and using information are not the same thing.

We conclude that Berkeley's argument that no information about objects in space could be certain has not yet been refuted. First, just as Brunswik's cues are uncertain indicators of the environment, so are Gibson's higher order variables. It is hard to see how the two-dimensional proximal information could stand in a one-to-one relationship to three-dimensional spatial objects. It is easy to point to examples where one-to-one relationships do not hold. For instance, motion parallax and other higher order stimuli that are usually produced by a three-dimensional layout may alternatively be produced, as in motion pictures and holograms, by lights on a two-dimensional screen. Second, there might be more than "pickup" in the brain. If we agree that neither illusions and

86   3. PERCEPTION

distortions nor spontaneous reversals in depth are properties of the objects themselves, then we must ask how these phenomena of perception can occur if perception is "direct." Typically, books on "direct" perception devote much space to the analysis of the array of light and tend to neglect the traditional phenomena such as visual illusions and logically impossible objects, whereas books in the Helmholtzian tradition show the reverse bias. What the Helmholtzians may learn from Gibson is that their processing analysis may be based on a simplistic stimulus description. What the Gibsonians may learn is that the "naive realism" of a pure stimulus analysis without specification of the process between retinal image and the percept is not sufficient. As Haber (1979) puts it, we might look forward to the breakthrough of "a truly Gibholtzian theory of space perception."

THE INDUCTIVE VIEW: HYPOTHESIS TESTING

In a severe critique of Gibson's "naive realism," Gregory (1974b) lists what he considers the challenging facts in perception and tests whether Gibson's "direct" theory and five competing theories can account for them. In this examination game, the "direct" theory gets the worst score, and, no surprise, Gregory's hypothesis testing version of Helmholtz's "unconscious inferences" wins the contest. [Hebb's (1949) theory of "phase sequences" wins silver. Phase sequences are developed by experience and can be seen as physiological embodiments of the "schema" concept of Sir Frederic Bartlett (1932), who was Gregory's teacher at Cambridge.] The "direct" theory even fell far behind Gestalt theory, since it could not provide answers for such questions as the following: How is skilled behavior maintained through (temporary) absence of sensory input? Why are highly improbable objects more difficult to see (or recognize) than probable objects of similar form (e.g. a hollow-mold face appearing as a normal face)? and How can perceptions be of (logically) impossible objects (e.g. the Penrose impossible triangle figure)? Of course, as in any real exam, the candidates' scores depend on who asks the questions.

Methods of Science as Metaphor

Gregory, like Helmholtz and Brunswik, rejects the reductionistic dream of a future in which all perceptual processes are explained by physiological processes. More than Brunswik, Gregory (1974a) emphasizes that both the methods of science and the process of perception might be based on the same principles.

THE INDUCTIVE VIEW: HYPOTHESIS TESTING   87

The cognitive strategy carried out by brains is not so like what physics *describes* as it is like the *methods* of physics. More specifically, it is surely scientific *method* which is the best paradigm we have of how data can be used for discovering the nature of things and predicting from past experience—by building and selecting predictive hypotheses. It is suggestive that discrepancies from the truth can be generated in science not only by loss of the calibration of instruments but also by applying inappropriate strategies to problems. This, I believe, is like many kinds of illusions, which cannot be understood from physiology alone. (pp. xxvii–xxviii)

Gregory's (1980) thesis is that "perception is similar to science itself" (p. 63)—but similar to which methods of science? Gregory does not, as Brunswik did, draw the analogy between perception and parameter estimation through Karl Pearson's correlational and regression statistics. He draws the parallel between perception and the small sample statistics of the inference revolution, where no parameters are estimated but hypotheses are accepted or rejected. To perceive an object means to accept a hypothesis, and Gregory states that he takes the notion of perceptions as hypotheses quite literally (p. 63). Like a statistician, the physiological mechanisms in the brain collect and store data and draw inferences from available sensory data to potential hypotheses concerning the state of the external world. The hypothesis accepted from among all the considered hypotheses is the perception. It is this hypothesis testing analogy to which Gregory refers when he talks of "active" and "passive" accounts of perception, an example of the latter being the "direct" theory. Both science and perception are irreducibly *cognitive* activities: constructing hypotheses in order to predict data, and collecting data in order to test hypotheses. And both activities are accompanied by errors, revisions, new errors, and new revisions rather than a veridical "pickup" of the external world. More than Brunswik, Gregory emphasizes the understanding of perception as *predictive* hypotheses. The following phenomenon illustrates the meaning of this term (Gregory 1974b).

Consider an eye/hand tracking experiment. The task is to move a joystick in order to keep a marker on a moving target displayed on a screen (similar to some video games). If the target is removed from time to time, no errors occur; successful behaviour can continue through gaps in the sensory input. In every day life, there are similar phenomena. We do not have to watch the ground or the steps continuously when we walk. And there are even phenomena where the missing sensory input itself is filled in. For instance, we are seldom aware of blinking, and there is no blank in the viewed world that corresponds to the blind spot in our eye; the blind spot is "filled in." The general question is, how can behaviour be maintained through steady temporary and local gaps in visual informa-

88   3. PERCEPTION

tion? The answer is that behaviour is not controlled by sensory input but by hypotheses. These are inferred from past data and predict the sensory input when gaps occur.

Like science, then, perception acts on the basis of hypotheses—on what is "believed"—and goes far beyond the sensory information given. "Behaviour is guided not by stimuli, but rather by guesses" (Gregory, 1974a, p. xxv). For instance, the success of a conjurer's illusions may be guaranteed by such inferences from sensory data to hypotheses.

The Betting Machine Metaphor

Is there more than metaphorical talk about methods of science here? Is there a precise "hypothesis testing" model? What exactly does Gregory mean when he calls the perceptual system a "betting machine" or an "induction machine"? To answer these questions, we shall start where Gregory starts, with Helmholtz's "unconscious inferences," which we now rewrite using the new language of "data" and "hypothesis":

Major premise: This retinal shape D ("data") has nearly always occurred when external object H *("hypothesis") is present.*
Minor premise: The retinal shape D is present.
Conclusion: Therefore the external object H is present.

Recall that the major premise is arrived at from past experience and the minor premise is the proximal information. The perception of the object H *is* the inference that the hypothesis H is valid. Gregory goes beyond the syllogism metaphor in explicitly considering perception as hypothesis testing, that is, as the selection of hypotheses by sensory data: "Perception is a matter of selecting the most likely object. But what are the possible objects selected from? Not from the actual world of objects. Retinal images evidently serve to select from a stored repertoire of objects represented symbolically in the "visual" brain. Perception must, it seems, be a matter of seeing the present with stored objects from the past" (Gregory 1970, p. 36).

The question, which object is there? is answered by testing a number of hypotheses (possible objects) against the data available. This view implies, of course, more than a single syllogism, since we are dealing with many object hypotheses, H_1, H_2, and so forth, and the mechanism of the testing (selection) process must be explicated. The only hint about the mechanism we may get out of the syllogism analogy, as stated earlier, is that the perceptual system takes the likelihoods into account (the probabilities $p(D|H)$ of a retinal information D given some hypothesis H). These are referred to in the major premise. Does the betting machine also

THE INDUCTIVE VIEW: HYPOTHESIS TESTING 89

consider prior probabilities $p(H)$, or does it neglect empirical base rates? How does it set the decision criterion to decide between competing possible objects, and how does it learn to balance the errors in testing? In short, what kind of intuitive statistician is the betting machine?

To begin with, there is no precise quantitative model. But we find statements of analogy that show the perspective. First, we may ask, what is the nature of that uncertainty that forces Gregory (as opposed to Gibson) to think about the perceptual system as a betting machine? Like Brunswik (1955b), Gregory (1974a) sees the external world as deterministic and certain; "neither generalizations nor probabilities exist, except in brains; for they are not properties of the world of events" (p. xxv). The betting machine is not confronted with a god who throws dice; its raison d'être is a Laplacean epistemic probabilism, human ignorance caused by unreliable information. Brunswik's intuitive statistician plays the game of the brain against the world by multiple regression; Gregory's betting machine plays the brain game by the instruments of hypotheses testing, the new post-inference revolution statistics.

Gregory (1974a, p. 525) refers to R. A. Fisher's empiricist dictum, quoted earlier, that inductive inference is the only way to get new knowledge about the world. Fisher's concepts of null hypothesis and significance are introduced to illuminate the way the betting machine functions. Consider the question, why in the presence of competing hypotheses can we perceive an object having only *one* form and can achieve stability in perceiving exactly this form? "We may account for the stability of perceptual forms by suggesting that there is something akin to statistical significance which must be exceeded by the rival interpretation and the rival hypothesis before they are allowed to supersede the present perceptual hypothesis." (Gregory 1974a, p. 528). Significance testing of null hypotheses is also used as an analogy of how the betting machine learns that objects have different base rates in an environment. The analogy is that the betting machine starts with assuming no difference (the null hypothesis) and rejects the null if the actual base rates of the objects deviate far enough from equality. The deviation between the null and the actual base rates necessary for abandoning the null "could be interpreted as a measure of the criterion of 'significance' which the organism adopts, or demands, in this situation" (Gregory, 1974a, pp. 534–535).

Two remarks are necessary. First, Gregory (1974b) does not go into more detail with respect to the null hypothesis testing analogy, although he seems to be convinced that the analogy with hypothesis testing in particular and methods of science in general is more than only metaphorical language. Second, not all examples of perception as a selection between hypotheses can be properly explained by the null hypotheses

90   3. PERCEPTION

testing analogy. The reason is that the analogy poses the question, "Is object H_0 present or *anything else?*" whereas "selection" means to pose the question, "Which one of objects H_0, H_1, H_2, etc., is present?". The difference is that between asymmetric and symmetric testing of hypotheses, as pointed out in chapter 1. The mechanism of the betting machine may be more adequately described in terms of Neyman and Pearson's symmetric testing procedure, although generalized to more than two hypotheses. Such a view would assume that the mind calculates the likelihoods $p(D|H_0)$, $p(D|H_1)$, $p(D|H_2)$, and so on, for all possible objects (hypotheses) and adopts a decision criterion such as perceiving the object with the maximum likelihood.

Gregory (1974a) seems to imply exactly this when he explains the instability of ambiguous figures such as the Necker cube and the various and famous figure–ground reversals. "The jump from one perceptual experience to the other represents, on our theory, the putting up of alternative hypotheses for testing, both hypotheses having equal probability on the evidence. First one then the other hypothesis is accepted" (p. 527). Here, the betting machine must have adopted a symmetric testing procedure, otherwise $p(D|H_0)$ and $p(D|H_1)$ could not be calculated. However, whereas the stability of a perceived form, as mentioned, is consistent with assuming testing procedures as in science, the *instability* of these ambiguous figures, switching back and forth, seems not to be. The latter would be consistent with a symmetric test of hypotheses that is based on a decision criterion that *oscillates* over time. These oscillations, random or systematic, would force the betting machine to select one possible object for a time, then the other, then turn back to the first, and so on. Such a mechanism would also be consistent with the phenomenon that the alternative objects are never seen simultaneously, only successively. It would, however, no longer be consistent with an explicit hypothesis testing model in science, and this argument shows one boundary of the analogy between mechanisms of perception and methods of science.

To go a little further in elaborating the meaning of the hypothesis testing analogy of perception, let us pose the following question: Is the betting machine a Bayesian statistician? Consider one of the challenging facts in Gregory's examination game, the fact that a hollow mold of a face appears as a normal face, with the nose sticking out and not as it is, with the nose receding in. The betting machine gives us this percept, despite depth cues available in normal lighting such as texture and some stereopsis from the two eyes. Such phenomena should not exist according to a pickup theory, since higher order stimuli such as texture gradients should specify depth completely. Then why are improbable objects such as the hollow face more difficult to see than probable objects (of similar form)?

Gregory's (1974b) answer is: "We should expect on several grounds that hypotheses of high prior probability will be selected by less evidence than will hypotheses of low prior probability, if any reasonable efficient Bayesian selection procedure is adopted" (pp. 276f.). Thus, the betting machine seems to weight prior probabilities (values of $p(H)$) against likelihoods (values of $p(D|H)$) in some instances, as Bayes' theorem suggests; whereas in others, when it follows null hypothesis testing and the like, it is implied that it does not. If Bayes' theorem is used as the model, the notorious Nativist–Empiricist controversy turns into the question of whether the perceptual system starts from the very beginning with unequal prior probabilities or whether, in accordance with Laplace's (1774/1878-1912) principle of indifference, it starts with uniform priors, which are later modified by experience. An example for the first nativist view is the Gestalt thesis that the perceptual system favours certain objects, for example, objects with a "good Gestalt," over others.

What is the answer to our question concerning the nature of the hypotheses testing mechanism in the betting machine? The answer is that there is no single theory of hypotheses testing that functions as an explicit model. Instead there are references to Fisher's null hypothesis testing, to symmetric hypotheses testing *sensu* Neyman and Pearson, and to Bayesian statistics. Such a heterogeneous picture does not allow for quantitative predictions and falsification of a specific meaning of the "betting machine," but it does provide a conceptual repertoire that enables Gregory to articulate the unconscious inference tradition in the language of the new instruments of psychology after the inference revolution. And, interestingly, the hybrid character of inferential statistics in psychology is reflected in the hybrid nature of Gregory's betting machine. But since Gregory's main claim is that perception operates like a scientist, perhaps we should not be surprised at the statistical inconsistencies, for they are typical of real scientific practice.

THE DEDUCTIVE VIEW: COGNITIVE ALGEBRA

In the deductive view, perception means calculating. However, in contrast to the inductive view, these calculations are algebraic rather than probabilistic; they have a single solution and do not involve uncertain inferences from data to hypotheses. Since inductive inferences are not part of the perceptual process, techniques of statistical inference, in this view, are meaningless as an explanation. But deductive theories also differ from the realist view because the mind may perform the wrong calculation, and therefore perception need not be veridical. How closely a deductive view may be connected with a Helmholtzian view can be

92   3. PERCEPTION

illustrated by Irvin Rock, who was originally an ardent advocate of the Gestalt point of view but converted to Helmholtz' idea that perception functions like conscious reasoning. Rock (1977, 1983) considers many but not all kinds of perception as problem solving but identifies problem solving with a kind of cognitive algebra, where uncertain inferences are not involved. For example, consider how Rock (1983) explains why an observer whose head is laterally tilted 50° clockwise can nevertheless perceive a horizontal line as being horizontal. What Rock calls an unconscious inference is the following calculation:

> 1.   The line is perceived as egocentrically oblique at a 40-degree clockwise angle with respect to the head (proximal mode).
> 2.   Information is available that the head is tilted 50 degrees clockwise with respect to gravity.
> 3.   Therefore, the line in the environment producing the image must be 90 degrees from the direction of gravity, or horizontal (world mode percept) (p. 273).

Rock calls this unconscious adding of two angles a "transitive deductive inference": perceiving means adding or multiplying numbers (and, as we shall see, for most cases, only two such numbers). This example illustrates the range in the use of the term unconscious inference.

In this section we show how even the deductive theory was influenced by the inference revolution. This is a particularly interesting kind of influence, since deductive theories by definition do *not* use the metaphor of perception as an intuitive statistician of whatever school. In the following we conduct a case study on Norman H. Anderson's deductive approach, which he calls "cognitive algebra" or "information integration theory" (Anderson, 1970, 1981, 1982). Standing neither in the Helmholtzian nor in the Gibsonian tradition, cognitive algebra tends to be neglected by authors in these traditions (e.g. Gibson, 1979; Gregory, 1974a, b; Hochberg, 1979; Rock, 1983) but has found resonance in neo-Brunswikean approaches (e.g. Brehmer, 1979, 1984).

Some authors even consider Anderson "an intellectual descendant of Brunswik's probabilistic functionalism" (Massaro, 1984, p. 12). Of course, Brunswik's theoretical perspective is meant here rather than his methods, representative design, and correlation statistics. We shall, however, soon make clear that even here the differences are fundamental: for instance, the proximal–distal distinction, the uncertainty of cues, and the statistical metaphor of perception are nonexistent in cognitive algebra. Cognitive algebra combines a deductive view of cognitive processes with what Anderson calls an "inductive research philosophy," which is wholly dependent on techniques of the inference revolution, namely, on null hypotheses testing by way of Fisher's analysis of variance. Probably

THE DEDUCTIVE VIEW: COGNITIVE ALGEBRA   93

because of the popularity of this instrument, Anderson's research program is making inroads into almost every area of psychology.

We shall concentrate on the question, how do we perceive the area of rectangular objects? We have selected this issue for the case study because (a) it is here that proponents of cognitive algebra claim one of their greatest "discoveries," the so-called Height + Width rule used by children; (b) it parallels our discussion of the program of the Vienna Brunswik; and (c) the issue has the advantage of being relatively simple, thus clarifying the argument. With this case study we shall show, at a concrete level, the impact of the inference revolution on a deductive view. Our arguments will be the following:

1. *Hypotheses Considered.* Hypotheses considered for cognitive (deductive) processes are restricted to those which are expressible in the language of analysis of variance. That is, analysis of variance functions as an implicit tool for hypothesis construction.

2. *Hypothesis Testing.* Since null hypothesis testing, like analysis of variance, rejects and accepts hypotheses by an asymmetric procedure (see chapter 1), empirical results depend on what has been defined as the null hypothesis.

3. *The Danger of Circular Conclusions.* Biases both in hypotheses construction and testing can combine: A hypothesis that can be expressed in terms of analysis of variance is more likely to be confirmed by the analysis of variance.

Perception as Cognitive Algebra

Figure 3.5 illustrates the analysis of the perception of area of rectangular objects by information integration theory. The judgment of area is considered as a sequence of three transformations: (a) the psychophysical functions V and V' transforming physical height H and width W into subjective height h and width w, respectively, (b) the integration process I that combines h and w into subjective area a, and (c) the psychomotor or response function M that transforms a into the judged area A on a rating scale. Note that only H, W, and A can be measured directly; everything else must be inferred.

Let us consider the first transformation on the left side of Fig. 3.5. Note first that there is no distinction made between distal variables and proximal cues, which is essential for the inductive view. No proximal cues mediate between physical height and width and the subjective values for these. With this, cue uncertainty and inductive inference are eliminated, as in Gibson's theory. The assumption is that there exist for height and width subjective values that are monotonic functions of the physical

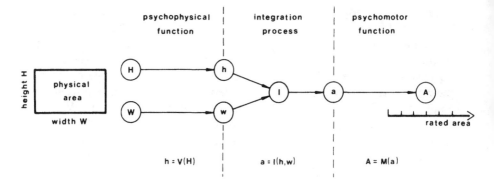

FIGURE 3.5. Analysis of area judgments by information integration theory. H and W denote physical values for height and width; h and w denote subjective values for height and width, a and A stand for the subjective value for area and the judgment of area on a rating scale, respectively.

values. Anderson calls these "psychophysical" functions but does not specify them, since this is not essential for his further argument (note that the use of the term deviates from Stevens'). Second, Brunswik and Anderson start with different answers to the question, what are the dimensions attended to? Whereas Brunswik assumes that these are area (because of the instruction to judge area) and shape (as covarying information), Anderson first decomposes the rectangular object into height and width and postulates that the mind integrates them again. Since the subjective values of height are assumed independent of width (and vice versa), as can be seen from the two psychophysical functions, context independence (see chapter 3) is assumed. The main focus, however, is on the nature of the integration process (in the middle of Fig. 3.5), and it is from this emphasis that the term cognitive algebra comes. What does integration mean? It is assumed that a percept such as subjective area is calculated from independent cognitive units, h and w, by means of a cognitive algebra. But what kind of algebra is cognitive algebra? The claim is made (Anderson & Cuneo, 1978; Cuneo, 1980; Wilkening, 1979) that children around the age of 5 perceive area by *adding* subjective height and width, whereas adults *multiply:*

Area = Height + Width (children),
Area = Height × Width (adults).

The 'discovery' of the hitherto unknown Height + Width rule used by children stimulated a large amount of developmental research. The final and general thesis was that cognitive development means a change in integration rules (Anderson, 1980).

We turn now to the response function on the right side of Fig. 3.5.

THE DEDUCTIVE VIEW: COGNITIVE ALGEBRA   **95**

Whereas Brunswik does not distinguish between perception (subjective values) and judgment, information integration theory does. Recall Brunswik's opposition to introspection, which forced him to choose a judgmental task that reduces introspection to the unavoidable minimum. The task of the Vienna Brunswik was the judgment of equality, either by matching a comparison to a standard or by pointing to equal objects. Judgments of this kind demand neither responses with numbers nor responses in a verbal mode. In contrast, information integration theory relies on numerical responses generated by rating scales. This is the data appropriate for the subsequent analysis of variance. Of course, the question concerning the meaningfulness and reliability of numerical answers must be raised, particularly with children's ratings, and we shall come back to this issue.

However, the focus of the research program is on the nature of neither the response function nor the psychophysical function, but of the integration process. The claim is that numerous experiments throughout cognitive psychology have shown that humans—children as well as adults—integrate information mostly by simply *adding, multiplying,* or *averaging*. Of course, there seem to be some exceptions (e.g. Anderson, 1982, p. 299), but the general claim is that it has been discovered that these simple algebraic operations explain how perception functions. Adding, multiplying, and averaging are considered as the very essence of cognitive functioning; they "lay bare the underlying structure of information processing" and represent not only form, but process. (Anderson, 1981, p. 80; 1982, pp. 298–300).

As early as 1965 Anderson (1981) already believed that "it was clear that a simple, unified account of a complex of data had emerged" (pp. xiii, 3). According to this account, most human judgment is simple cognitive algebra such as

Deservingness = Achievement + Need,
Heaviness   = Weight + Appearance, and
Performance = Motivation × Ability.

Because of the ubiquity of such conclusions, Anderson makes the proposal that the adding and multiplying operations should be considered as *general-purpose integration processes,* which operate in many contexts and contents.

The Fisherian Perspective in Hypothesis Construction

Consider a two-factorial design with height and width as factors. What questions can we answer if we apply analysis of variance to the design? We can pose the following questions: whether one or both of the factors

96   3. PERCEPTION

are significant, and whether the interaction between the two factors is significant. This vocabulary gives *all* the hypotheses that have been constructed and examined by information integration theory (Anderson, 1980; Anderson & Cuneo, 1978; Cuneo, 1980; Wilkening, 1979, 1980):

(1) Area = Height, or Area = Width   (only one factor significant)
(2) Area = Height + Width   (both factors significant)
(3) Area = Height × Width   (interaction significant)

There are three points to make concerning hypothesis construction: (a) the hypotheses constructed are those expressible in combinations of significant main factor and interaction effects, as shown in the foregoing; (b) hypotheses not expressible in these terms are no longer considered; (c) the new language is used as a Procrustean bed for Piaget's theory on the issue—his ideas are pressed into the categories supplied by the new language, at the price of some distortion. This point must be elaborated.

The simplest species of cognitive algebra hypotheses, the Height-only and Width-only rules (only one factor significant) can be used to illustrate the Procrustean effect of the analysis of variance terminology. Anderson and Cuneo (1978) believe that these represent Piaget's theory of centration, and consequently they claim to have disproved Piaget's theory. However, Piaget's (1969) *law of relative centrations* predicts that the perceived height is *dependent* on the width, and vice versa, in the sense that a physical height is overestimated when paired with a shorter width and underestimated when paired with a longer width. Such a dependence contradicts the context independence assumption (independent functions V and V'), and all of the previously cited simple cognitive algebra hypotheses. Of course, it is fair to say that Piaget's concept of centration has more than one meaning, but it is with this "law" that Piaget actually studied the perceived height in rectangular objects. This law is clearly not what a single significant factor in analysis of variance expresses; it even contradicts the basic assumption of independent values for height and width, which are implied by the height-only and width-only rules.

To summarize, the hypotheses considered are limited to a narrow spectrum, namely those that can be expressed by the vocabulary of analysis of variance: hypotheses are combinations of main and interaction effects. Hypotheses that would need a different vocabulary, such as the cue learning principle, the perceptual compromise principle, or Piaget's law of relative centration are either not considered or assimilated into the Procrustean bed of analysis of variance.

The Fisherian Perspective in Hypothesis Testing

There would be no objection against a narrow principle of hypotheses construction, if the resulting hypothesis were correct. But how can we know? Anderson's tool for testing is, again, Fisher's analysis of variance.

THE DEDUCTIVE VIEW: COGNITIVE ALGEBRA   97

He rejects Karl Pearson's correlation and regression analysis as a tool for testing goodness of fit. Here he is absolutely correct in pointing out the many problems arising from multiple regression as suggested by Brunswik (1956) and used by Neo-Brunswikeans (e.g. Hammond, Stewart, Brehmer, & Steinmann, 1975). Any justification of hypotheses based on calculating correlations between predicted and observed values is now called "weak inference" (Anderson & Shanteau, 1977), whereas null hypothesis testing is "strong inference." But how strong is strong inference? We have already pointed out the limitations and blind spots in Fisher's asymmetric testing of competing hypotheses by rejecting a null hypothesis (as opposed to Neyman and Pearson's symmetric test of hypotheses, see chapter 1). We shall now point out the blind spots as they reappear in cognitive algebra.

How was the Height + Width rule inferred from the ratings of 5-year-old children? The key argument is the following *parallelism theorem:*

Parallelism Theorem: If subjective height and width are integrated by an adding operation *and* if the response (i.e. psychomotor) function is linear, then the factorial data plot will form a set of parallel curves.

Figure 3.6a illustrates the predicted parallel curves. Each point corresponds to one rectangle. If we replace "adding" by "multiplying" in the above theorem, than we get a diverging fan of curves, as shown in Fig. 3.6b. For comparison, we have added the predictions of the cue learning principle, assuming that squarelike shapes (as opposed to elongated shapes) are taken as cues for indicating larger area. Therefore, the squares (4×4, 8×8, 12×12, and 16×16) are overestimated, as can be seen in Fig. 3.6c.

Three points can be made concerning hypothesis testing. First, the *joint* impact of analysis of variance on hypothesis construction and testing tends to "validate" the constructed hypotheses, even if others hold. This can be seen in Fig. 3.6c, where the predictions of the cue learning principle are made explicit. This hypothesis cannot be expressed by the vocabulary of significant main and interaction effects, and such data would be easily mistaken for "random" deviation from "simple" cognitive algebra such as "multiplying."

Second, the "validation" of the Height + Width rule rests on the *confirmation of the null hypothesis* of no interaction. The significance of the interaction is the criterion by which the decision between the two major models, adding and multiplying, is made. If the two major main effects (height and width) are significant, but not the interaction, then it is concluded that the child uses the Height + Width rule; if, however, the interaction is significant (more precisely, its bilinear component), it is concluded that a multiplying rule is used. Therefore, the more "error" the

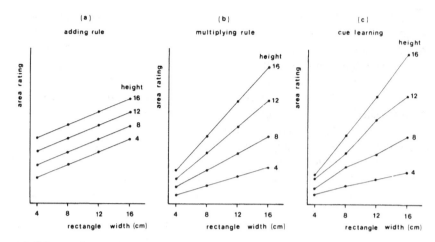

FIGURE 3.6. Predictions for area ratings if the perceptual system (a) adds subjective height and width, (b) multiplies subjective height and width, and (c) uses the cue learning principle to infer the area. A linear response function is assumed in all three cases. For the cue learning principle, area ratings are assumed to be dependent on shape (i.e. shape is used as a cue for area): Elongated rectangles are underestimated; squarelike rectangles are overestimated. Of the 16 combinations of height and width shown in the figure, there results a total of 6 different shapes (ratio of smaller to larger side): 1/4, 1/3, 1/2, 2/3, 3/4, 1/1. To give quantitative predictions, the most elongated shape (1/4) was assumed to be underestimated by 10%, and the most square-like shape (1/1) was assumed to be overestimated by 10%. The shapes 1/3 and 3/4 were assumed to be underestimated and overestimated by 5%, respectively, while we assumed no deviation for the two remaining shapes. Of course, if we had assumed effects greater than 10%, the differences between (b) and (c) would have been more pronounced.

ratings of area contain (and the ratings of 5-year-old children are highly unreliable, see Gigerenzer 1983b, c), the larger the error term and the less likely it is that a significant interaction will be found. This gives apparent support to the adding rule. Note that the inference from the nonsignificance of the interaction to the Height + Width rule goes beyond what Fisher himself allowed: Fisher (1935) explicitly stated that we must not infer a hypothesis from a nonsignificant result (p. 16). We return later to this issue.

Third, can we infer at all that children add subjective values from observed parallel curves such as those in Fig. 3.6a? Of course not, since there are numerous alternative parallelism theorems. For instance, Birnbaum (1982, p. 451) gives four alternatives, one of which is the following: If subjective height and width are integrated by a multiplying operation, and if the response function is logarithmic, then the factorial plot will be a set of parallel curves. We realize now the fundamental dilemma: Parallel curves give us virtually no information about the nature of the supposed integration rule per se, and they give us no information about the nature

THE DEDUCTIVE VIEW: COGNITIVE ALGEBRA   99

of the response function per se. We may only conclude that some combinations, "integration rule *plus* response function," are in agreement with parallel curves, such as the two combinations mentioned earlier. Other combinations, *including the same integration rule* as in Anderson's parallelism theorem, such as "adding rule *plus* logarithmic response function", are in contradiction to parallel curves. This clearly shows that an inference from ratings (as in Fig. 3.6) to integration rules per se cannot be made.

Do the proponents of cognitive algebra now withdraw their claim (e.g. Anderson, 1981, pp. 81ff) that they inductively arrive at their discoveries through analysis of variance? No. Anderson's faith in inductive research echoes Fisher's (1935): "Inductive inference is the only process known to us by which essentially new knowledge comes into the world" (p. 7). Anderson clearly sees and discusses the problem that empirical answers are available only for combinations and not for integration rules. But like Fisher, he does not hesitate to assert in strong words thereafter that there is a solution: "Nevertheless, a rigorous, objective foundation for these three unobservables [*I, R*, and *V*, in Fig. 3.5] can be constructed from the observable stimuli and response. That is actually quite easy to do." (Anderson, 1981, p. 5). The "rigorous" foundation is analysis of variance. From significant main effects for height and width and a nonsignificant interaction, the Height + Width rule is claimed to hold: "Five-year-olds judge area of rectangles by an adding, Height + Width rule" and "Parallelism *implies* that 5-year-old children judge area of rectangle by Height + Width rule" (Anderson, 1981, p. 33, italics ours).

Of course, such conclusions are unwarranted, as we have stressed. The parallelism result is used to argue backwards toward an arbitrary affirmation of one of the two assumptions (i.e. the integration rule). Must we conclude that the inductive research philosophy which "discovered" the Height + Width rule is mainly faulty logic? Not yet, because there exists an experiment, designed to rule out *one* possible alternative explanation, the combination of a multiplying integration and a logarithmic response function (Anderson & Cuneo, 1978, Experiment 6). This single critical experiment illustrates our claim of circularity in hypothesis construction and testing, in particular the danger of "proving" whatever was put forward as the null hypothesis.

The Circle of Hypothesis Construction and Testing

The experiment is based on an interesting idea: If children must judge the *joint* area of two rectangles, then one can differentiate between the hypothesis "Height + Width rule *plus* linear response function" and an alternative, the "Height × Width rule *plus* logarithmic response func-

100   3. PERCEPTION

tion" hypothesis. According to the "adding/linear" hypothesis, the joint estimated area A_{1+2} of the two rectangles (assuming a rectangle + rectangle rule) is:

$$A_{1+2} = c_1(h_1 + w_1 + h_2 + w_2) + c_0$$

where c_1 and c_0 are the constants of the linear function. According to the "multiplying/logarithmic" hypothesis, the joint area is:

$$A_{1+2} = \log(h_1 w_1 + h_2 w_2).$$

The actual sizes of the rectangle pairs used in the decision experiment and the averaged ratings of their joint areas by 16 5-year-olds are shown in Fig. 3.7 (actual data). Each point corresponds to a pair of rectangles.

What can be concluded from these two crooked curves? Anderson and Cuneo follow Fisher's lead: They test a null hypothesis, and thus they test

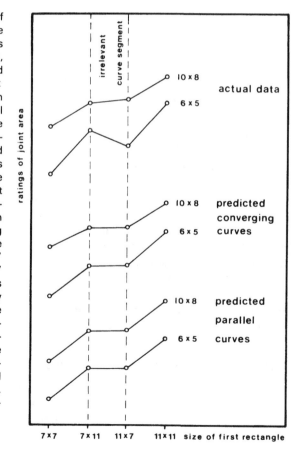

FIGURE 3.7. Analysis of asymmetric testing. The size of the first rectangle is specified on the abscissa, and the size of the second rectangle was either 10 × 8 or 6 × 5. The bottom graph shows the parallel curves predicted by the "adding/linear" hypothesis. The distance apart and the slope of these curves are chosen to approximate the data, as these are not specified by the hypothesis. The middle graph shows the converging curves predicted by the "multiplying/logarithmic" hypothesis. Since V and V' are not specified by this hypothesis, for simplicity we assumed them to be identity functions. The distances between corresponding points on the two curves can then be calculated as .213, .167, and .124 for the 7 × 7, 7 × 11, 11 × 7, and 11 × 11 rectangle, respectively.

THE DEDUCTIVE VIEW: COGNITIVE ALGEBRA **101**

asymmetrically. As in all tests of the adding rule, the null hypothesis is no interaction. Anderson and Cuneo (1978) find: "The curves are nearly parallel, and the interaction did not approach significance, $F(4,56) = 1.20$, showing that the adding rule did replicate" (p. 352). And finally they conclude that "these results *imply* that the judgments of single rectangles follow the height + width rule and that the judgments of the pairs follow the rectangle + rectangle rule" (p. 353, italics ours).

Note that Anderson and Cuneo did not, as Neyman and Pearson argued, specify the predictions of the competing hypothesis and determine the likelihoods of the data under both hypotheses. Therefore, *we* have specified these predictions in Fig. 3.7: the parallel curves predicted by the adding/linear hypothesis and the converging curves predicted by the multiplying/logarithmic hypothesis. (The predictions show, curiously enough, that two rectangles, 7×11 and 11×7, are used, which give the same predictions for both hypotheses, namely, parallel curves in either case. Incidentally, this artificially favours a nonsignificant interaction, but this is not our primary concern here. We shall not consider the irrelevant middle segment in Fig. 3.7 further.) With respect to the two outer segments, the adding/linear hypothesis predicts parallel curves, whereas the multiplying/logarithmic hypothesis predicts converging curves (converging from left to right).

Note that null hypothesis testing finds no significant difference between the actual data at the top of Fig. 3.7 and the predicted parallel lines at the bottom. However, it can be seen that the actual data is closer to the predicted converging curves than to the predicted parallel curves. (The actual data converge left to right, and to an even greater extent than do the predicted converging curves.) Imagine that the children had produced ratings coinciding exactly with the predicted converging curves; these imaginary ratings would not have yielded a signficant interaction either, since the actual data—more extreme than the imaginary ratings—did not do so. Hence, even if the children had conformed exactly to the multiplying/logarithmic hypothesis, the conclusion would still have been that they conformed to the adding/linear hypothesis.

The general point is that with Fisher's null hypothesis testing one of the two competing hypothesis is identified with the null hypothesis, whereas the other is not specified. Only when we specify the alternative, however, can we see the validity of the argument in the previous paragraph. It can also be seen that had we selected the multiplying/logarithmic hypothesis as the null hypothesis, we would have found no significant difference between the predicted and the actual data. Thus, we would have "confirmed" the multiplying/logarithmic hypothesis. But, from the perspective of the linear additive model underlying analysis of variance, the null hypothesis is always the adding rule.

102   3. PERCEPTION

The basic reason why analysis of variance was not able to detect the obvious difference between the actual data and the predicted parallel curves is the considerable amount of error in the ratings. In general, the greater the error, the greater the probability of survival for that hypothesis which has been selected as the null hypothesis.

The present argument is not restricted to the alternative of a multiplying rule plus a logarithmic response function. Children using any perceptual strategy that gives predictions within the range shown in Fig. 3.7, or even beyond, would have been found by analysis of variance to use the Height + Width rule.

If we were forced to conclude anything from this, the only crucial experiment extant, it would have to be that the data supports the multiplying/logarithmic hypothesis. Even this is in doubt, however, because of the large amount of error in the ratings. This amount of error results (a) from forced quantification by using rating scales, which produces highly unreliable data in 5-year-olds (Gigerenzer 1983b, 1984b); (b) from the difficulty of the task, that is, the judging of the joint area of two rectangles; and (c) from taking interindividual difference as error variability in the analysis of variance. In fact, it has been found that if children are given simpler tasks (paired comparison rather than ratings), the error is reduced to the low level of that of adults, and symmetric testing of competing hypotheses reveals no hint of a Height + Width rule but does indicate a dependence of judged area on shape (Gigerenzer, 1984b; Lohaus, in press; Richter & Gigerenzer, 1984). Recall that Gosset, who developed the t-test, said that the important thing is to have a low real error, not to have a significant result.

Let us summarize. We have used the Height + Width rule of 5-year-old children as a case study for evaluating the impact of the inference revolution on a deductive view of perception. In Norman H. Anderson's cognitive algebra, Fisher's analysis of variance provides both the conceptual language for constructing hypotheses and the instrument for testing them. This interdependence can lead, as we have shown, to circularity in the construction and subsequent "empirical" validation of the simple algebraic rules that the perceptual system is supposed to use.

The methodological moral of this tale is two-fold. In general, null hypothesis testing is inadequate to test competing hypotheses, as Neyman and Pearson showed (see chapter 1). In this particular case, there is the additional problem that the analysis of variance also controls hypothesis construction: Out of all the possible cognitive algebra hypotheses, only those that fit the linear, additive structure of the analysis of variance are even considered. This formal structure of the technique tends to replace a conceptual analysis specific to the subject matter—in this case, perception. Compare the theoretical richness of the other approaches

SUMMARY

discussed in this chapter with the pared down vocabulary of the cognitive algebra school, which could be (and is) applied to almost any other domain, from moral judgment to risk taking. However, this very generality may be responsible for the increasing popularity of the approach, even though that generality (and the simplification of research design that it implies) is purchased at the expense of subject-specific theoretical context.

SUMMARY

In this chapter we traced the transformation of the scientific explanation of how the perceptual system estimates the properties of objects. This question is subsequent to that treated in the previous chapter, how an object or a difference between objects is detected. In contrast to the detection process, the notion that the perceptual system performs inferences has been present in explanatory accounts of object perception since 1866, when the third volume of Helmholtz' *Physiological Optics* was published. The meaning of Helmholtz' unconscious inferences can be represented by a probabilistic syllogism: The perceived location, size, and so forth of an object is an uncertain inference based on proximal, sensory information (minor premise) and a generalization from experience (major premise).

For about 100 years, the idea of unconscious inference seemed to many psychologists to be self-contradictory. They assumed that consciousness is necessary for inferences. This belief changed with the inference revolution, when the techniques of the scientist, inferential statistics, and computers were applied to the way the mind works. The idea that unconscious inferences is a selfcontradicting explanation now appears as semantic inertia. Today, the perceptual system is assumed to set levels of significance and to test null hypotheses unconsciously.

Neo-Helmholtzians such as R.L. Gregory assert that Helmholtz' unconscious inferences were neglected for a century or more, during the reign of physiological theories and Gestalt theory. We have pointed out a major exception to that neglect, Egon Brunswik's intuitive statistician. Brunswik transformed the meaning of unconscious inferences from a probabilistic syllogism to correlation and regression statistics: The perceptual system estimates an object's size, distance, and the like by unconsciously calculating multiple regressions. Beginning in the late 1930s, Brunswik did the same thing, as many psychologists did after the inference revolution: He took the statistical instruments available at the time as a model of cognitive processes. But Karl Pearson's correlational statistics were not considered indispensable in experimental psychology:

104 3. PERCEPTION

instead they were the essential tools of the Galton–Pearson program, and the schism between the two programs was already deep (see Cronbach, 1957; Dashiell, 1939). Although Brunswik's metaphor of the intuitive statistician is widely used today, with many a meaning, at the time it was neither accepted nor for the most part even understood. We consider Brunswik's case, like Thurstone's, as historical events that support the *tools-to-theories hypothesis*. Only after inferential statistics had been institutionalized by the inference revolution and come to be seen as an indispensable instrument of the scientist could the link between the mind and the statistician be understood and accepted by the experimental community.[2]

Like signal detection theory, Brunswik's intuitive statistician was not a necessary consequence of experimental facts, as we have shown in detail. The same seems to hold for the significance testing and null hypotheses analogies after the inference revolution.

For the post-1955 period we have selected three theories that represent the three old, competing approaches to knowledge: inductive, deductive, and naive realism. Gibson's direct theory can be seen as the most influential incarnation of the naive realistic view: *We see what is there*. The best way to understand perception is to assume that it is immediate, certain, and veridical. Cognitive algebra may be seen as the representative of the deductive or mathematical approach to knowledge: *We compute what is there*. Perception means to perform calculations on mental numbers. The mental numbers are taken for certain; no statistics are needed, but perception may be nonveridical (such as with the Height + Width rule) since the wrong calculation may be performed on the correct numbers. We have shown by a case study on area judgment that Fisher's dogma of null hypothesis testing has had a great impact on cognitive algebra research. It shapes the hypotheses put forward and at the same time provides the criterion by which these are tested; we have pointed out the resulting danger of circular verification. As in Gibson's theory, there is no uncertainty besides measurement error. Finally, Gregory's version of unconscious inferences is a modern representative of the inductive

---

[2]With hindsight, Brunswik's intuitive statistician even appears similar to a Neyman and Pearsonian decision maker: "Perceiving, since it involves inference, rests upon a decision process, as Brunswik (. . .) and Tanner and Swets (. . .) and others have pointed out" (Bruner, 1973, p. 15). Although this may be intended to rehabilitate Brunswik's intuitive statistician by putting him hand in hand with the successful post-inference revolution metaphor of an "ideal observer" in TSD, it reflects the widespread condensation of *different* and *competing* statistical metaphors. (See also Peterson & Beach [1967, p. 29], who treat both Bayesian reasoning and the "ideal observer" in TSD as normative for their "intuitive statistician," although as shown in chapter 5, both statistical models may produce conflicting predictions.)

approach to knowledge: *We infer what is there*. Perception is based on induction and therefore is in principle incomplete. Gregory has been persuaded by the inference revolution that perceptual processes are best understood as statistical hypothesis testing. His view of the perceptual system as an induction machine, or betting machine, mirrors scientific practice: The induction machine is as eclectic as scientific practice in its choice of statistical theories and, in particular, as inconsistent as the hybrid theory of the inference revolution.

For all three approaches, perception still seems intimately tied to epistemology and thus to the question of what is the best way of knowing. In this sense, all three present-day approaches are normative. However, it is the inductive position that has been strengthened by the explosive evolution of statistical methods during the last hundred years. And this evolution is reflected in the evolution in the meaning of the inference metaphor, from Helmholtz' probabilistic syllogism to Brunswik's multiple regression to Gregory's inferential statistics.

There is a final parallel between visual perception and scientific practice concerning the certainty in which both present their products. We experience what we see as *certain*: We see that the moon is larger on the horizon than up in the sky; we see the Swiss mountains arising immediately behind Lake Constance when the view is very clear, but under normal viewing conditions we see them far away. We do not see the size of the moon and the location of the Swiss mountains oscillating according to the degree of uncertainty involved in the perceptual inference. Here, the perceptual system seems to proceed like the average scientist: A conclusion based on many uncertainties, from sampling to inductive inference, is finally presented as a fact, as something that approaches certainty. This aim of both seems to be to deemphasize uncertainty and to generate certainty.

4 Memory: From Association to Decision Making

In this chapter we ask how far the metaphor of the intuitive statistician can be, and has been, applied to the study of human memory.

There are few areas of psychological study that are so full of competing models and collections of data, which are not always properly understood, as memory. As mentioned in chapter 1, metaphors have been applied to memory since the time of the Greeks. One feature standing in the way of the application of the metaphor of the intuitive statistician is that memory storage has sometimes been considered a passive process in which decision-making is hardly called for. According to those who believe that memory is a passive process, the organism possesses a cluster of habits or memories which are evoked by appropriate stimuli or retrieval cues, and processes such as decision making and hypothesis testing are relatively unimportant. This was the traditional view until the time of the inference revolution, but it is worth asking whether there were any writers prior to the inference revolution who did conceive of the retrieval process as involving inference. First, then, let us briefly survey memory theory as it existed before the inference revolution.

HISTORY: BEFORE THE INFERENCE REVOLUTION

The Behaviorist Legacy

Classical learning theory can be considered to have started before Pavlov, because from the 17th to the 19th centuries (and even earlier) the view was commonly put forward that the individual is, so to speak, propelled by habit to do one thing rather than another in a situation when choice must be made. In the 17th century, an English anatomist, Thomas Willis (1672/1971) described how a horse feeling hungry will experience changes in his nervous system—a flow of "animal spirits" down particular channels of the brain—of such a nature that the thought of food arouses the thought of a field associated with food, which in turn initiates a movement toward that field. It was stressed by several French writers of the 17th century that learning could be inculcated by association of a movement with a reward and that punishment could be used to decrease undesired behavior (Diamond, 1969). When "habits" were so instilled by associations with reward, or were decreased by association with punishment, the model emerged of the animal or person being motivated to action by whichever associations were strongest at a particular time. The great tradition of associationist psychology presented this model for the next three centuries. In James (1890/1950), the "flow of animal spirits" has been replaced by a model according to which nervous "excitement" can be selectively channelled in one direction or another. But the idea is the same as Willis's; habits themselves, for example, are ingrained by virtue of the following law: "When two elementary brain-processes have been active together or in immediate succession, one of them, on reoccurring, tends to propagate its excitement into the other" (p.566).

The discovery of classical conditioning by Pavlov, and, independently, by Twitmyer in the United States in 1902 (see Coon, 1982), gave credibility to this model. Pavlov himself developed an elaborate account of how nervous excitation and nervous inhibition—an important addition to the associationist armory—spread from one brain area to another during the course of conditioning. Excitation and inhibition were also incorporated into Hull's (1943) model of the course of animal learning, and throughout this period the notion seems to have been firmly entrenched that repetition of two stimuli together or successively will somehow strengthen the association between the brain representations of two stimuli.

The relationship between the connectionist theories of how habits were strengthened in animals and theories of memory processes in humans was not always clearly specified, and even now the matter is ambiguous. At the outset of behaviorism, Watson (1919, 1924) argued that language itself was a habit, with speech responses being motor conditioned reflexes elicited by stimuli or by previous motor responses (as in inner speech) and that therefore there was no strong reason to think of memory as separate from that of habit. In fact, Watson avoided the use of the word memory, partly because it has associations with consciousness, a topic he wished to banish from psychology. Instead one was to refer to habits or skills, which could be strengthened by use or weakened by disuse. In this context, there was little room for such processes as inference. Watson, if confronted with the question of how far retrieving or recognizing involves

108   4. MEMORY

inference, would probably have considered the question misleading or anthropomorphic: if a "memory" was hard to retrieve, it was because other responses were prepotent given the stimulus circumstances; and the statement that "one is searching" for the correct response is only a metaphor best avoided. If a subject was engaged in evaluating the hypothesis, "I have seen X before" and claims that he used inference in the process, it was better described, for Watson, by saying that X has aroused a number of competing responses and vacillation is occurring. But simply because it is convenient for the human to say "I have decided so-and-so," it is not necessarily appropriate to speak of an animal's having decided something. This has overtones of conscious activity. Instead competing habit strengths determine the outcome in a choice situation, and there is no need for the language of decision making in the scientific vocabulary describing behaviour in a choice or conflict situation.

These views were given additional support by the success of models of human learning based on competition between verbal response tendencies. The most extreme expression of this view was the *Mathematico-deductive Theory of Rote Learning* of Hull and his colleagues (1940), a book that offered an exactly worked out theory of response competition based on a few hypotheses about excitation and inhibition in the nervous correlates of the verbal responses being studied. A number of phenomena were explained by this theory, including why distributed learning is more efficient than massed learning—because there is more time for inhibition to die away between trials in distributed learning. Another phenomenon only recently reinvestigated is reminiscence, where something that has been forgotten early after original learning "comes back" at a later time. The early forgetting was seen as due to a buildup of inhibition, which, when it faded away, allowed the learned response to reappear. From 1940 to about 1965, the development of theories of response competition became very sophisticated, yet in all of this there was little mention of cognitive activity other than the raw and unanalyzed process of rote learning itself.

This belief in the essential passivity of the animal or human had its critics however. In the 1930s, Tolman believed that animals could conjure a mental representation of a stimulus in its absence and that certain rather clever behaviours by animals could be explained if they had "cognitive maps" of the environment.

Tolman (1932) was quite explicit that when a stimulus was presented, it does not merely release a habit (as Watson and Hull had implied) but can arouse an expectation. An expectation was defined by Tolman as "an immanent cognitive determinant aroused by actually presented stimuli"

(p. 446). An expectation can have three moods or aspects. One is "perception," when a present stimulus leads to the expectation that another stimulus is also present, because they are both concurrently present. Another is "mnemonization," when a present stimulus leads to the expectation that another stimulus is also present, because the stimuli have been perceived together in the past. A third is "inference," when a present stimulus leads to the expectation that another stimulus is present, even though the two have not been perceived together before. In this instance the present stimulus is called the "sign-object": "Nevertheless (perhaps because of past experience with "relatively similar" situations, or because of pure creativity) the organism is led to invent the sort of signified object and sort of direction-distance relations to this signified object which will result from commerce with the given sign-object" (p. 446).

For Tolman, animals use inference chiefly as a means of making novel associations, which can lead to the acquisition of new skills and allow for much greater adaptability in new situations than the passive behavioristic model allowed for—in fact, he devoted a whole chapter to examples of inferential behavior in rats. Tolman and Honzik (1930) showed that rats would develop a preference for route A in a maze, followed by route B (longer than A, but sharing a final common segment with A), followed by route C (the longest route, not sharing a final common segment with A). This hierarchy of habits was, however, not followed unreasoningly. If the final segment common to A and B was blocked, a rat who found it could not use A would then follow path C; it did not follow B, presumably because it could infer that B was also blocked. For Tolman, therefore, inference was an intrinsic part of the learning process, and in turn the ability to infer depended on the animal's having a cognitive representation of the world.

But Tolman was not always heeded, and it is only lately that he has received his proper credit. Gleitman (1981) has written a popular introductory text in which he clearly presents Tolman's notion that, on the basis of previous experience, an animal can form an *expectation* about what will happen when it sees a stimulus and that even classical conditioning can therefore contain a cognitive element. But in the heyday of classical learning theory, from about 1935 to 1960, animals were usually seen as bundles of potential responses, which were elicited passively by stimuli, and the emphasis was on how they would move in a given situation. The notion that the animal possesses mental representations was assumed to be suspect because anthropomorphic, and even Köhler's 1917 evidence for intelligent behavior in chimpanzees was seen as ultimately reducible to concatenations of previously learned habits.

110   4. MEMORY

Studies of Human Memory: Semon and Bartlett

During the peak years of behaviorism, from about 1920 to 1965, a great deal of research was carried out on human rote memorizing, the classic work in this endeavor being the monograph on rote learning by Hull *et al.* (1940). Following Watson, it was accepted that "consciousness" was a term to be avoided, and little mention was made of "decision-making" or "inference." Two workers on memory, however, stressed that memory does not consist of fixed, lifeless traces but that the process of retrieving involves cognitive activities such as inference. Both wrote before the inference revolution, and their conception of inference did not include statistical inference. Because their theories depend heavily on new concepts of memory storage, we shall discuss these concepts in each case. Richard Semon (1904/1921; 1909/1923) argued for a model of memory in which the very act of retrieving a memory changes the memory itself; Sir Frederic C. Bartlett (1932) proposed a comprehensive account of memory in which each memory is not judged in isolation but only in the context of a mass of memories.

In Semon's account, a memory is called an *engram*, which refers to a change in neurological encoding that occurs when the stimulus is first encountered. But this change is such that if the stimulus, or a similar one, is encountered again, the original engram can be aroused by a process unique to nervous systems and to which Semon gave the name *synergistic ecphory*. The effect of re-presenting a stimulus is that an old engram can be revived, giving rise to an experience of recognition. In turn, the re-presented stimulus can lay down its own engram, which will be associated by contiguity with the rearoused engram of the first experience. Thus, memory consists of a mass of associated engrams, and, in contrast to the behavioristic view that a fixed trace can be strengthened, engrams relating to several reoccurrences of a stimulus are themselves separate; thus, in the mass of engrams, there will be many corresponding to what we call a familiar stimulus and few corresponding to what we could call an unfamiliar stimulus. Moreover, when an engram is revived it is linked with a cluster of new engrams associated with the present moment, so that the contents of a person's memory can not be considered as static but in a state of continuous flux. These two concepts—that multiple traces may represent what we think of as the same stimulus presented several times and that revival of an engram alters it—have important implications for the modern study of memory, as has been stressed by Schacter (1982, pp. 189–195).

If, however, we search Semon's two books, *The Mneme* (1904) and *Mnemic Psychology* (1909) for references to hypothesis testing or inference at the time of storage or, more particularly, at the time of retrieval,

HISTORY: BEFORE THE INFERENCE REVOLUTION   111

we search in vain. Semon's theory essentially described how a present stimulus could ecphorise a past engram; the theory was not meant to be a phenomenological account of the process of memorizing or of searching for memories. Nevertheless, Semon (1904, p. 174) makes an important point that anticipates later remarks by Bartlett. According to Semon, if one engram is ecphorised at about the same time as another, the two evoked engrams can combine into a new complex, which in turn may be ecphorised at a later date. Semon's example was the following: In a hotel, he noticed, to his annoyance, that the newspaper had been taken by a tall man. This reminded him of a similar occasion in the past, when, in a different place 10 years earlier, the newspaper had been taken by a short man. This chain of thoughts is enough to cause the formulation of a new complex in which the tall and the short men are thought of together, a combination that psychologists of an earlier generation called an association. Semon's point is that this tendency for the simultaneous ecphory of engrams to result in new combinations seems to be characteristic of humans, not of animals, and "this peculiarity forms the starting-point of the highest achievements of which the sensory organization on its so-called 'spiritual' side is capable" (p. 174).

Later in the book Semon (1904/1921) discusses how abstract concepts arise from the simultaneous ecphory of engrams with similar contents. With this ability to form abstract representations and new combinations of ideas, human beings given a retrieval cue ought therefore to be more flexible in their behavior than animals. In the animal, a cue either ecphorises an engram or does not; in the human, a failure of immediate ecphory may nevertheless give rise to a search process, through a process of association, until ecphory occurs. In the case of recognition, a stimulus may ecphorise an engram to the extent that a feeling of familiarity is evoked, but further association processes may be necessary before the subject can identify where the stimulus was first met or why the stimulus seems to be changed from the original. In discussing recognition, Semon is, however, more concerned with establishing the ecphoric theory than with elaborating the cognitive processes accompanying the experience. But his examples illustrate that he was aware that the process of recognition can be accompanied by considerable uncertainty.

Bartlett's idea is equally interesting. Bartlett (1932) showed in a series of experiments that a subject asked to describe a picture of an object presented very briefly will seize on details and then construct a picture, using inference combined with his memory for the details and a general grasp of the overall form of the presented stimulus. Much the same process occurs when a subject is trying to recall a story or draw a picture from memory. There will be a general grasp of the overall form; isolated details will stand out in memory; and the story will be constructed from

112 4. MEMORY

these fragments, using inferences based on everyday experiences and from the need to give coherence to the story. If the story contains elements that were unusual, given the participants' cultural background, these elements will be rationalized or conventionalized. Bartlett therefore argues that all memories are embedded in a general schema, or a mass of traces, and that each retrieval of part of the schema alters the totality of the schema, so that successive retrievals will show a progression of changes. He believes that, in this system, consciousness is *essential,* because it allows the subject to "turn round" on his own schemata, examine them, and pick out items in an order different from that in which they were laid down. Because consciousness plays such a large part in retrieval and inference plays such a large part in the construction process during perceiving and memorizing, Bartlett strongly criticized the behaviorists for ignoring these processes. He also criticized them for not understanding that what pulls schemata together is not just order in time (association by contiguity) but rather "appetites, instincts, interests and ideals" (p. 210), with the first two being crucial in the development of schemata in animals and the last two being more important in the development of schemata in human adults.

Because the greatest impact of the inference revolution was on the subject of recognition, we should ask what Bartlett wrote on the subject. In chapter 9 of *Remembering* (1932) he deals especially with recognition and argues that it plays an important part in determining perception generally. He describes the case of a boy who, after a traumatic operation, seemed to be deaf but was later found to be able to imitate animal noises. He was then given special instruction by a teacher and came to understand the speech she uttered and eventually that of others. Bartlett describes this as a case where "he heard sounds; but, for psychological reasons, he failed to listen to them" (p. 190). By extension of the argument, Bartlett believed that recognition had two components: (a) a specific sensory reaction; and (b) an attitude or orientation, which Bartlett believed to belong to the whole subject reacting. Only if this attitude is carried over to the re-presentation of the stimulus will the stimulus be recognized. Theories of recognition that restrict themselves to the notion that the stimulus simply "fires" the memory, with no concomitant psychological processing such as judgment, are bound to be fruitless. Bartlett suggested that this psychological processing might be by "comparison and judgment, sometimes by feeling, and sometimes, apparently, by direct 'knowing' of relations" (p. 192). Like Semon, Bartlett saw that a study of recognition would involve more than the study of passive ecphorization or arousal. But their concept of "inference" in the context of memory does not include the kind of statistical inference we associate with the inference revolution.

THE EMERGENCE OF THE DECISION METAPHOR

Research During the 1960s and Early 1970s

The voices of Semon and Bartlett were relatively isolated; the main engine of behaviorism rolled forward unimpeded until the 1950s, when, from a variety of sources, the cognitive revolution began. The history of the revolution has been traced in detail by Gardner (1985), who shows that it was not only new ideas in psychology that were used to challenge behaviorism, but also ideas from philosophy, anthropology, and computer science. But Gardner acknowledges the influence of Bartlett in particular in stressing that the actions of retrieval from memory are not to be separated from the actions of perception or thinking.

There were other events in the area of memory research, such as the distinction between short-term and long-term memory, which represented the beginnings of the break from the view that human memory is a string of "habits." This distinction was important because the transition from short- to long-term memory was assumed to be mediated by conscious, elaborative, cognitive processes (Broadbent, 1958). Similarly, those who argued that memorizing was facilitated if the new material could be incorporated into an ongoing schema or plan, and those who argued that memorizing involved the formation of cohesive groups, or "chunks," of material, were in the vanguard of the cognitive revolution. For memory theory, the essence of the cognitive revolution was that memorizing became a process listed under cognition and not an isolated corner of learning theory; cognitive processes, such as imaging, organizing, and constructing, were part of the total task of memorization.

In the 1960s and early 1970s most research on memory focused on the storage phase; later, research was centered on the retrieval phase, and "searching" became a popular, if controversial, topic for study. Semon's (1904/1921) model was given new life when Tulving (1983) and his colleagues produced experimental evidence about the nature of ecphoric arousal. Recognition was seen to occur when the retrieval cue was identical to a stimulus perceived before; recall, when the retrieval cue was an associate of an item perceived before. Particularly for recognition, and to a lesser extent for recall, it became accepted that the total process of retrieval involved not merely arousal of the engram but also a statistical decision-making procedure. In recognition we ask, is this retrieval cue identical to one I perceived before? In recall, we ask, is this association that I have to the retrieval cue the one I require?

Prior to the cognitive revolution, the inference revolution occurred, as has been outlined in previous chapters. One main effect on theory construction in psychology was the development of signal detection

114   4. MEMORY

theory; and it was at the onset of the cognitive revolution, when it was realized that recognition in particular involved more than just ecphoric arousal but also decision-making, that signal detection theory was first applied to the analysis of recognition data. Just as in the study of detection and discrimination (see chapter 2), the application of Neyman and Pearson's theory of statistical decision making gave rise to new concepts and questions in the study of recognition. In particular, a new question was asked that Bartlett, writing prior to the inference revolution, had not discussed. Given that a stimulus arouses a certain feeling, how shall I decide that this feeling is one associated with a stimulus I have perceived before? Bartlett had indicated that the feeling of familiarity itself is related to psychological, as well as purely sensory, processes; now a third variable is added, the variable of uncertainty about how to evaluate the feeling once it is aroused. In situations involving uncertainty, a decision must be made before a response is made and the notion that the retrieval process involves decision making as well as ecphoric arousal was propagated only after the inference revolution. Decisions involve uncertainty: they can be mistaken, they can be based on subjective evaluations just as much as on objective rules, and they may be subject to the influence of such variables as payoffs, expectations, and biases. That performance in recognition experiments was in part the outcome of such decisions, as occurs in hypothesis testing, was clearly understood in the 1960s.

Furthermore, recognition leads naturally to a signal detection analysis. In a typical recognition experiment, a sequence of stimuli are presented (the "target" stimuli) and then a particular stimulus is shown (the "probe" stimulus) that may either be "new" or "old" (i.e. a representation of one of the target stimuli). A correct recognition, or "hit," plays the same role in a recognition experiment as detection of a signal does in a psychophysical experiment. If the probe is new but the subject says "yes, I recognize it," this is equivalent to the false alarm of psychophysics and the false alarm rate can be measured by the probability p ("yes"|new probe). The equivalent of a signal is the presentation of an old probe, and the equivalent of a noise is the presentation of a new probe. The probe will arouse an internal representation and the subject must decide whether it came from the signal distribution (was an old item) or from the noise distribution (was a new item). The decision is determined by the setting of a criterion (see chapter 2). However, in most recognition experiments, criterion settings have not been manipulated either by payoffs or by variations in the probability of old probes. Rather, they are measured by asking subjects to give confidence ratings. For each response of yes or no, the subject is asked to give a numerical rating of his

THE EMERGENCE OF THE DECISION METAPHOR 115

confidence that he is correct. It is assumed that each confidence rating represents a criterion setting, so that from a series of ratings, each associated with a hit and false alarm rate, one can derive an ROC curve. Each point on this curve represents a confidence rating.

Among the first and most influential attempts to apply signal detection theory to recognition was that of Wickelgren and Norman (1966).

The Wickelgren and Norman Model

Donald Norman (1966a) presented a paper in which he described how, with Wayne Wickelgren, he had extended the study of memory from only the study of acquisition and retention to the study of the decision process at retrieval as well. He suggested that recognition was the study of memory for items that could be conceived of as having a certain "strength" in memory, whereas recall was a means for retrieving items by way of association. In recall, what determined successful retrieval was the strength of the various associations to the item: if the retrieval cue involved a strong association, recall would be more efficient than if a cue of lesser association strength to the target had been presented. For recognition, the advantage of taking the view that items had different strengths in memory was that the dimension of strength could be represented as a feeling (later, Atkinson and Juola, 1974, used the word "familiarity") and the subject's task was to decide whether a particular feeling he had when he saw a recognition probe had come from an old item or a new item. From the pattern of correct and false recognitions, d' could be calculated as a measure of the distance between the distributions of new and old items, and in the detailed model put forward by Wickelgren and Norman (1966), d' was taken to represent memory strength, exactly as d' in psychophysics was taken to represent the distance between noise and signal distributions.

Wickelgren and Norman (1966) extended this argument in detail to an experiment in which they varied the number of target stimuli from 2 to 7 and obtained confidence ratings on a 5–point scale for both yes and no judgments. At the outset of the paper, they discussed the signal detection model (as shown in Fig. 2.2) and contrasted it with a model based on the choice axiom of Luce (1959, 1977b). They showed certain important connections between the two and went on to compare several different possible models of how memory strength might be affected by the delay between input of the target item and the presentation of the probe. The model that best fit the data was one in which the strength of a target item was determined by the attention it received when it was first heard, with this strength being reduced by a fixed proportion as each later target item

116   4. MEMORY

was presented. Target items at the start of the list were particularly well encoded (the primacy effect). This model, called the Acquisition-Primacy model, was supported by graphs showing how d' for an item decreased as more items intervened between it and its re-presentation as a probe. (Incidentally, d' was derived from ROC curves whose slope and symmetry suggested that the normal distribution, equal variance assumption of signal and noise was appropriate in most cases here.)

They postulated that if i is the number of interfering items,

$$d' = d_0 \phi^i \tag{4.1}$$

where d_0 is the level of d' at the moment of encoding (registration) and ϕ is the strength to which the item is reduced following one interfering item (the forgetting rate). For example, immediately after presentation, d_0 might be 2, and after one interfering item its strength might be reduced by $\phi = .7$ to 70% of its starting strength, that is $d' = 1.4$.

It was quickly discovered that different variables affected d_0 and ϕ independently (Norman, 1966b): d_0, the initial registration strength in the recognition task, varied with subjects and with the type of material (being highest for single digits and lowest for nonsense sounds). Norman also devised a way of measuring d_0 and ϕ from recall probabilities and found that, for both visual and auditory digits presented for probed recall, d_0 decreased systematically, the faster the digits were presented, whereas ϕ changed erratically but not significantly with presentation rate.

The Wickelgren and Norman model was greatly elaborated by Wickelgren and Berian (1974) to include the distinction between short-term and long-term memory. The starting equation became

$$d' = s + l + X \tag{4.2}$$

where s is the strength of the short-term trace, l is the strength of the long-term trace, and X represents uncontrolled noise, which is a random variable with zero mean and unit standard deviation. The strength was presumed to decay exponentially with time, but it is argued that a trace needs to be consolidated before it is retrievable, so retrieval from long-term memory is held to be possible only after a consolidation period. The strength of an item in long-term memory also decays, very slowly over the course of years, but Wickelgren and Berian assumed that even over the course of a few minutes the long-term trace can also be described as fading exponentially. In this study, the independent variables were the retention interval (3 sec–5 min) and the storage load (1- or 6-letter lists). Storage load had a large effect on the degree of acquisition (a measure corresponding to d_0 in the earlier model) for both short- and long-term

THE EMERGENCE OF THE DECISION METAPHOR   117

traces, but little effect on the decay rate in short-term memory. The study of the retention interval indicated that the short-term memory trace was usable for about 8–10 sec, whereas long-term memory underwent a consolidation that began about 10 sec after input and was complete after about 30 sec.

Again, we have evidence that at the time of intake some sort of encoding procedure assures a certain degree of strength, whereas we have not found a variable that effects the forgetting rate. It should, however, be stated that in this task rehearsal is not encouraged, and we know that intralist rehearsal can facilitate short-term recall—if it is prevented *between* items, for example, recall decreases (Murray, 1966). It is possible therefore that only studies varying the degree of intralist rehearsal would find effects on ϕ or some other measure of decay or the effect of interference. Another change in the two models is also noteworthy: In the Wickelgren and Norman (1966) model, forgetting is presumed to occur when new items come in, whereas in the Wickelgren and Berian (1971) model, forgetting can occur as a function of time. Wickelgren (1970) had already published a study that he believed provided evidence that time decay could occur in addition to item decay. The question of knockout versus time decay is still not resolved, though both Wickelgren and Norman were heavily influenced by the demonstration of Waugh and Norman (1965) that forgetting in short-term memory seems due to knockout rather than time decay.

The idea that encoding at intake influences memory strength has been supported by other demonstrations that d_0 rather than ϕ is affected by certain experimental manipulations. For example, Elkin and Murray (1974) studied the effect of sleep loss on short-term recognition performance and found that the longer a subject went without sleep, the lower the level of d_0, initial recognition strength, when d' measures were taken during performance of a recognition task; ϕ was unaffected by sleep loss. Murray and Hitchcock (1974) studied recognition memory in patients with Korsakoff's psychosis, severe memory loss due to alcoholism. Such patients have normal memory spans but seem to be incapable of putting information from short-term memory into long-term memory. In a short-term recognition paradigm, the mean value of d_0 for the group with Korsakoff's psychosis was lower than that for an alcoholic control group without evidence of memory impairment; ϕ was the same for the two groups. The lowered recognition strength in the group with Korsakoff's psychosis may have resulted because they persisted in thinking about the first item of the list throughout the list. Emerging from these studies— which are based, it must be repeated, on evaluations of d'—is a picture of memory as consisting of an early acquisition phase, in which a memory

118   4. MEMORY

may be registered with more or less strength depending on circumstances, followed by a retention phase, followed by a decision phase in which the subject can be seen as a tester of hypotheses.[1]

The Return of Signal Detection Theory in the 1980s

During the late 1970s and early 1980s not much new research appeared using the basic Wickelgren and Norman (1966) model, although in the late 1970s a few investigators moved away from models in which items were viewed as being in "locations" that could be "searched through," and instead offered a new metaphor of memory that both involved an analysis of "activation" or "resonance" and also laid great stress on the metaphor of retrieval as involving statistical decisions. One of the starting points for this inquiry was the intuition that retrieval latencies might offer means for distinguishing between different theories of retrieval. Townsend and Ashby (1983) have recently shown that retrieval latencies are not as useful as they might seem for distinguishing between serial and parallel search processes, but throughout the 1970s there was an optimism that retrieval latencies could be used to make inferences about internal processes. Norman and Wickelgren (1969) had suggested that "retrieval latency is related to trace strength in exactly the same way that confidence judgments are related to trace strengths, namely, that extreme values of latency or confidence reflect extreme values of strength or strength differences" (p. 195). In their paper, they show typical results for one subject, in which response latencies became faster, the more confident the subject was in his response of either "yes, the probe is old" or "no, the probe is new." But there was no systematic attempt to predict how strength would influence retrieval latency apart from this.

---

[1]Murray and Smith (in preparation) have examined d_0 and ϕ in a probe recognition experiment in which three-digit numbers were the targets. The numbers were either voiced aloud at presentation; or viewed passively as the word "the" was articulated; or viewed passively as the subject spelled a word aloud. The value of d_0 was highest for the 'Voice' condition, less for the 'The' condition, and lowest for the 'Spell' condition. But ϕ, the decay parameter, indicated less forgetting for the 'The' condition than for the other two conditions: A tentative explanation is that the degree of forgetting is in part determined by how often one must switch attention to what is to be enunciated next. In the 'Voice' and 'Spell' conditions, attention has to be continually switched onto new items to be articulated; in the 'The' condition, the same sound is repeated. If this hypothesis can be confirmed, the failure to find changes in ϕ in previous experiments could be ascribed to the fact that they all involved tasks demanding about the same amount of attention-switching during the presentation phase.

Murdock's Model

Wickelgren and Norman were not the only writers to make use of signal detection theory to study memory. Murdock (1966) was among the first to show that although d' might vary with serial position in probed recognition, it does not necessarily do so in a paired-associate recall task. He also found that the criterion placement became stricter, the earlier the items were in the list. Murdock and Duffy (1972) confirmed Wickelgren and Norman's finding concerning latencies, namely that extreme confidence ratings of new and old were associated with the fastest responses; but at the same time they raised the question of whether the strength concept was adequate for the prediction of the behavior of response latencies. They claimed that strength theory predicted that the variability of latencies associated with correct responses should exceed the variability of latencies associated with errors, but the data did not support this. However, Murdock (1985a) has shown this claim may have been erroneous; it is only a simple version of strength theory that predicts this. In a more elaborate version, in which various parameters are allowed to vary with conditions, (such as list length or serial position), strength theory can generate explicit predictions about latencies. In Murdock's (1985a) version of strength theory, it is assumed that there is a "transfer function" in which reaction times decrease the more removed they are from the criterion setting, but that each point on the transfer function is weighted by a strength density to obtain a resulting *distribution* of latencies. By assuming values for the means and standard deviations of the old and new distributions, and assuming the strength-latency transfer function to be exponential, predictions were generated concerning the size and distribution of latencies in certain experimental tasks. One such task involved recognition after a probe delay where strength was presumed to vary from item to item—in this task, strength is presumed to decrease with the greater distance of the target item from the probe. We shall show shortly that even this model may have been superceded.

Ratcliff's Model

The desire to extract the maximal information from reaction latency data also led to at least one major model of memory that took as its starting point the resonance metaphor, namely, the model of Ratcliff (1978). Ratcliff began, like others, by considering short-term recognition and by assuming that the task of the modeler was to predict reaction latencies. He considered that a "comparison" process took place in which the probe was matched to a set of items in memory, the search set:

120   4. MEMORY

> I will adopt the notion of search set suggested by a resonance metaphor (Neisser, 1967, p. 65). Suppose each item in memory corresponds to a tuning fork and the information on which comparisons are made corresponds to latency. Then, the comparison process can be viewed as the probe tuning fork ringing and evoking sympathetic vibrations in memory tuning forks of similar frequencies. Whether or not the probe evokes sympathetic vibrations in a memory-set item depends only on the similarity of frequencies and is independent of whether or not the memory item is in the experimenter-designated memory set. The amplitude or resonance drives the random-walk comparison process: The greater the amplitude (better match), the more bias there is toward a "yes" response; the smaller the amplitude (poorer match), the more bias toward a "no" response. (p. 60)

By the random walk process is meant here that a process, which can be considered mathematically as a counter, is invoked in which features of the target and features of the probe are matched, so that for a feature match, a counter is incremented, and for a feature nonmatch, a counter is decremented. The ratio of the number of matching features to the total number of features is called the relatedness of the probe and target; and it is assumed that on a dimension of relatedness, nontarget items form one distribution, and target items form another, in a way similar to the usual noise and signal distributions of signal detection theory. The distance between the means of the distributions, d', now does not reflect a simple strength but instead measures how much more related a target is than a nontarget to the probe. The parameters of the model include the means and variances of the two distributions and measures of the mean and variance of the relatedness between target and probe. From a combination of these parameters, Ratcliff predicted distributions of reaction time latencies as a function of relatedness. In particular, if relatedness decreases there will be a surplus of slow responses yielding an asymmetrical distribution of reaction times. The model is applied to the prediction of accuracy and latency results in a number of tasks, including the probe recognition task of Sternberg (1966) in which latencies are studied; a feature unique to the model is its prediction of response latencies not only for hits, but also for errors.

Ratcliff's model is the most comprehensive in this chapter in which extensive use is made of metaphor of the intuitive statistician. It is a model of both retrieval and storage and involves a counting mechanism, the assumption that relatedness is a determinant of retrieval quite as much as is the setting of a decision criterion; and it predicts reaction latencies, continuous measures that fluctuate widely both with memory parameters and decision parameters. The model was perhaps rather restricted in application to short-term memory but paid more attention

THE EMERGENCE OF THE DECISION METAPHOR **121**

than other models to the effects of shifting the criterion setting upon both accuracy and latency. In particular, there is a careful discussion of the speed-accuracy tradeoff, in which a speeding up of response is accomplished only at the expense of accuracy. It is assumed that to speed up responding, the subject essentially shifts the boundary at which he or she accepts that the counter has reached a sufficient total of positive matches to warrant a yes response.

Distributed Memory Models

Nevertheless, by assuming that relatedness is the dimension along which the distributions of new items and old items are assumed to lie, sight is lost of the older notions that memories have strengths whether or not a retrieval is given. There has recently arisen a new concept of the nature of forgetting that contains within it a theory of retrieval, in which both the resonance and relatedness concepts are subsumed, and that maintains the idea that retrieval involves a decision. In 1982, Murdock presented a paper involving the concept of "distributed memory." Until then, memories had often been thought of as being items "in" a location or store, and retrieval involved a search. In models of distributed memory, it is presumed that at the moment of registration a memory leaves a trace; another item presented afterwards leaves another trace. The two traces combine to make a separate product; each of the original traces is no longer an entity in itself, but information about the original events leaving the traces can be obtained from the new compound. Murdock (1982) offers an intriguing analogy:

> A good metaphor would be to imagine what the waves on the surface of a pond would look like after various objects had been dropped in the pond. Say the objects were an automobile tire, a beer bottle, the kitchen sink, and a telephone. The wave action on the surface of the pond shows traces of all but is specific to none. However, by the proper comparison process, one could determine that the telephone had been thrown in but a pair of skis has not. Furthermore, one could "retrieve" a beer bottle rather than a kitchen table, telephone or skis given tire as the cue for recall. However, what is retrieved is not the object itself but information sufficient to support veridical recall or recognition. (p. 611)

As the mathematics for representing the behavior of a distributed memory system like this, Murdock chose the language of vector analysis originally suggested by J. A. Anderson (1973), although Pike (1984) has argued that a language involving matrices would have been more suitable to the task (for this see Murdock's (1985b) reply to Pike). In Murdock's model, memories are related to vectors as follows.

122   4. MEMORY

As usually defined, a vector is a line with a particular direction. If the start of the line be taken as the origin of a set of axes (say, three for three-dimensional space), the line can be specified by giving the three coordinates for the other end of the line, say (x_1, y_1, z_1). If we have another line also starting at the origin whose end point is (x_2, y_2, z_2), we can talk about the relationship between the two lines by a single figure combining them. This figure, called the "dot product," represents the length of one of the lines multiplied by the distance the second line would project onto that line; it would be maximum if the second line projected entirely onto the first. The dot product is obtained by multiplying the two coordinates of each line on each dimension and summing them. In our example, the dot product would be $(x_1x_2 + y_1y_2 + z_1z_2)$.

In Murdock's model, the memory for an item is represented by a listing of features, for example, (0, 1, 0). This can be handled mathematically as if it were the description of a vector. Suppose we have a probe whose features are (0, 1, 0) and we wish to decide whether the probe is the same as the target. The dot product is taken of the two, in this case, $(0 + 1 + 0)$ = 1, and this particular value is the one that would have been obtained given maximum similarity of the two vectors. Lesser degrees of similarity would have yielded different dot products. The dot product is then fed into a decision mechanism, which in Murdock's model differed from those of Wickelgren and Norman (1966) and of Ratcliff (1978) in having two criteria (Fig. 4.1). It is assumed that noise is inherent in the memory comparison and that noise can be added to the result of the comparison of the two vectors. If the input to the decision system is above a certain value, the subject says yes; but it is assumed that the subject will say no only if the input is below a different value—there are thus two criterion settings. This idea was not original with Murdock and has even been found in psychophysics (see Murdock, 1982, p. 264) and was initially proposed by Neyman and Pearson. If the input lies between the two settings the subject will wait. The important aspect of this waiting feature is that we can predict that recognition latencies will be longer for inputs in between the two criterion settings—note that it is in the same area as that associated with long reaction times in the Wickelgren and Norman model.

The task for a distributed memory model is to say how *anything* can be retrieved from a single store in which essentially all memories are mishmashed together. According to Murdock (1982) one memory item following another causes the vectors of the two to become convolved into a new vector; the process of recall (as opposed to recognition, which was described earlier) involves finding a correlation between the retrieval cue and the vector containing the (convolved) target item. It is impossible here to give the derivations of the convolutions and the correlations, but Murdock maintains that a model of the storage of items and associative

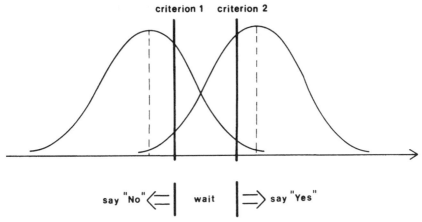

FIGURE 4.1. Murdock's two-criteria model of short-term recognition. A recognition response is the result of calculating the dot product of the probe vector and the target vector, adding noise, and feeding the result into the decision system. The dot product measures the degree of similarity between probe and target, and the abscissa represents degrees of similarity. Recognition is interpreted as a statistical decision whether a given similarity measure (dot product) arose from a new item (left hand distribution) or an old item (right hand distribution). It is assumed that there are two criteria rather than one: if the similarity measure falls between the two, no response will be given until a change in the noise levels shifts the similarity measure to one yielding a response; alternatively, the two criteria might be shifted closer together.

information can be built up in which we can be precise about the contents of the vector with which the probe, or recall cue, can be matched. Intrinsic to the model were predictions not only about means but also about variances of the dot products that featured in the mathematical development of the model. In 1983 Murdock extended the scope of the model to encompass serial order information. In particular (pp. 332–334), Murdock showed that a distributed memory model gave a better fit to certain data from an experiment on recognition memory for trigrams than did a discrete memory model in which each item is subject to forgetting through the addition of noise and in which order information can be lost.

OTHER METAPHORS

It would of course be misleading to state that the metaphor of the intuitive statistician has played a dominant role in recent memory research. But in the study of the restricted topic of recognition, it has been all important, as can be seen from the foregoing and from the extensive discussion of signal detection concepts in Murdock's (1974) summary of research on memory up to the mid-1970s. Of course, other concepts and metaphors have been equally important, particularly in the study of recall as op-

124   4. MEMORY

posed to recognition. In this section, we briefly consider some other models of memory and ask explicitly how they can be reconciled, if at all, with the metaphor of the intuitive statistician. Two concepts (which themselves are often treated not as metaphors but as direct descriptions of what occurs) of importance in modern theorizing on memory are *short-term memory* and *search*.

Short-Term Memory

The transition from the behaviorist to the cognitive approach to memory was epitomized in Broadbent's *Perception and Communication* (1958) in which short-term memory was introduced as a structure in a flowchart describing the throughput of information from the senses into long-term memory. For Broadbent, short-term memory was a device that allowed sensory information to persist above or near the threshold of consciousness while other information was being responded to. But from being a subsidiary store, short-term memory rapidly grew to become a central "box" allowing several items of information to be processed in parallel and then either kept in consciousness by being rehearsed or put out of consciousness into long-term memory (LTM). We have no hesitation in invoking the word consciousness in this context: it was William James (1890/1950) who first distinguished between "primary memory," as he called it, and "secondary memory"; the former represented a persistence in awareness of something just perceived or thought about. In 1960, Broadbent's single "short-term store" was replaced by two stores, pure sensory storage of an iconic (visual) or echoic kind (as Broadbent had first demonstrated in his studies of dichotic listening), and a store essentially occupied by speech-coded material (Sperling, 1960). Much later, it was realized that three stores might be necessary: a sensory store, a speech store (or articulatory loop), and a store concerned with processing the contents of the other stores. This last type of store was called working memory (Baddeley & Hitch, 1974). In Broadbent's (1984) most recent flowchart working memory has come to occupy a major position; and information from sensory or motor output stores, or from long-term memory, may enter a central processor that integrates this information with the contents of working memory. Perhaps the most striking feature of these differences in opinion has been the growing appreciation that a model involving a purely serial flow of information is too limited. The mind can handle a great deal of information at once and, as Gardner (1985) points out, one of the latest opinions in cognitive science is that if the mind is to be modeled mechanically, it must be by a bank of computers processing information in parallel.

The recent evidence for the parallel operation of a sensory memory, an

THE EMERGENCE OF THE DECISION METAPHOR   125

articulatory memory, and a working memory has not been the impetus for mathematical modeling. But the serial transfer of information from sensory to auditory-verbal-linguistic memory, and the serial transfer of information from the latter to long-term memory, were the subject of intensive investigation, particularly during the 1960s. One can trace a distinguished lineage of stochastic models during this period, models whose essence was predicting the probability of various cognitive events, such as the probability of entering short-term or long-term memory. These models have not been contradicted, but it is possible to argue that the reason is their range of application is rather restricted.

All-or-None Learning

The transition from short-term memory to long-term memory was modeled in two ways. The earlier literature on this topic was heavily influenced by a discovery that posed an unexpected threat to Pavlovian and Hullian models according to which learning was the strengthening of "excitatory" responses initiated by a stimulus. Repetition of the stimulus, for example, was held to be one means of strengthening responses to it. But in a paired-associate paradigm, Rock (1957) showed that if, while a series of paired associate words were being learned, pairs *not* recalled on trial n were dropped from trial $n + 1$ and new ones substituted, learning to criterion took the same number of trials as if the old unrecalled pairs had been left in the list on trial $n + 1$. The suggestion was that an item was not half-learned on a trial, waiting to have its strength boosted on the next presentation until its excitatory level allowed for successful recall; the suggestion instead was that an item was either learned or not learned, in all-or-none fashion, on a single trial. It is perhaps worth mentioning that Murray (1980) has shown that if confidence ratings are obtained of how correct one thinks one is in a standard paired associate paradigm, there are very few incidences of intermediate levels of confidence or of "tip-of-the-tongue" reports: as far as one can judge oneself, one either knows or does not know the correct response on a trial. As learning progresses, judgments of "very confident" increase and judgments of "not confident" decrease in a straightforward manner.

The postulate of all-or-none learning had a more devastating effect than is often realized. The first mathematical model of paired associate acquisition to incorporate this assumption (Bower, 1961) has become, because of its success in predicting the learning curve, almost a cause célèbre. But Bush and Mosteller (1959), as Bower emphasizes, were the first to explore the implications of the postulate that an item is either learned or not learned on a given trial, with no immediate levels of learning being needed. These authors, however, had earlier been respon-

126   4. MEMORY

sible (Bush & Mosteller, 1951) for some of the most elegant and far-reaching developments of operator theory as applied to learning, in which it was assumed that the probability of giving a learned response on trial n + 1 was the result of an operation applied to a different probability as evinced on trial n. In the new stochastic models, the probability of reporting a response correctly on a given trial was a function of a fixed probability that the item entered the learned state. Galanter and Luce (1974), in their eulogy of Bush, note that all-or-none Markov models very rapidly superceded operator models in the literature of mathematical psychology. Be that as it may, the fact is that the *Journal of Mathematical Psychology* in the 1960s published a series of articles (Atkinson & Crothers, 1964; Calfee & Atkinson, 1965; see also Suppes & Ginsberg 1963), each essentially an elaboration of Bower's model, in which the inadequacies of the simple model were handled by elaborations of the stages by which an association was transferred from being the object of perception to being an object in long-term memory. Some of these models incorporated the probability that an item might be forgotten from a particular store.

These models are reviewed in several well-known texts of mathematical psychology that appeared in the early 1970s (Coombs, Dawes, & Tversky, 1970; Laming, 1973; Restle & Greeno, 1970). The question here is not so much whether they fit the data as what implications they have for our metaphor of the intuitive statistician. In almost all these models the unknown parameters are the transition probabilities of going from state to state, and little is said about inferential and decision procedures. As shown earlier, this is in part because of the relative certainty subjects have that they are right or wrong. With the very simple two- or three-choice response alternatives used in this task, there is little room for uncertainty, and what there is can be handled by the assumption that forgetting can occur from short-term memory. None of the models dealt with recognition, a situation that is more easily modeled than is recall by signal detection assumptions.

The Atkinson and Shiffrin Model

A different assumption about the transition of information from short-term memory to long-term memory was incorporated into the model of Atkinson and Shiffrin (1968). The model involved three stages, a sensory store, a short-term auditory-verbal-linguistic store, and a long-term store. There were four parameters to the model: (a) the probability of transfer from sensory store to short-term store; (b) the number of items that can be held in short-term store, a value believed to vary with the kind of material; (c) the rate of transfer of information from the short-term to the long-term store; and (d) if an item has been knocked out of short-term

THE EMERGENCE OF THE DECISION METAPHOR   127

store, but resides in long-term store, each new trial causes the information stored in long-term store to decrease by a constant proportion. A fifth parameter was added later: it was assumed that a new item entering the short-term store knocked out an item already there: the fifth parameter was the probability that the oldest item in the buffer (the first in) was knocked out.

The method of evaluating the model is standard. The data are collected, and an iterative computer search finds those values of the five parameters that when inserted into the equations resulting from the model yield a curve deviating least from the obtained curve. It was concluded for example that the probable capacity of short-term store for the letter–number pairs was about two items. The criticism can be made of this, and similar models involving several parameters to be estimated, that being able to obtain a single curve that "best" fits the data is not a proof that the resulting values of the parameters are the *only* values of the parameters that could achieve a similar result. This model received so little criticism that, 12 years later, Raaijmakers and Shiffrin (1980) would tentatively adopt it as the starting point for their model of retrieval from long-term memory.

The success of these models of the transition from short-term memory to long-term memory depends largely on their being restricted to recall. With simple materials, recall is generally all-or-none, that is, it is correct or not correct, and there is little opportunity for shades of uncertainty to be measured, in contrast with the case where confidence ratings are used in recognition studies. The metaphor of the intuitive statistician is difficult to apply to recall because there is room for latitude and arbitrariness in trying to relate the recall task to the signal detection paradigm. There is, for example, a model of recall, the generation-recognition model, according to which a retrieval cue leads to a search procedure until a response comes to mind and the response is then recognised as correct or not. The latter phase might be modeled by signal detection, but the generation phase seems independent of the decision process. In the following sections, we consider this model more carefully, as research on it has revealed important insights into recall that will help us to be more precise about the limitations of the metaphor of the intuitive statistician.

Search

Nonstatistical Search

By the early 1970s the impression was that both short-term memory and long-term memory could be represented as holding structures, or stores, in which elements resided at a location. A particular boost to this

128   4. MEMORY

store metaphor was given by Lindsay and Norman (1972), who were among the first to offer pictures representing long-term memory in which particular items were seen as nodes in a space with connections to other nodes by association. It was even speculated that consciousness could be considered as a searchlight, which, so to speak, illuminated a set of nodes, thus making them the object of a present thought. The width of the beam could be varied to encompass variations in how much one could think about in a given moment, and a great deal of ingenuity was exercised by Norman and his colleagues in delineating the basic kinds of association that existed between nodes. This effort culminated in the ELINOR model of long-term memory (Norman & Rumelhart, 1975).

The notion that retrieval from long-term memory consisted of a search through a set of nodes permeated thinking about memory in this period, although search theory, which is an autonomous branch of probability theory (Gal, 1980; Stone, 1975), was seldom if ever applied to the problem. Moreover there was no suggestion that the search was the kind a statistician might undertake, taking random samples and searching them to see if a particular element or value of an element was present. Instead, researchers had a fairly deterministic view of search in mind. For example, the generation-recognition model of recall held that in seeking a forgotten item, a sequence of possible responses is generated and when the correct one appears, it is recognized as the item sought. It was held that search is common in recall tasks but rare in recognition tasks. Classical interference theory, of course, had no difficulty explaining temporary forgetting: other responses compete with the target response, and the cognitive efforts of the subject to retrieve the desired item need no special descriptions as is implied by the word search. Gillund and Shiffrin (1984) have classified models for recall and recognition in terms of the extent to which search is involved. The quintessence of the search phenomenon is held to be the activity involved in the task of free recall, where subjects typically recall a few items out of a list of say, 20, quite quickly and then produce extra items with increasing intervals between successful retrievals.

Nonstatistical Decisions

Because search takes time, the concept has often been invoked when response latencies are to be discussed. In contrast to stochastic models, where response probabilities are predicted, models involving search typically try to model a sequence of decisions. Historically, the origin of this endeavor may be taken to be Meyer's paper of 1970, in which it was argued that the time it took to identify whether a sequence of letters, such as DOCTOR, formed a word was a function of whether it had been preceded by a word related in meaning (e.g. NURSE). We can move quickly to Meyer (1973) in which it was claimed that, concerning an earlier experiment, "the data supported the view that words are stored at separate "locations" in long-term memory, that proximity of words in the memory structure varies with their closeness of meaning, and that the derivation of successive retrieval operations increases with the "semantic distance" between words" (p. 124).

In the 1973 paper Meyer describes a task in which the subjects judged whether or not a stimulus word belonged in either of two distinct semantic categories (e.g. Does PIGEON belong to the category BIRD or IN-SECT?). It was found that the closer in meaning the two categories were, the faster were both positive and negative decisions, and the results were interpreted in terms of a search through the two categories. The stimulus word (e.g. PIGEON) was first encoded; then a search was made through members of BIRDS: if PIGEON was a member, a yes response was given; if it was not, search proceeded through the category of INSECTS. In this case, a fast yes response would be given, but had the BIRDS been searched second, responding would have taken longer. For negative instances (e.g. Is JAPAN a BIRD or a CITY?), reaction time was longer if the semantic distance between the categories was wide rather than narrow. Thus, reaction times needed to access information in long-term memory were held to be the outcome of several processes, each of which took time—search through first category, decision, shift to second category, search through second category, decision.

The decisions involved in models of these kind were of the yes/no kind, and it was nowhere suggested that decisions were based on the weighting of evidence—a task was carried out and the decision in question could be phrased as an algorithm. If PIGEON was in the list of BIRDS searched through, the subject responded Yes; otherwise he went on searching. The role played by the decisions in the model was essentially to determine reaction time: the more decisions, the longer the reaction time. This is quite different from saying that the human operator was deciding between hypotheses on the weight of evidence, and indeed the decisions in the categorization task were of a nonstatistical kind.

Activation Rather Than Search

What seems to have reduced the popularity of this search metaphor is its replacement by a metaphor of resonance, or activation. It was Semon (1904/1921) who first stressed that no memory exists in isolation but is laid down at a certain time in association with other items and in a given context. Each of these other items, and the context itself, furnishes a *cue* to the re-arousal of the engram, or stores representation of the object, by

130   4. MEMORY

the process Semon called synergistic ecphory. In the 1970s Tulving and his colleagues at the University of Toronto did many experiments, which all pointed in the same direction: you cannot divorce the engram from the cues that arouse it. Any theory of memory has to speak not only of the stored trace, or memory representation, but also of the cues that arouse it. This arousal takes place by a process variously called resonance or activation (we have already discussed Ratcliff's use of resonance), and the image of search is to some extent replaced by the idea of cue efficiency, although, as we shall see, not entirely.

The essence of both the activation and the resonance models was that a given cue could cause the experience we call memory arousal. For activation, the process was perhaps slower and more mediated by intervening associations than for resonance, where access to the memory was assumed to be direct and unmediated. In both cases, the implication was that the encoded engram and the retrieval cue formed a complex or constellation: to discuss a memory event, both had to be specified. Tulving and his associates (Thomson & Tulving, 1970), in particular, did a number of demonstration experiments showing, for example, that if a target word such as STEAK was presented in a free recall task, along with a weak retrieval cue such as knife, knife was a more effective retrieval cue than a strong association, such as meat, which had not been presented at the time of learning. Tulving has also demonstrated the following effect at conferences, and one of the authors (Murray) has used it frequently as a classroom demonstration. If a list of 20 words such as JACKET, TIGER, BRIDGE, . . . is presented for immediate free recall (the words can be recalled in any order), a class of undergraduates will typically recall about 10–12 words each. If, however, each of the 20 words is presented with a retrieval cue (e.g. JACKET—an article of clothing; TIGER—an animal; BRIDGE—a construction), and recall is then required at each cue (e.g., What was the article of clothing?) recall increases to about 18–20 items per subject. The subjects, however, can be tricked by being given an inappropriate retrieval cue, for example, What was the game?, a cue not given at any time during the original presentation. The subject cannot give an answer, not recalling that cue, and the appropriate answer, BRIDGE, is seldom given because the appropriate retrieval cue for BRIDGE was "a construction." These results indicate that the most effective retrieval cues are those associated with the target at the time of storage.

The SAM Model

One of the most rigorous models incorporating notions both of search and of activation by a retrieval cue is SAM, an acronym for Search through Associative Memory, which was introduced by Raaijmakers and

THE EMERGENCE OF THE DECISION METAPHOR 131

Shiffrin (1980, 1981). Later Gillund and Shiffrin (1984) extended the theory to recognition and, as mentioned earlier, classified other models in terms of the extent to which search was involved. This model is described briefly here because it also incorporates Tulving's notion that a memory theory cannot deal with isolated memory items, but only with items linked indissolubly with appropriate retrieval cues. It can be considered as a model that deals with activation because its central concept is that a cue can activate a stored item directly, but that in reality there are several retrieval cues to an item, which differ in the strength of the association with that item. What the classic learning theorists called response competition is epitomized here in the notion that some cues are stronger than others when it comes to eliciting a particular target item. The model borrows from previous research in several ways: It is assumed that items first enter a retrieval buffer of size r in the manner specified in Atkinson and Shiffrin's model (1968) and that information is then encoded into LTM. In LTM an item can be seen as consisting of many components (here called features), but associations are made between items (or clusters of components) and (a) other items, (b) retrieval cues, and (c) the general context. Each item in memory is called an image, so that any image may be activated by another image, by a retrieval cue, or by the surrounding context.

When an item is presented, it is encoded/rehearsed. The greater the amount of this activity, the stronger is the resulting associative strength between that item and the context and also between that item and the image of itself (the self-strength). If the item is rehearsed along with others, then the associative strength relating that item to each of these others will also be increased. These strengths are established during rehearsal, and the model postulates that four parameters determine various strengths: a determines the strength of the context-to-item association, this strength being a function of a multiplied by the amount of time in the rehearsal buffer; analogously, b determines the strength of the association between any two items rehearsed together; c determines the amount of self-strength; and d determines the strength of the association between any two items not rehearsed together. It is also assumed that if an item is recovered, the strength of the association between that and other items is incremented: After a recovery, the strength of the association between context and item is incremented by e units, the strength of the association between two items rehearsed together is incremented by f units, and the self-strength is incremented by g units.

It is also assumed that when a cue is given, there is a search through LTM in which items are sampled and evaluated; if it is decided that the recovered item is not the sought item the search is begun again. One such search cycle is called a loop and L_{MAX} is the number of consecutive loops

132   4. MEMORY

of the search carried out with a given cue before deciding to change to a new retrieval cue. The parameter K_{MAX} is the total number of failed loops in the total search.

As is customary, the value of the model was tested by finding whether, if suitable estimates of the parameters were available, the predicted patterns of results could fit obtained patterns of results. Murdock (1962), for instance, obtained what are often quoted as the standard data on serial position effects in free recall as a function of list length: The first item of a list is usually well recalled, as are the last four items or so, with all the remaining items being recalled at a low level, with roughly equal probability. For 20 and 40 word lists, the SAM model fit Murdock's data well with $r = 4$, $K_{MAX} = 30$, $a = c = .055$, $b = .02$, $d = .004$, and $e = f = g = 6$. Of course, the same cautionary remark as we made concerning the work of Atkinson and Shiffrin (1968) is appropriate here: Because of the large number of theoretical parameters, there may be more than one reasonable solution.

The SAM model, in dealing with recall, tries to be precise about the determinants of the generation process. It assumes that various associative strengths determine recall. In support of this, Murray (1980, 1982) had subjects rate the associative strength of word pairs on a scale of 1 to 7. When lists were constructed of these pairs, such that each list had a different level of mean rated associative strength, correct recall rose with the level of rated associative strength of the list.

When they developed their model to encompass recognition, Gillund and Shiffrin (1984) had no hesitation in adopting the signal detection model. The target item is presumed to elicit a range of values of familiarity; the distractor items elicit a lower range of familiarity values. These can be represented as two distributions with some degree of overlap. The subject, as in standard signal detection theory, sets a criterion for testing the hypothesis that his present feeling of familiarity results from a target rather than a distractor. Gillund and Shiffrin generated supposed distributions of internal states associated with distractors and targets from their recognition data by inserting particular values of the parameters of the model. It was found that the variance of familiarity associated with the targets appeared to be greater than that due to noise.

CONCLUSIONS

In this chapter we have tried to evaluate the role of the metaphor of the intuitive statistician in the context of memory. We saw that in the behavioristic period both Semon and Bartlett, basing their ideas on their theories of ecphory and schemata respectively, argued that retrieval by

CONCLUSIONS 133

humans was subject to the operation of such cognitive processes as abstraction and construction. Semon realized that seldom does a recognition event occur *in vacuo,* so to speak, whereas Bartlett stressed that recognition involved a linkage, not just with a sensory trace, but with a highly developed schema. Although they suggested that inference might be included in an account of memory processes, there is no indication that they thought about inference as statistical inference. After the inference revolution, recognition was analyzed into two phases, one that Semon would have called ecphorization, and a decision phase modeled after Neyman and Pearson's theory. In a later development, Murdock qualified the new understanding of recognition by suggesting that there might be two criteria, one set so that states of familiarity below that criterion would be judged as new, one set so that states of familiarity above that criterion would be judged as old, with vacillation occurring for familiarity states between the two criteria. Signal detection models of recognition have been integrated into Ratcliff's model, Murdock's distributed memory model and Gillund and Shiffrin's SAM model.

Intuitive Statistics and Recall

It is less clear how useful the model is for describing the process of recall. In the SAM model, recall proficiency is described entirely in terms of associative strength, and there is a clear affinity between this approach and older connectionist models, such as that of Hull, or newer associationistic models, such as Anderson and Bower (1973) described. Nevertheless, the generation-recognition model prescribes that after an item has been found, it must be judged as correct or not correct, a process often called recognition. But care must be taken here. The subject who retrieves Napoleon as the name of a French Emperor, even after a search, does not merely recognize the word Napoleon as one seen before; it has to be recognized as fitting under the rubric French Emperor. Similarly, in the recognition tasks we have been considering, one does not recognize a particular probe digit merely as having been seen before, but as having been seen before in a particular context, namely, the list of target items. If the hypothesis testing metaphor is applied in the recognition phase of a generation-recognition procedure, it is reasonable to suppose that the generation process actually occurs. Introspection suggests it does, but a different theory, proposed by Tulving, postulates that if a cue fails to evoke a desired recall response, it is because the cue is ineffective and not because the subject is mainly generating responses. It is important therefore to consider the evidence against the generation-recognition hypothesis.

This evidence was put forward by Tulving and Thomson (1973) and

134   4. MEMORY

Watkins and Tulving (1975), who argued that parsimony could be attained if we maintained that there was only a single variable that needed to be considered, namely the nature of the cue. In the case of recognition, the cue was a copy or replica of the item represented in memory. In the case of recall, the cue was an associate of the item and thereby a less effective elicitor of the item stored in memory. Tulving and Thomson, and Watkins and Tulving, carried out supporting experiments. They presented a list of target words to which they then gave strong associates. For example, if the target word was TABLE, they later presented the subjects with the word CHAIR. The subjects typically generated TABLE as an associate to CHAIR. But when they were asked to judge whether TABLE, as generated to CHAIR, had also been present in the target list, they were not always able to do so. On the other hand, they could recall TABLE from the target list, given the recall cue that had also been presented with TABLE in the target list. Tulving's point was that we can have a recognition task (recognizing TABLE as an item on a target list) that is harder than a recall task and that this is evidence that the difference between recognition and recall can best be described in terms of cue effectiveness rather than in terms of differences in search processes. There is, however, a difference between simply recognizing something as being familiar and assigning something recognized as familiar to a particular context; subjects, for example, certainly recognized TABLE as familiar, but they were unable to assign it to the context of the target list. The generation-recognition model also assumes that recognition of the searched-out item as being correct is a case of recognition in a context: the item is recognized as correct in the context of the original question. Tulving has shown that this is a fallible step in the generation-recognition process. But it is not clear that by showing this, he has invalidated the notion that a recall cue, which we agree is an associate and not a copy of the stored item, cannot also be described as a cue leading to a search process in which a sequence of possible answers to the question are evoked and rejected before the correct answer is found. We approach here the metaphor of the hypothesis tester: in the search process, each item that comes to mind is tested against the hypothesis that it is the correct answer, and there can be missed signals and false alarms in this process. But the influence of Tulving is so strong that research on the search process and on the rejection of competing items has been neglected, and research on the efficacy of particular kinds of recall cues has been elaborated.

We conclude therefore that the phase of recognizing a response as being a correct recall is open to uncertainty and that the hypothesis that a response is correct can be seen as a hypothesis of a signal to be evaluated against competing hypotheses. But Tulving's point that retrieval, or

CONCLUSIONS 135

ecphorization, depends on the appropriateness of the cue remains unchallenged. Since this is a key part of the retrieval process, it must be admitted that hypothesis evaluation occurs as a process secondary to ecphorization. Just as there is an energy threshold in psychophysics, so an engram might require a specific cue to arouse it; otherwise it would never provide memory content requiring evaluation.

Extensions of the Signal Detection Model in Recall

One matter meriting further discussion is the role of similarity between a stimulus and a memory in determining how the stimulus will be responded to. If a stimulus is identical to a stored content of memory, ecphorization will normally yield a recognition response. But if the stimulus is similar only in certain respects, there will be uncertainty about whether the stimulus should be responded to as if it were identical with the stored content. Similarity of features is a key parameter in Ratcliff's (1978) and Murdock's (1982) models of recognition, and Wickelgren and Norman (1966) showed how their theory of recognition could be expanded to include a dimension of similarity. It plays an important part in determining animal behavior. A baby gull will peck on a spot on the bill of a wooden model, presumably because it is so similar to an innate releasing stimulus normally found on the mother gull's bill. A dog will show vacillation and emotional behavior if presented with a stimulus halfway between a circle (associated with food) and an oval (associated with shock), and thus similar to both. All such situations can probably be described as forcing the organism to decide between two hypotheses, "the stimulus is A" and "the stimulus is B," but we have not found this hypothesis testing view in the literature on memory. The nearest equivalents perhaps are models of concept formation, in which subjects must evaluate whether particular stimuli are examples of particular concepts. These models depend heavily on the idea that weights are attached to particular hypotheses in making decisions and are not usually presented as problems in statistical decision-making (Bower & Trabasso, 1964). But as a starting point for thinking about such matters, it should be observed that in some problems it will not be very important whether a given stimulus is an *A* or a *B*, whereas in other problems (such as the dog confronted with the ambiguous stimulus) the costs of errors could be considerable. This is the sort of situation that can be modeled by a variable criterion, or perhaps even by two criteria.

We should like to end this chapter by discussing the relation of the foregoing to the distinction between procedural, episodic, and semantic memory promulgated so vigorously by Tulving (1983). We have talked so far as if the discussion of memory had two aspects, an ecphoric aspect

136 4. MEMORY

and a decision aspect. Tulving has divided the totality of engrams into three classes: (a) those concerned with knowledge of how to do things (procedural memory, for example, knowledge of how to swim or tie shoelaces); (b) knowledge concerning one's own biography in which episodes are time tagged (episodic memory—note that the stimuli presented in recall and recognition tasks are stored in episodic memory because one must recall or recognize them as being in particular contexts); and (c) semantic, or abstract memory, including knowledge of language, history, nature, and the like. The production of a response based on any of these categories, we believe, can be associated with uncertainty, so it seems unlikely that there is a need for separate models of how uncertainty interacts with ecphory for the three classes of memory. Recognizing that a probe digit occurred in a target list or that a person you meet at a party has been encountered before are both examples of episodic memory that can be modeled according to Neyman–Pearson principles. But semantic memory can also be probed by using alleged *facts* as the probe material. You could ask "Napoleon was the French Emperor—true or false?" with true replacing yes in the signal detection diagram, false replacing no, the assumption being that there is a distribution of states of familiarity associated with the assertion "Napoleon was the French Emperor" and a different distribution of states of familiarity associated with the assertion "Napoleon was not the French Emperor." As with the case for similarity, we do not know of a signal detection modeling of true–false judgments, which presumably probe semantic memory, but there is no a priori reason one should not be developed. We believe that the metaphor of the intuitive statistician can be applied to semantic as well as to episodic memory. Nevertheless, we foresee one problem: We suspect that if, say, confidence ratings were used to establish criterion settings, there might be many cases where judgments of certain I'm right and certain I'm wrong predominated, with very few judgments of uncertain. If this is the case, the value of a signal detection analysis as a means of exploring semantic memory would be greatly diminished. As mentioned earlier in connection with paired-associate recall, certainty rather than doubt characterises many tasks involving recall, and in these cases the applicability of a model based on statistical hypothesis testing might be limited.

5 Thinking: From Insight to Intuitive Statistics

Attempts to understand how we think, as well as how we perceive, historically have been linked to epistemology. Ever since Locke's *Essay Concerning Human Understanding* (1906/1959), how we *should* think has been conflated by philosophers and psychologists with how, in fact, we *do* think. The relationship between probability theory and thought is a case in point: History has witnessed the attempt to make probability theory coherent with what was believed to be rational thought, and it has seen efforts to reduce rational thought to probability theory. For instance, what was believed to be rational judicial and economic thought actually determined the way in which probability theory developed mathematically, as was shown by Daston (1980). From the theory's inception until the middle of the 19th century, probability was regarded by mathematicians and philosophers as being, in Laplace's famous phrase, "only common sense reduced to calculus" (Laplace, 1814/1951, p. 196). The title that George Boole (1854/1958) gave to his famous book on logic and probability was *An Investigation of The Laws of Thought*.

This circular relationship between probability theory and rational thought has been an continual source of confusion. After the inference revolution, when probability theory entered theories of thinking, this confusion was imported into psychology. As we shall see, Daniel Kahneman and Amos Tversky and their followers (e.g. Tversky & Kahneman, 1980, 1982b) implicitly define rational thought by the laws of probability theory. In the first, historical section, we show that this link between thinking and probability theory did not exist for the German psychologists who started the experimental study of human thought around 1900

138   5. THINKING

and dominated the field until the 1930s, when their leading lights were forced to leave Germany. Although many of them emigrated to the United States at this time, the strength of the indigenous behaviorist tradition virtually extinguished psychological interest in the topic in the 1940s and 1950s. The main event described in this section is the shift from the Würzburg school to the Gestalt school, which resulted in the fading of associationism and in a change in the experimenter–subject relationship. These German schools offer a sharp contrast to post-inference revolution approaches to human thinking that are strongly imprinted by probability theory. As we shall see, thinking was not identified with calculation, and the problems considered relevant could be solved with insight, but not with probability theory.

HISTORY: BEFORE THE INFERENCE REVOLUTION

Aristotle set forth the three principles—temporal and spatial contiguity, similarity, and contrast—that state the conditions under which ideas are associated in memory. He is the father of associationism, which flowered again in the 17th–19th centuries with the British school of Thomas Hobbes, John Locke, David Hume, David Hartley, James Mill and others. Ideas and sensations were the elements of the mind: sensations were the elements of sensory experience; ideas, those of nonsensory, higher mental processes such as thought; and ideas were composed from sensations. Associationism provided the framework for the emerging experimental psychology of the late 19th century. However, Wilhelm Wundt, the father of experimental psychology, believed that the experimental method should be limited to the study of simple psychical processes, that higher mental processes must be approached by different methods, as in his *Völkerpsychologie* (cultural psychology). Wundt (1897) argued that since thought processes are as variable as they are and gain a degree of constancy only when they become collective, their study is the subject matter of social psychology. The experimental method cannot decompose human thinking, which is strongly dependent on language and culture.

The Fading of Associationism

In the early 1900s, in opposition to Wundt's dogma, one of his students, Oswald Külpe, and his coworkers at the University of Würzburg (e.g. Ach 1905; Bühler, 1907; Külpe, 1912; Marbe, 1901; Messer, 1906) began the experimental study of thinking. A central question posed by the Würzburg school was whether Aristotle (1941) was correct when he

HISTORY: BEFORE THE INFERENCE REVOLUTION   139

postulated in *De Anima* and *De Memoria* that the mind thinks in the form of images. From their experiments they concluded that, contrary to common belief since Aristotle, imageless thought does exist, that is, thought devoid of such sensory characteristics as colour and sound. But we must ask, what was an "experiment" at that time? The experimental procedure consisted typically of three steps. First a stimulus such as a word or a question was presented to the subject. Second, the subject was asked for a response such as an association to the word or an answer to the question. Finally, after the response was obtained, the subject described introspectively the thought processes that had occurred in between the stimulus and the response.

It is essential to grasp how the respective roles of the subject and the experimenter have changed since the time of the Würzburg school. Then, under the assumption that the thought process is introspectively penetrable, the subject, not the experimenter, was assumed to provide the theoretical description. Consequently, the selection of subjects was important; they had to be trained observers of themselves. In fact, the main experimental contribution of Külpe, the founder of the school, was to serve as a subject, not as an experimenter. But, as we shall see, the results obtained soon forced the experimenter to supply the theoretical constructs.

Consider, for example, the experiments of Bühler (1907), who confronted his subjects with unusually sophisticated tasks. He posed such questions as Does monism really signify the negation of personality? and Can we capture by our thoughts the nature of thinking? Bühler's subjects—professors and Ph.Ds only, no undergraduates—were asked for a yes-or-no answer and thereafter to describe introspectively the thought process that led to the answer. As we have mentioned, the subject was expected to reveal the laws of thought through introspection, functioning as an objective observer of his own thought flow. To give an impression of the introspective reports, here is Külpe's report of how he came to say yes to the question about whether we can capture the nature of thinking by our thoughts:

> The question at first struck me as odd; I thought it might be a trick question. Then it suddenly occurred to me how Hegel had criticized Kant, and then I answered decisively: Yes. The thought about Hegel's critique was quite rich, I knew at this moment exactly what it amounted to, I didn't say anything about it, and also didn't imagine anything, only the word "Hegel" resounded to me subsequently (acoustic-motoric). . . . (Bühler, 1907, p. 305)

Of course, Külpe could hardly have answered no to this question, since it concerned the very issue that divided the Würzburg school from Wundt.

140   5. THINKING

Wundt (1907) condemned such experiments as naive introspectionism, denied that such introspective reports could reveal the nature of thoughts, claimed that this research had produced no results, and accused the researchers of taking experimental psychology back to the scholastics with their arbitrary interpretations of the reports. Külpe (1912) and his coworkers, however, interpreted their experimental results as driving a wedge into the closed ranks of the associationists. They were struck with the fact that introspection revealed thoughts that seemed to be neither images nor sensations nor feelings. However, Külpe and his school never proposed a mechanism for the imageless thought they had discovered. There was the additional finding that subjects were unable to report introspectively how they had arrived at their answers. The early experimenters (Mayer & Orth, 1901) seemed to be quite surprised by this inability and found themselves helpless in their new role as inventors of explanatory concepts of their own. (For these attempts and the parallel attempts of Alfred Binet in France, see Humphrey, 1963, and Mandler & Mandler, 1964). We have here a turning point in our conception of the role of the experimental subject: Since the thought process is not conscious, only the subject's behaviour, not his (introspective) explanation remains of interest to the experimenter. The burden and power of explanation has shifted to the experimenter, and this seems to us one factor leading to the gradual replacement of professors by undergraduates and the resulting asymmetry in the contemporary experimenter–subject relationship (see Danziger, 1985).

The Würzburg school thus helped undermine the supremacy of the conscious mind by their conclusion that even the process of thinking occurs mostly at an unconscious level. The conscious mind was under attack from all sides in early 20th century psychology: Freud's Id contributed to it along with the behaviorists' reduction of higher mental processes to reflexes. The belittling of consciousness, and with this, of the belief in rationality, gained ground steadily.

Another major contribution, in particular by Ach (1905) and Messer (1906), was the extension of the associationist theory to a two-factor theory of thinking: Thought is directed both by a reproductive tendency, which is a function of the number of repeated associations, and by a "determining tendency," which is a function of the particular task or instruction given. The latter induces an "attitude" in the subject, which favours the reproduction of certain associations and inhibits others. We shall deal with this second force, the direction of thought given by the task, in the next section, as it reappeared in the Gestalt psychology of thinking. The continuous transition from the Würzburg school to the Gestalt psychology of thinking is exemplified in the contribution of Otto Selz (1913, 1922), who was the first experimenter to propose an explicit

HISTORY: BEFORE THE INFERENCE REVOLUTION   141

alternative to the classical associationist doctrine of thinking. The continuity between the two schools is nicely illustrated by Karl Bühler and Otto Selz, who accused Kurt Koffka of having simply stolen the new Gestalt view of thinking from Selz (see Humphrey, 1963).[1]

Insight and Restructuring

About 1920 the Gestalt psychologists started to become concerned with the nature of human and animal thinking and joined Selz' experimental attack on associationism. The two principles established at that time—the existence of unconscious thought processes and the importance of the task—could easily be assimilated into the Gestalt view. Since thought was explained by analogy to perception, and the laws of perception or Gestalt laws were not consciously penetrable but rather had to be discovered by the psychologist, unconsciousness provided no problem, and the emphasis on the task was in analogy to the importance of the layout in the perceptual field. Problem solving came to be understood analogously to the restructuring of the perceptual field, that is, as a restructuring of the original problem task.

Wertheimer (1945) wrote on the nature of what was called productive thinking, and Köhler's (1917) notion of insight to explain how his chimpanzees suddenly solved problems is a well-known rejoinder to the trial-and-error explanation of the behaviorists. But it seems to us that a disciple of Wertheimer and Köhler, Karl Duncker (1903–1940) gave the most thorough exposition of the Gestalt theory of thinking. We shall illustrate the Gestalt approach with Duncker's experiments (1926, 1935/ 1945).

In a typical experiment, a problem was posed and the subject was asked to "think aloud" while trying to solve the problem. A protocol was taken from what the subject thought aloud. These protocols were the data from which Duncker (1935/1945) drew his conclusions about the nature of

---

[1]The Würzburg school had a direct influence on the development of behaviourism. J. B. Watson sought to banish the study of consciousness from psychology. In his 1913 address "Psychology as the behaviourist views it," he made it clear that one of the reasons for his disillusionment with consciousness was his belief that the introspective method, as practised by the Würzburg school, had led into a blind alley. For example, he wrote:

> The time seems to have come when psychology must discard all reference to consciousness; when it need no longer delude itself into thinking that it is making mental states the object of observation. We have become so enmeshed in speculative questions concerning the elements of mind, the nature of conscious content (for example, imageless thought, attitudes, and *Bewusseinslage* [sic], etc.) that I, as an experimental student, feel that something is wrong with our premises and the types of problem which develop from them. (p. 163)

142   5. THINKING

thought. The problems posed were of two kinds, practical and mathematical. Here are examples of both kinds:

"Given a human being with an inoperable stomach tumor, and rays which destroy organic tissue at sufficient intensity, by what procedure can one free him of the tumor by these rays and at the same time avoid destroying the healthy tissue which surrounds it?" (p. 1)

"Prove that there is an infinite number of prime numbers". (p. 9)

Duncker's subjects were no longer university professors, but anonymous university and college students. Here is an excerpt from the beginning and the end of the protocoled thinking aloud of a subject confronted with the tumor problem:

1. Send rays through the esophagus. 2. Desensitize the healthy tissues by means of a chemical injection. 3. Expose the tumor by operating. 4. One ought to decrease the intensity of the rays on their way; for example— would this work?—turn the rays on at full strength only after the tumor has been reached. . . . 12. . . . I see no more than two possibilities: either to protect the body or to make the rays harmless. 13. . . . Somehow divert . . . diffuse rays . . . disperse . . . stop! Send a broad and weak bundle of rays through a lens in such a way that the tumor lies at the local point and thus receives intensive radiation.

From such protocols Duncker concluded that solutions are typically not achieved in a single step, but are mediated by successive reformulations or restructurings of the original problem. In the foregoing protocol, the original problem, How to free the patient from the tumor without destroying the healthy tissue?, has been reformulated in various ways, such as How to decrease the sensitivity of the tissue? and How to decrease the intensity of the radiation on the way? The latter formulation was decisive for the eventual solution. Since every problem can be reformulated in more than one way, and these reformulations need still further reformulations to arrive at a solution, Duncker represented the flow of thought as a tree. The original problem was the trunk, and the successive reformulations were the branches. The flow of thought was compared with a back-and-forth movement in the branches. For instance, Duncker (1935/1945) gave the following example of moving back from a solution to the preceding reformulation, in order to start again therefrom to find a second solution: "From the ingenious proposal, to apply the rays in adequate amounts by rotation of the body around the tumor as a center, a [subject] made a prompt transition to the neighboring proposal: 'One could also have the radiation apparatus rotate around the body' " (p. 13).

HISTORY: BEFORE THE INFERENCE REVOLUTION 143

In the prime number problem, the original task was to prove that there is an infinite number of prime numbers. The decisive reformulation is, I must prove that for any prime number p there exists a greater one. One subject arrived at the subsequent reformulation, I must construct a number greater than p which cannot be represented as a product, and from there to the "solution": to calculate the product of all numbers from 1 to p and to add 1—a solution close to a correct one, which is calculating the product of all prime numbers from 1 to p and adding 1.

Duncker's theoretical conclusion from the protocols followed those of Selz (1913, 1922), who found similar transformations of the original task and spoke of thinking as the exchange of the original goal for a more specific one. These successive reformulations were understood by Duncker in terms of Gestalt theory: the reformulations constitute a restructuring or reorganization of the situation as a whole. Parts and elements that, before the restructuring, were hardly perceived or were in the background become afterwards the new center of attention, the "figure," and vice versa. But that restructuring involves a *change in the functions* of the parts was emphasized even more than was the occurrence of figure–ground reversals: For Duncker's students, the esophagus became a "passage for rays" in the above protocol; for Köhler's chimpanzees, the boxes lying around acquired the new function of tools (platforms) to reach the fruit.

Thus, productive thinking was the step-by-step restructuring of an original task, and restructuring was identified with the transformation of functions within a system. But how are these restructurings arrived at? Duncker claimed that it is the use of heuristic methods that permits restructurings. "Inspection of the situation," "looking over the situation," and "paying attention" are examples of such heuristic methods. These can be observed "even in the most primitive animal experiment" (Duncker, 1935/1945, p. 24) such as Thorndike's experiments on cats locked in cages, where blind struggling was soon replaced by looking over the situation. However, exactly how a particular heuristic method leads to a particular restructuring was not spelled out.

Insight is the term applied by Gestalt theorists to the final, often sudden restructuring of the problem into a solution, possibly accompanied by an "aha-experience." However, the relationship between restructuring and insight was left undecided by Köhler and others (see Humphrey, 1963). Is insight the cause of restructuring, its consequence, the experience accompanying it? Or is insight synonymous with restructuring? Duncker attempted to sort out different meanings, and, among others, distinguished between insight of the first and second degree. The distinction is whether an animal or human suddenly knows *what* to do in a situation, or whether it knows both *what* to do and *why* (the latter is called

144   5. THINKING

insight of the first degree). Thus, the sudden drop in the curve of errors—the main empirical criterion for insight (Hartmann, 1931; Yerkes, 1929)—may indicate either; if it indicates insight of the second degree only, then, to put it paradoxically, there is insight into a connection (what to do) that is totally inaccessible to insight (with respect to why).

The Emphasis on the Task

We consider the emphasis on the task, from the Würzburg to the Gestalt school, as a major contribution to a theory of thinking, and beyond that, to cognitive psychology itself. As we shall point out, in many contemporary approaches to thinking, the tasks, or the instructions, or the examples given in the instructions are understood as mere neutral tools to elicit the thought process. The latter is often assumed to exist independently of these tools, which open the "mind's door" so that we can observe the process. Variations of the instruction or of the example given are assumed not to be important for theory construction, as long as these fulfill their only supposed purpose—to specify clearly what the experimenter wants.

Recall that the formulation of the task or problem is, from a Gestalt point of view, analogous to the layout of objects in the visual field. Köhler (1917) showed that the particular layout of objects in the visual field of the chimpanzees directed their problem-solving behavior. For instance, it was hard for the ape to see a box, a stick, and a fruit in a new functional relationship (to climb on the box and pull the fruit down with the stick) if one of these was behind him and the others in front of him. Seeing new functions proved easier when the elements were present in the same visual field, that is, on the same side. Therefore, for the human subject, the visually or acoustically presented instruction, like the layout of objects in the visual field, was not considered neutral; it gives the thought process a particular impulse. Some restructurings are facilitated; others, inhibited.

Duncker (1935/1945) varied the instruction concerning the tumor problem. The only change was from the active case to the passive in the last two sentences. The active version was: The rays would thus destroy healthy tissue, too. How could one prevent the rays from injuring the healthy tissue? The passive version was: Healthy tissue, too, would thus be destroyed. How could one protect the healthy tissue from being injured by the rays? In the first version, the emphasis lies on the rays; in the second, on the tissue. Duncker reported that in the group that received the active version, 43% ($n = 23$) of the subjects dealt with the intensity of radiation, whereas only 14% ($n = 21$) of the subjects who heard the passive version did so.

HISTORY: BEFORE THE INFERENCE REVOLUTION   145

Moreover, Duncker emphasized that not only the instruction, but the example that illustrates the problem directs the thought process. Consider the following problem: "Why is it that all six-place numbers of the type *abcabc*, for example 276276, 591591, and 112112, are divisible by thirteen?" When Duncker changed the example into "276276, 277277, and 278278," more subjects solved the problem. He claimed that the neighbor-relation in the second example facilitates the appropriate restructuring of *abcabc* into "abc times 1001" and the final realization that 1001 is divisible by 13. Incidentally, this conclusion was based on two groups with 5 and 4 subjects only, and 0 and 3 correct solutions, respectively. Nevertheless, Duncker (1935/1945) concluded that although the numbers "appear too small, they are not so" (p. 35)—as befits a good German experimental psychologist at the time, untouched by statistical thinking.

The Lost Program

The new programmatic perspective was directed against the reduction of thought to the association of elementary ideas, and it robbed Wundt of his monopoly over psychological experimentation. Of course, the theoretical explanation of how restructurings and insight were arrived at, was not clearly worked out in Duncker's writings, and even less so in Wertheimer's famous *Productive Thinking,* published posthumously in 1945. But there were precise experimental questions such as those concerning the selective role of the task and the functional fixedness that hinders productive thinking. However, the program did not develop into maturity; on the contrary, it came more or less to an end after around 1935, after Duncker had published his book.

What were the reasons for this premature end of the new experimental program? As has been repeatedly pointed out, a main reason was the launching of behaviorism in America, which reduced thinking to subvocal speech and revitalized associationism through its marriage with behaviorism. But the question must still be posed, why did the program cease also in Germany? Here we find a second answer unrelated to behaviorism: the fatal impact of Nazism. This was an accident of history, for we cannot see any specific opposition between experimental studies of thinking and Nazism. Nevertheless, most of the main figures ran foul of the Nazi regime, either because they or their wives were Jews or because of political reasons. Key figures of the Würzburg school like Marbe, who at the time held the chair in Würzburg, and Messer, who held the chair in Giessen, were retired early. Karl Bühler, Max Wertheimer, Kurt Koffka, and Wolfgang Köhler all emigrated to the United States. Koffka and Wertheimer died rather early, as did so many emigré intellectuals, during the war. Bühler never found an appropriate position, although he had an

146   5. THINKING

offer from Harvard around 1930, which he declined. Otto Selz fell into the hands of his persecutors in the Netherlands and was killed in a concentration camp in 1943. At about the time of the publication of his book in 1935, the promising Karl Duncker was forced to escape to England. A few years later he was invited to Swarthmore College, where Köhler taught. There, depressed by the outbreak of the war, he committed suicide in 1940.[2]

Summary

The mechanism of thought was understood by 19th century associationists as the association of ideas, which result in what was called reproductive tendencies. The Würzburg school supplemented the reproductive tendencies by the concept of determining tendency, the directional force of the task, which brings order to the chaos of the many possible associations. Gestalt theory retained the concept of a direction in thinking but rejected the Würzburg dichotomy derived from associationism. Thinking was understood as the successive restructuring of a task into a solution, or, as it was often put, as a transformation of a state of disequilibrium into one of equilibrium. We have shown that some important changes in the idea of experiment occurred as a consequence of these changing theoretical assumptions. Understanding of the subject changed and, consequently, the experimenter–subject relationship; and introspection (including explanation) turned into thinking aloud (without explanation). With the rise of behaviorism in America and of Nazism in Germany the new experimental program came to a premature end, although there are certainly traces left today. Thinking aloud protocols reemerged in the cognitive science studies of thought (e.g. Simon, 1979), and the concept of restructuring, or reorganization, became the cornerstone of Thomas Kuhn's famous *The Structure of Scientific Revolutions* (1970).

The German psychologists of thinking believed neither that the mind was an intuitive statistician, nor that it should be one. The metaphor seems never to have occurred to them. They did not construct problems that could be answered by probability theory. If the problems were numerical, they were of a mathematical rather than a calculational nature, such as finding a proof for the existence of an infinite number of prime numbers. The mind was not yet seen as a calculator, but rather as an agent that restructures the given by seeing new functional relationships between the parts. As we shall see, problems have changed with the new

---

[2]The sad story of the forced migration of these German-speaking intellectuals as a consequence of the Nazi regime has been traced by Wellek (1968) and Mandler and Mandler (1969). For the situation of psychologists in general during the Nazi regime see Geuter (1984). On the historical context of the controversy between Wundt and the Würzburg school see Ash (1980) and Danziger (1980).

metaphor of the mind as an intuitive statistician. And, after the inference revolution, the experiments of Duncker and others were considered methodologically suspect particularly because "no statistical analysis was performed" (e.g. Mayer, 1977, pp. 64, 79).

IS THE MIND A BAYESIAN?

After the inference revolution, a new question arose: Are the long sought-after laws of thought the laws of probability theory? And, to answer the new question, a new kind of problem was posed. These problems were constructed so that they could be answered by *calculating* probabilities, means, variances, or correlations. Restructuring was seldom necessary for the solution of such problems, and so this aspect of the theory of thought was held in abeyance. Consequently, the new vocabulary for understanding human reasoning was the vocabulary of the statistician; the new elements of thinking were numbers (probabilities), and the process of thinking itself was explained by statistical operations such as calculating likelihood ratios. The theoretical questions asked by experimenters, the problems posed to the subjects, and the explanations sought all reflected the fascination with probability theory and statistics.

The new vocabulary made the study of inductive thinking into one of the fastest growing areas of the new psychology of thinking, revitalized by the cognitive revolution. Our concentration here is on the link between inductive thinking and probability theory to the exclusion of other issues such as deductive thinking (e.g. Johnson-Laird, 1983; Wason & Johnson-Laird, 1972) and computer models of problem solving (e.g. Dörner, 1983; Newell & Simon, 1972; Simon, 1979). In this section we deal with the question whether the mind is a Bayesian statistician.

Conservatism

Urns and balls have long been the stock-in-trade of the probabilists. For instance, when Laplace (1774/1878–1912) proved Bayes' theorem, he used the well-known urn filled with white and black balls as his illustration. In the 1960s, the urn-and-balls problems made their way into the laboratories of experimental psychologists, although often in a more contemporary terminology, as bookbag-and-poker chips problems (e.g. Edwards, 1966; Edwards, Lindman & Phillips, 1965). Consider for instance a typical problem posed to the subjects:

> Imagine yourself in the following experiment. Two urns are filled with a large number of poker chips. The first urn contains 70% red chips and 30% blue. The second contains 70% blue chips and 30% red. The experimenter flips a fair coin to select one of the two urns, so the prior probability for

148   5. THINKING

each urn is .50. He then draws a succession of chips from the selected urn. Suppose that the sample contains eight red and four blue chips. What is your revised probability that the selected urn is the predominantly red one? (Peterson & Beach, 1967, p. 32).

If your answer is around .75, you agree with most of the subjects. Compare the new bookbag-and-poker chips problems with those of the Würzburg school and Gestalt psychology. In Bühler's and Duncker's problems, calculation was seldom a useful tool; and if it was, it was not sufficient to find a solution. Now the answer asked for is a number, and calculation rather than restructuring is sufficient to go from the problem to the answer. How is that calculation done? Bayes' theorem gives an answer.

Bayes' theorem is an elementary consequence of the definition of conditional probability given a mutually exclusive and exhaustive set of hypotheses. In the foregoing problem, there are two hypotheses: H_1 that the selected urn is the predominantly red one; and H_2 that it is the predominantly blue one. The answer asked for is the *posterior probability* $p(H_1|D)$ that H_1 is true given the data D, that is, eight red and four blue chips. According to Bayes' theorem, the posterior probability is:

$$p(H_1|D) = p(H_1)p(D|H_1)/p(D) \qquad (5.1)$$

with

$$p(D) = p(H_1)p(D|H_1) + p(H_2)p(D|H_2).$$

As described in chapter 1, $p(H_1)$ and $p(H_2)$ are the *prior probabilities* of the hypotheses H_1 and H_2, respectively, and $p(D|H_1)$ and $p(D|H_2)$ are called the *likelihoods* of the data D if H_1 and H_2, respectively, are true. Thus, Bayes' theorem gives a rule for revising a prior probability (or, *base rate*, as it is often called) into a posterior probability after new data has been observed. The posterior probability will be greater than the prior, if the ratio $p(D|H_1)/p(D)$ exceeds 1, which is the case if the data has a high probability if the hypothesis H_1 is true. For the present problem, the likelihood of getting $x = 8$ red chips in a sample of $n = 12$ if H_1 holds is given by

$$p(D|H_1) = \binom{n}{x}p_1{}^x(1-p_1)^{n-x} \qquad (5.2)$$

In words, $p_1{}^x$ is the probability of drawing a sequence of x red chips (p_1 is the percentage of red chips in the urn H_1), and $(1-p_1)^{n-x}$ is the probability of drawing a sequence of $(n-x)$ blue chips. Therefore, the product of $p_1{}^x(1-p_1)^{n-x}$ is the probability of a sequence of x red and $(n-x)$ blue chips. The number $\binom{n}{x}$ denotes the number of different orderings in which x red and $(n-x)$ blue chips can occur. Thus, we can calculate the likelihoods:

$$p(D|H_1) = (\tbinom{12}{8}).7^8 \times .3^4 = .231$$
$$p(D|H_2) = (\tbinom{12}{8}).3^8 \times .7^4 = .008.$$

Inserting the likelihoods and the prior probabilities into Bayes' theorem, we calculate the posterior probability:

$$p(H_1|D) = .5 \times .231/(.5 \times .231 + .5 \times .008) = .967$$

Thus, after having observed eight red chips in a sample of twelve, we should revise the prior probability from .50 to around .97. Compared with this, the average subject was more conservative, revising from .50 to only .75. This "cautious" revision of the prior probability was called *conservatism* and was the main finding of that early research. Incidentally, the calculations for this simple bookbag-and-poker chip problem illustrate the complexity of the mental calculations that the reasoning mind is supposed to perform.

By the late 1960s, it was concluded that conservatism was a persistent phenomenon, although some variables, such as the sequential order of the data and the introduction of incentives, influenced the degree of conservatism (Peterson & Beach, 1967; Peterson & DuCharme, 1967; Phillips & Edwards, 1966). In Edwards' (1968) words, "It takes anywhere from two to five observations to do one observation's worth of work in inducing a subject to change his opinions" (p. 18). The question whether the mind reasons like a Bayesian seemed to have found a consistent answer: The mind is a quasi-Bayesian, that is, a very conservative one. The mind mistrusts new data and gives greater weight to the prior probabilities.

How to Explain Conservatism?

Peterson and Beach (1967) proposed that the mind systematically miscalculates equation (5.2), but not (5.1). That is, the mind first miscalculates the likelihoods, but then correctly uses Bayes' theorem, although with the wrong likelihoods. Edwards (1968) proposed the opposite explanation— that the mind correctly calculates equation (5.2) but miscalculates (5.1). In other words, the likelihoods are correct, but the mind misaggregates them with the prior probabilities instead of combining them according to Bayes' theorem. There were other interesting attempts to explain the phenomenon, such as the idea that the mind considers as relevant data the ratio of red to blue chips rather than their difference. Bayes' theorem, however, implies that only the difference counts: eight red and four blue chips (a difference of four) in a sample of twelve give the same result as five red and one blue chips in a sample of six (see Manz, 1970).

The important point here is to see *where the explanatory concepts come from* rather than to speculate which explanation might be correct. The psychological explanations now come from the vocabulary of probability theory and, in particular, from Bayes' theorem, like the research

150   5. THINKING

question and the problems posed. First, the facts that require explanation are the deviations from Bayesian reasoning: Had the subjects followed Bayes' theorem, no explanation would have been necessary. Bayes' theorem has become the frame of reference. Second, although human reasoning does deviate from Bayesian reasoning, the explanation is still sought in the vocabulary of Bayes' theorem, such as "miscalculating" likelihoods or "misaggregation." Like textbook problems in probability theory, these explanations ignore the content and context of the specific problem: it is the mathematical structure that counts. It is ironic that the whole phenomenon of conservatism disappeared when in the early 1970s Daniel Kahneman and Amos Tversky posed Bayesian problems with a content different from bookbags and poker chips. Subjects no longer seemed to reason conservatively about the new problems; indeed, they even seemed to neglect the prior probabilities.

Base Rate Neglect: The Kahneman and Tversky Program

There is an important difference between the kind of problems posed by Edwards, on one hand, and Kahneman and Tversky, on the other. Edwards' problems were pure application of probability theory, whereas Kahneman and Tversky's problems, while still of the textbook sort, approximated real-life situations. The latter thus became simultaneously more interesting and, as we shall see, more ambiguous in their interpretation.

Kahneman and Tversky (1973) started with the unquestioned belief that Bayes' theorem would give a single correct answer to the problems they investigated. Their problems were typically presented in questionnaires and distributed in classrooms and other group settings; subjects were typically high school students and college undergraduates. One of the best known problems is the Engineer-Lawyer Problem. Kahneman and Tversky (1973) told the following cover story to a group of students:

> A panel of psychologists have interviewed and administered personality tests to 30 engineers and 70 lawyers, all successful in their respective fields. On the basis of this information, thumbnail descriptions of the 30 engineers and 70 lawyers have been written. You will find on your forms five descriptions, chosen at random from the 100 available descriptions. For each description, please indicate your probability that the person described is an engineer, on a scale from 0 to 100.
>
> The same task has been performed by a panel of experts, who were highly accurate in assigning probabilities to the various descriptions. You will be paid a bonus to the extent that your estimates come close to those of the expert panel. (p. 241)

A second group of students received the same instruction with inverted base rates (prior probabilities), namely, 70 engineers and 30 lawyers. All subjects were given the same personality descriptions. One of these thumbnail descriptions follows:

> Jack is a 45-year-old man. He is married and has four children. He is generally conservative, careful, and ambitious. He shows no interest in political and social issues and spends most of his free time on his many hobbies which include home carpentry, sailing, and mathematical puzzles. The probability that Jack is one of the 30 engineers in the sample of 100 is ____%. (p. 241)

Although the likelihoods—p(description|Engineer) and p(description|Lawyer)—are not specified here, the experimental situation is set up in such a way that it is still possible for Kahneman and Tversky to use Bayes' theorem to compute the posterior probabilities: They calculate the ratios of the odds in both groups, so that the likelihoods cancel out.[3] Bayes' theorem predicts that the posterior probabilities should be different for the two groups. Kahneman and Tversky found, however, that the mean responses in the two groups were for the most part the same and concluded that base rates were largely ignored.[4] The explanation was that

---

[3]The likelihoods are cancelled out in the following way: The "prior odds" p(Engineer)/p(Lawyer) are 30/70 in the first and 70/30 in the second group. The likelihood ratios p(description|Engineer)/p(description|Lawyer) are assumed to be the same in both groups. If we use the symbol O_1 and O_2 for the prior odds in the two groups, respectively, and L for the likelihood ratio, then the ratio of the posterior odds Q_1 and Q_2 in the two groups is given as follows:

$$\frac{Q_1}{Q_2} = \frac{O_1}{O_2} \times \frac{L}{L_1} = \frac{O_1}{O_2} = \frac{3/7}{7/3} = .18$$

This means that the posterior odds p(Engineer|description)/p(Lawyer|description) in the first group should be only 18% of those in the second, or equivalently, the odds in the second should be more than five times as high as in the first (see Kahneman & Tversky, 1973).

[4]In fact, however, Kahneman and Tversky (1983) found a statistically significant difference between the two groups ($p < .01$). Nevertheless, they subsequently ignored this and concluded that the manipulation of the information about base rates had only a "minimal effect" and therefore that base rates were "largely ignored." Of course, they were quite right to forget about their null hypothesis test, since null hypothesis testing in this situation, with two competing predictions, is useless. Both Bayes' theorem and the "neglect of base rates" hypothesis specify predictions, and it is nonsensical to identify one with a null hypothesis. In fact, Kahneman and Tversky came to their conclusion by eyeballing (the results lie much closer to the predictions of the "base rate neglect" hypothesis than to those of Bayes' theorem); alternatively one might have adopted a symmetric hypothesis testing procedure such as Neyman & Pearsons'. This example, like that of cognitive algebra in chapter 3, shows that null hypothesis testing not only may be useless, but may actually be misleading. In contrast to Anderson, Kahneman & Tversky realized this, but it is still a question why they performed the null hypothesis testing ritual in the first place.

152   5. THINKING

the subjects had arrived at the probability judgments by judging only the similarity between the description and the stereotype of an engineer, or, in order words, the degree to which the description is representative of the stereotype. This strategy was called the *representativeness heuristic.*

The five personality descriptions included the following nondiagnostic sketch, which is particularly interesting because it was constructed to be totally uninformative with respect to the question whether the person is an engineer or a lawyer: "Dick is a 30-year-old man. He is married with no children. A man of high ability and high motivation, he promises to be quite successful in his field. He is well liked by his colleagues." (Kahneman & Tversky, 1973, p. 242). The median probability judgments for Dick being an engineer were 50% in each group, and the authors concluded that the subjects had ignored base rates even when the description was totally uninformative.

The representativeness heuristic again reveals the dream of universal laws of thought—if not Bayes' theorem, then at least such universal heuristics as representativeness. This search for a few simple laws plays down the importance of the *task* for structuring thought. For instance, Ginosar and Trope (1980) repeated the Engineer-Lawyer study, but gave only one of the five personality descriptions (including the nondiagnostic sketch) to each subject. They concluded that in this situation the nondiagnostic sketch *was* assessed by the base rate. It seems that one particular feature of Kahneman and Tversky's task, namely the presentation of diagnostic descriptions *before* the nondiagnostic sketch, directed the reasoning about the nondiagnostic sketch. A second feature of Kahneman and Tversky's task was that no subject was given different base rates. But Fischhoff, Slovic, and Lichtenstein (1979) report that base rates have more impact if they are varied in the problem posed to a subject. The general structure of the task, and not only some general "law of thought," appears to determine performance.

Representativeness

What is the explanation for the new phenomenon, the so-called neglect of base rates? Kahneman and Tversky (1973, Tversky & Kahneman, 1982a) offer two major explanations, the representativeness heuristic and causal versus incidental base rates. The first explanation is derived from the Engineer-Lawyer Problem and similar problems. Kahneman and Tversky claim that their subjects arrived at their answer by a heuristic, or short-hand, strategy rather than by Bayes' theorem. This heuristic is called representativeness and is identified with the similarity between the description and the stereotype of an engineer. In their early writings, they seemed to imply that the base rate fallacy necessarily results from the use of the representativeness heuristic. But soon it became clear that other problems, such as the Cab Problem (see below), could not be dealt with by a representativeness heuristic. Thus, representativeness might be only one condition for the neglect of base rates. As Kahneman and Tversky (1972) put it, "Representativeness, like perceptual similarity, is easier to assess than to characterize. In both cases, no general definition is available, yet there are many situations where people agree which of two stimuli is more similar to a standard" (p. 431). The term representativeness was used in the early writings with more than one meaning, as the authors themselves later realized (Tversky & Kahneman, 1982b). We shall therefore confine our discussion to the use of the term representativeness in the context of Bayesian-type problems of probability revision such as the Engineer-Lawyer Problem.

Kahneman and Tversky (1973) distinguish between formal rules like Bayes', which specify how we should determine probabilities, and non-formal heuristics like "representativeness," which describe how we actually determine probabilities. Bayes' theorem is correct and is about probability; heuristics are mostly misleading and not influenced by probability. But as we shall show, this distinction is illusory. In fact, the representativeness heuristic boils down to computing probabilities using only likelihoods, without prior probabilities. It is therefore just as formal and potentially quantitative as Bayes' theorem itself, though not normative. We submit that this formal nature of a purportedly informal, qualitative heuristic shows the extent to which probability theory has permeated contemporary theory construction in this area of psychology.

In the following section we show that the concept of a representativeness heuristic can be reduced to the concept of likelihood in Bayes' theory.

The Skeleton of a Heuristic

How can we show that representativeness is a redescription of base rate neglect rather than an explanation? It seems to us that in most, if not all, cases, representativeness or similarity is synonymous with likelihood. If this is true, the explanation will turn out to be merely a redescription of the phenomenon in Bayesian terms. What basis do we have for this claim? Let us consult Tversky and Kahneman (1982b), who dissect their original use of the term representativeness into two different senses; judgments *by* representativeness, the heuristic used for inference and prediction; and judgments *of* representativeness, the finding that people judge and expect samples to be highly representative of their parent

154 5. THINKING

populations. It is the first meaning we are concerned with. They differentiate four basic cases of judgment *by* representativeness. For each, they characterize representativeness as a directional relation between a model or population and an instance or sample. This means that a sample is more or less representative of a particular population, but not vice versa. This general characterization is in accordance with that of a likelihood, which is a directional relation, $p(D|H)$ between a sample D and a population or hypothesis H. Although Kahneman and Tversky believe that their subjects use representativeness as an alternative to probabilistic thinking, they themselves characterize at least the first three kinds of judgments by representativeness in terms of distributions (Tversky & Kahneman, 1982b, p.87). Let us look at the four basic kinds in which the concept of representativeness is invoked.

In the first case, representativeness is defined as a relation between a class H and the value D of a variable defined in this class. The given example speaks of (more or less) representative values of the income of college professors. The authors state that representativeness is determined here mainly by what the subject knows about the frequency distribution, and that a value D will be most representative if it is close to the mean. In this first case, representativeness is identical with the likelihood of an observed value D given a subjective distribution H, that is of a likelihood $p(D|H)$, where H is a one-dimensional distribution and D is a single observation.

In the second and third cases, representativeness is defined as a relation between a class and an element or subset, respectively. Since Kahneman and Tversky see the second case as a special case of the third, we shall deal only with the latter. To use one of the authors' examples, students of astronomy are less representative of the entire student body than are students of psychology. Kahneman and Tversky contrast this to the first case by pointing out that we now deal with more than one attribute in the population and with more than one element in the sample. Thus, the first can be regarded as the unidimensional version of the third, as the authors themselves state. Therefore, representativeness is for case 3 identical with the notion of a likelihood $p(D|H)$, where D is a sample rather a single event and H is an unknown, subjective multidimensional distribution rather than a unidimensional one.

In the last case, representativeness is defined as a relation between a causal system and a possible consequence. Here, it is no longer a class but a system that may produce a consequence D. For example, let H be pneumonia and D be high fever, which is frequently associated with pneumonia. This case seems to be equivalent to the unidimensional case 1, except that the subjective distribution of effects which specifies the likelihoods is now interpreted as "caused" by a system H. This specific interpretation does not, however, change the formal identity of case 4 with case 1 and can therefore be subsumed under case 1.[5]

To summarize, representativeness seems to be in all cases reducible to likelihood. Thus, to say that the subject uses a representativeness heuristic for probability revision seems to be equivalent to saying that the subject uses the likelihood in Bayes' theorem, but not the prior probability. Our conclusion, therefore, is that Bayes' theorem provides the vocabulary for the explanation of the phenomenon, as it also did for the phenomenon itself. This clarifies our point that the explanation offered is but a redescription of the phenomenon. The phenomenon that is called "neglect of base rates" could just as well be called "neglect of base rates and nonneglect of likelihoods." The explanation, judgment by representativeness, can be now rephrased as "use of likelihoods and neglect of base rates." The explanation is a redescription of the phenomenon.

Although Bayes' theorem has been dismissed by Kahneman and Tversky as a fundamental law of human thinking, the new candidate, representativeness, has inherited major attributes, since it stems from the same framework, as we have shown. These attributes are typical of formal and calculational approaches to human thinking: it is held that the representativeness heuristic operates independently of the content and the context of the problem; the heuristic has nothing to say about the process of information search; and it emphasizes rationality rather than passion.

Independence of Human Thinking from Content. The assumption is that human thinking should be directed by the formal structure of the problem, not by the content. Along with their conviction that Bayes' theorem should be used in all problems that seem to have a Bayesian structure, independent of the actual content, Kahneman and Tversky (1972) have the parallel conviction that people use a representativeness heuristic for all contents: "Although our experimental examples were confined to well-defined sampling processes (where objective probability is readily computable), we conjecture that the same heuristic plays an important role in the evaluation of uncertainty in essentially unique situations where no 'correct' answer is available" (p. 451). Examples that follow are the judgment of the probability that a particular 12-year-old boy will become a scientist, that a company will go out of business, and that a politician will be elected for office. However, in the recent past it has become more and more evident that if the structure of the problem

---

[5]The problem with Tversky and Kahneman's (1982b) distinction into four kinds of judgments *by* representativeness is that their own formal structure (p. 87) does not make sense in the light of all the examples they give. Here we have concentrated on those examples which fit into their own formal structure.

156   5. THINKING

posed is held constant, but the content is changed, responses differ. That content is crucial for the laws of human reasoning has been found in problems concerning both inductive and deductive thinking (e.g., see Einhorn, 1980; Evans, 1984; Griggs, 1983; Pollard, 1982; Wason, 1983). For instance, in their research on deductive thinking and the understanding of negations, Wason and Johnson-Laird (1972) also started with the assumption that the content they invented to illustrate a structure, say a syllogism or a double negation, would not affect the operation of the laws of thought: "For some considerable time we cherished the illusion that this was the way to proceed, and that only the structural characteristics of the problem mattered. Only gradually did we realize first that there was no existing formal calculus which correctly modelled our subjects' inferences" (pp. 244f.). Kahneman and Tversky (1982) also made a retreat, realizing that content is crucial and that, consequently, human reasoning cannot be described by content-independent formal rules. However, what has not been clarified is that judgments by representativeness—because they are in essence judgments by likelihood—are as content independent as formal Bayesian reasoning.

Independence of Human Thinking from Context. To claim that human thinking is directed by a general-purpose heuristic such as representativeness implies that the context of the problem is not very important for a theory of thinking. For instance, the wording of the problem and the particular example given are contextual variables. As we pointed out earlier, the proponents of the Würzburg and the Gestalt school concluded from their experiments that these contextual variables give an impulse or a direction to the flow of thought. Recently, the role of these "irrelevant" variables has again come to be appreciated (e.g. Berkeley & Humphreys, 1982; Crocker, 1981; Einhorn, 1980). For instance, consider the additional information in the Engineer-Lawyer problem that a panel of experts were "highly accurate" in the same task and that "you will be paid a bonus to the extent that your estimates come close to those of the expert panel." It seems that Kahneman and Tversky added this paragraph to increase the motivation of their students to fill out their questionnaires more carefully. In fact, the impact may be far greater. The subjects may understand from the success of the experts that the personality descriptions are highly informative if only one knows how to read them. Thus they might conclude that there is only one strategy to win the bonus, namely, to concentrate on the description and to forget about the base rates. Whether this explanation of the base rate neglect in terms of contextual variables rather than general heuristics is true or not can be easily checked by repeating the experiment with different information. The general point, however, is that the representativeness heuristic, like Bayes' theorem, seduces one into believing that thinking is directed by a few universal laws of thought. But it is becoming increasingly evident that thinking, like perception (see e.g. Birnbaum, 1982), is directed by the specific context in which a problem is presented.

The Blind Spot: Information Search. Statistical hypothesis testing does not start until the variables and numbers needed for the formulas are available. It is not concerned with the preceding measurement process, with the questions, what is the relevant information we shall look for? and how shall we measure the variables which we consider relevant? Like statistical theories, the representativeness heuristic does not deal with the process of information search. We have shown that it stands in the framework of statistical problems, where thinking means mental work on prepackaged information. When the subject enters the laboratory, most if not all of the process of information search has already been done by the experimenter. In contrast, the older meaning of heuristic tool in Duncker's theory was confined to search for new information and new functional relationships. Heuristic tools were "looking around," "inspection," and "selection," and the outcome of heuristic processes were "restructurings" or "judgments of relevance," as recently reemphasized by Evans (1984).

Passionless Irrationality. The belief that Bayes' theorem is the manifestation of rationality has its mirror image in the link between representativeness and irrationality. Since the representativeness heuristic was assumed to be used in almost every content and context, it seemed to provide a cognitive explanation for many a human error, even those usually explained by people's emotions and passions. From base rate fallacy to self-serving attributions to ethnocentric prejudices—such phenomena were now understood as the result of a relatively passionless mind, handicapped by its ignorance of the laws of probability (e.g. Nisbett & Ross, 1980). The parsimonious heuristic user is seen as "governed by a consistent misperception of the world rather than by opportunistic wishful thinking. Given some editorial prodding, he may be willing to regard his statistical intuitions with proper suspicion and replace impression formation by computation whenever possible" (Tversky & Kahneman, 1971, p. 110).

Causal versus Incidental Base Rates

Kahneman and Tversky posed a second type of problem to their subjects, also of a Bayesian structure, but one in which the likelihood could not be easily interpreted as similarity. Therefore, the supposed base rate neglect could not be explained by representativeness. One of the best known examples is the Cab Problem. Since the publication of the first results around 1972, different versions have appeared; the present one is from Tversky and Kahneman (1980).

158 5. THINKING

A cab was involved in a hit-and-run accident at night. Two cab companies, the Green and the Blue, operate in the city. You are given the following data:

(i) 85% of the cabs in the city are Green and 15% are Blue.

(ii) A witness identified the cab as a Blue cab. The court tested his ability to identify cabs under the appropriate visibility conditions. When presented with a sample of cabs (half of which were Blue and half of which were Green) the witness made correct identifications in 80% of the cases and erred in 20% of the cases.

Question: What is the probability that the cab involved in the accident was Blue rather than Green?" (p. 162)

This problem has the same formal Bayesian structure as the urn-and-pokerchip problems, only the content has changed. The predominantly blue urn became the Blue cab company, and the chips drawn became the witness report. In contrast to the pokerchip problem, the likelihoods are already numerically given (.80 and .20). From Bayes' theorem, Tversky and Kahneman calculated a probability $p(B|"B") = .41$ that the cab was Blue (B) given the witness report "Blue" ("B"). If the subjects were "conservative" Bayesians, they should answer about .25–.30, in between the prior probability (base rate) for Blue (.15) and the Bayesian solution. Tversky and Kahneman (1980), however, report that several hundred subjects gave a modal and median response of .80. Since this median answer coincides with the credibility of the witness (the likelihood $p("B"|B)$, they conclude that their subjects ignored the relevant base rates.

The same conclusion was drawn in several studies (see Tversky & Kahneman, 1982a), for undergraduates as well as for professionals. For example, Casscells, Schoenberger and Grayboys (1978, cited in Tversky & Kahneman, 1982a) posed the following problem to 60 students and staff at Harvard Medical School: "If a test to detect a disease whose prevalence is $1/1000$ has a false positive rate of 5%, what is the chance that a person found to have a positive result actually has the disease, assuming you know nothing about the person's symptoms or signs?" (p. 154).

If one assumes that the test correctly diagnoses this disease in everyone who has it, one can calculate the posterior probability by Bayes' theorem, which is 2%. Of the 60 students and staff members, 11 gave this answer, whereas the average answer (mean) was 56% and the most common answer (mode) was 95%!. This range amply illustrates the large interindividual differences often found in such studies. The conclusion drawn was that "even highly educated respondents often fail to appreciate the significance of outcome base rate in relatively simple formal problems" (Tversky & Kahneman, 1982a, p. 154).

What is the explanation of this phenomenon? First, it is necessary to be clear about what the phenomenon itself is. The phenomenon observed is the mean, median, or modal probability judgment. The phenomenon is not the neglect of base rates. Like "conservativism," the latter is already an interpretation of the observed judgments in terms of Bayes' theorem. Nevertheless, Tversky and Kahneman (e.g. 1980, pp. 61ff) talk about "the phenomenon of base-rate neglect." This phrasing is quite interesting, suggesting that Bayes' theorem has become such a ubiquitous background to theorizing that the observed fact is immediately interpreted in terms of Bayes' theorem. This interpretation now appears as the fact itself; any observed median probability can be immediately located on a scale with the base rate and the likelihood on the extremes, where the observation appears as either neglect of base rates or overweighting base rates (conservatism). Thus, the fascination with probability theory has already penetrated the facts observed.

The "Explanation" Analyzed.

What is the explanation for the phenomenon called the neglect of base rates? Since the reliability of the witness can be hardly called a similarity, Kahneman and Tversky cannot explain this supposed neglect of base rates by a representativeness heuristic. Instead they offer a second explanation: "We propose that the phenomenon of base-rate neglect largely depends on whether or not the evidence is given a causal interpretation" (Tversky & Kahneman, 1980). What does this mean? For illustration, the authors give the following variation of the Cab Problem, where information (i) in the previous Cab Problem is replaced by the following information: (i') "Although the two companies are roughly equal in size, 85% of cab accidents in the city involve Green cabs, and 15% involve Blue cabs" (p. 63).

The difference concerns the question, base rate of what? In the original instructions, base rates of Blue cabs in the *city* were specified, whereas in the new instruction base rates of Blue cabs that were involved in *accidents* were also specified. With this new base rate, the median answer of subjects was .60, as compared with .80 previously. Intraindividual variability again was large. Since this median answer lay in between the reliability of the witness (.80) and Bayes' solution (.41), the authors concluded that the base rate was no longer ignored.

The explanation given is that there are two different types of base rates, causal and incidental. The "city" base rate in (i) is called incidental because the greater base rate of Green cabs in the city "does not justify a causal inference that makes any particular Green cab more likely to be involved in an accident than any particular Blue cab." The "accident" base rate in (i') is "causal because the difference in rates of accidents

160 5. THINKING

between companies of equal size readily elicits the inference that the drivers of the Green cabs are more reckless and/or less competent than the drivers of the Blue cabs." (Tversky & Kahneman 1982a, pp. 157–158)

But is there *also* a causal link between a driver's competence and the criminality of fleeing the scene of the accident? A lack of a causal link would imply that the "accident" base rate is also "incidental." One subject's incidental rate might be another's causal rate. We shall return to this question shortly.

What does it mean to explain the neglect of base rates by saying that the base rate was incidental? An urn analogy may be helpful here. Imagine there are Blue and Green urns, each filled with a mixture of witness reports "B" or "G." There are different possible experiments, two of which are called "urns in the city" and "urns in accidents." In each experiment, first one urn is randomly drawn from all urns, and then a witness report is randomly drawn from that urn. The experiments differ only in that different populations of Green and Blue urns are used. Imagine you are the subject in the accident experiment. Your task is to guess the color of the urn from which the witness report has been drawn. We tell you that a report B was drawn, and we tell you the proportion of reports B and G in the Blue and Green urns, respectively. We do not give you the base rates of Blue and Green urns in the accident experiment, but, by mistake, we inform you about the base rates in the city experiment. The latter do not refer to your experiment. This is exactly the meaning of incidental base rates, and you may be well advised to ignore such base rates.

We now repeat the accident experiment with another subject, correct our mistake, and give the subject information about the appropriate accident base rate. This is the situation to which Kahneman and Tversky refer as causal base rates. Thus, it becomes clear that the distinction between causal and incidental base rates boils down to whether the relevant base rates for one experiment or another are given. This simple analysis of the nature of the new explanation has an interesting consequence: The phenomenon disappears, and the subjects may even be rehabilitated as good Bayesians.

The Phenomenon Disappears. Tversky and Kahneman (1980) still believe that a posterior probability of .41 is "the correct answer" to the original version of the Cab Problem, where the city base rates were given. However, as we have argued, they did not specify the relevant base rate "cabs involved in hit-and-run accidents," but only those of a different "experiment." In this situation, a Bayesian might either use the base rates of the city experiment as the unknown prior probabilities and hope that both happen to be equal, or, for lack of better knowledge, fall back on the principle of indifference and assume that as many Green drivers as Blue drivers may commit hit-and-run crimes. In the latter case, a Bayesian would calculate a posterior probability of .80, which, surprisingly, is identical to the median answer given by the subjects. The conclusion from this would be that the subjects in fact behaved like Bayesians who were forced to apply the principle of indifference. The phenomenon therewith disappears. The point is, however, that there is no way to decide about the correct answer.

Let us turn to the revised Cab Problem, where the base rates of cab accidents were given. Kahneman and Tversky now insert the accident base rate instead of, as before, the city base rate into the formula and again calculate .41 as the correct answer (since the numbers of two base rates have been simply exchanged). Note again that the posterior probability asked for is concerned with the hypothesis that a Blue cab was in a hit-and-run situation, not in just any accident or in the city. The relevant hit-and-run prior probability is again unspecified. Why do the authors estimate the missing prior probability using the base rates of accidents rather than of cabs in the city, or by applying the principle of indifference? There is no discussion of this choice. As we pointed out earlier this choice means inferring lack of honesty from lack of competence. This may be true, or it may not be. For instance, drivers who constantly have accidents may be so well adapted as not to panic and drive off, whereas the driver who never had an accident may be nervous and excited and prone to speed away. In these cases, it would be unreasonable to insert the accident base rates into the formula. But we do not know. The point is not the plausibility of such alternative causal accounts, but rather the choice of *which* base rate to use must be defended—otherwise we risk mixing up experiments, as in the urn analogy. Consequently, there is no unique way to calculate the posterior probability in this experiment, since the prior probability is unspecified. Kahneman and Tversky's calculation of .41 is only one alternative. Therefore, the phenomenon disappears again in this second study, since one cannot conclude that subjects neglect base rates or that they neglect them to a lesser degree, if the base rate itself is not specified. Finally, if we assume that the subjects should apply the principle of indifference, then the median judgment of .60 even appears as an instance of conservatism.

The general lesson to be learned from this is twofold. First, the explanation of the neglect of base rates by incidental versus causal base rates can be reduced to an elementary rephrasing of Bayes' theorem: To revise a prior probability into a posterior probability and to assume that this has a *single* correct answer implies that the *relevant* base rate is specified. If not, as in "incidental" base rates, it is nonsensical to talk about a neglect of the base rate. Second, the more the urns in the example take on a specific content, the more ambiguity arises about which base

162   5. THINKING

rate is the relevant one and therefore the more doubtful it is that there exists a single correct Bayesian answer. We shall return to this fundamental issue in the next section.

To summarize, this new psychology of thinking is saturated with probability theory; Bayes' theorem gives the framework for the question posed, the problems constructed and even the vocabulary for the phenomenon "observed." Prior probabilities and likelihoods are the new elements of human reasoning. From this perspective, if the mind is not a Bayesian, there are only two possible alternatives: the neglect of base rates, or the neglect of the likelihoods. The former is the result presented by Kahneman and Tversky; the latter has been concluded from the earlier bookbag-and-poker chips studies. In fact, Kahneman and Tversky's explanations, although they appear informal, can also be reduced to these two new elements of the mind. To explain the neglect of base rates by saying that the subject uses a representativeness heuristic is in essence saying that the subject uses the likelihood in Bayes' formula, but not the base rate. Therefore, the supposed explanation is simply a redescription of the supposed phenomenon. The second explanation, causal versus incidental base rates, also boils down to Bayes' formula: To explain the neglect of base rates by saying that the base rates specified in the problem were incidental rather than causal is in essence saying that the relevant prior probabilities were not specified in the first place. We have repeatedly pointed out how the descriptive and explanatory conclusions hinge on Bayes' formula as the normative background. We have also repeatedly shown how this entire perspective depends on the assumption that Bayes' theorem is normative. Not only the explanations, but the descriptions of the phenomena themselves are colored by this assumption, as we have seen. However, it is only by neglecting content, context, and information search that this normative assumption is made tenable. In sum, Bayes' theorem has become the framework for reasoning about reasoning.

FUNDAMENTAL ASSUMPTIONS IN THE NORMATIVE PROGRAM

Essential for the conclusions drawn about how human reasoning functions and should function are two assumptions, which we call the *isomorphism assumption* and the *unambiguous answer assumption*. These assumptions are never made explicit in Kahneman and Tversky's reasoning about reasoning. However, both assumptions must hold for a given problem in order for the descriptive and normative conclusions drawn to be conclusive, as we shall show. We shall deal again only with Bayesian

FUNDAMENTAL ASSUMPTIONS IN THE NORMATIVE PROGRAM   163

statistics, but the argument applies to other kinds of statistical models as well.

Is There an Isomorphism Between the World and Bayes' Theorem?

The isomorphism assumption states that a problem can be mapped in a one-to-one fashion into Bayes' theorem. The problem can be either of the textbook type, like those presented earlier, or any "real-world" problem. We shall say that an isomorphism exists if the following two conditions hold:

1. Concept Isomorphism. The assumption is that each of the two formal concepts in Bayes' theorem is unequivocally matched with one semantic concept concerning the problem. The formal concepts are the prior probabilities and the likelihoods. This implies, for instance, that there are not two different candidates for the prior probability.

2. Structural Isomorphism. The assumption is that the formal structure underlying Bayes' theorem is represented by a similar structure of the problem. The structural assumptions include that the hypotheses considered are mutually exclusive and exhaustive, that the data D has been obtained by random sampling from the population H to which the prior probability refers, and that successive data sampled are mutually independent. For instance, if successive pieces of information are redundant rather than independent, Bayes' theorem is inappropriate for the successive revision of probabilities, and conservatism might be more appropriate.

Concept Isomorphism

The first question is whether concept isomorphism exists for a given problem. The most elementary kind of violation can be illustrated by the Cab Problem, where the two likelihoods needed, $p(``B"|B)$ and $p(``B"|G)$, are *not* specified. We are told only that "the witness made correct identifications in 80% of the cases and erred in 20%." This means that the *two* kinds of correct identification, those of Green and Blue, respectively, average to 80%. This, however, does not unambiguously determine $p(``B"|B)$; therefore, depending on whether the witness did better for either Blue or Green, any posterior probability between .31 and 1.00 can be calculated. As a consequence, the phenomenon—neglect of base rates—either appears or disappears, since it is defined *relative* to the "correct" answer. This kind of violation of concept isomorphism is the simplest variety, since it can be easily avoided by phrasing the problem carefully, as Tversky and Kahneman themselves (1982a) recently did:

164 5. THINKING

"The witness correctly identified *each one* of the two colors 80% of the time and failed 20% of the time" (p. 156, italics ours).

We turn now to a deeper issue concerning concept isomorphism, to be illustrated by the prior probabilities. We make the following conjecture: The more the urns are filled with content, the more candidates emerge for the prior probabilities. In other words, the essential question becomes, which base rate is the relevant one? Recall our discussion of that question for the Cab Problem. The posterior probability asked for is the probability, given the witness report, that a Blue cab was involved in a *hit-and-run accident at night*. There are several candidates for the prior probability, two of which were considered by Kahneman and Tversky: the base rate of Blue cabs in the *city,* and the base rate of Blue cabs involved in *accidents*. There is a third base rate considered earlier by us, the base rate of Blue cabs involved in *hit-and-run accidents*. Which one is the relevant one? Kahneman and Tversky use the city base rate, if given, the accident base rate, if both are given, but claim in each case that the solution is the only correct one. The hit-and-run base rate may, however, be considered as the only relevant one and might be as different from the accident base rate as the latter is from the city base rate. Therefore, one might better ignore both the city and the accident base rates and, since the hit-and-run base rate is not known, apply instead the principle of indifference and set the relevant prior probabilities as .50 each, owing to a lack of better knowledge. Only a fourth base rate permits a consensus about which is the relevant one: the rate of Blue cabs involved in *hit-and-run accidents at night*. This solution will work for the textbook problems because it exhausts all the already specified dimensions of content contained therein, but not as we shall see, for real situations.

Thus, one solution to the base rate quandary is to rephrase the posterior by the prior probability given in the problem, using the same wording. However, this problem of when to call a base rate incidental rather than causal or relevant is not the most important concern. The main point is that by reducing thinking to calculation on *specified* probabilities, a broad range of thought processes are eliminated from consideration, which concern information search and evaluation. In fact, the foregoing solution is possible only in textbook situations, since there the experimenter *has already decided* what information is relevant. In a real-world situation the subjects must themselves *search for the relevant information* and decide for themselves which features of the problem situation might be relevant. Thus, the features to which the base rate refers must be decided at first hand by a judgment of relevance in the course of information search. For instance, imagine a judge at court dealing with the hit-and-run accident. And let us assume that she is a

FUNDAMENTAL ASSUMPTIONS IN THE NORMATIVE PROGRAM   165

Bayesian. In contrast to the subjects, she must decide for herself which base rate is relevant for this case. For instance, she may search for information to decide whether the time and location of the accident matters for the base rate; she may ask whether the percentage of Blue cabs is greater at night than at daytime, or greater in this area of the city where the accident happened. The decision about which is the relevant base rate depends, first, on which variables are looked for and, second, which are evaluated as relevant. There is, however, no formal rationale for the process of information search and consequently no single answer to the question of which base rate is the best candidate for the prior probability.

To summarize: For textbook problems such as the Cab Problem, the inherent ambiguity about the relevant base rate could be resolved by rephrasing the content to which the posterior probability refers. This solution is possible only because the process of information search is excluded as a part of the subject's reasoning. In situations where the information search has not already been made by someone else (e.g. the experimenter), the subject must decide what features to look for and which feature to consider relevant. Since the questions of how to search and how to judge relevance have no single or formal answer, alternative candidates for the prior probability exist. This does not exclude the possibility that for some problems a consensus may be achieved, but in principle there is no unique way to arrive at a single answer.

Structural Isomorphism

Whether the world is stable enough and regular enough for the application of probability and statistics to make sense has been debated since the very beginning of the theory in the mid-17th century. Although mathematicians like Jakob Bernoulli and Abraham DeMoivre posited such stability and regularity on metaphysical grounds, practitioners of risk, like insurers, were more skeptical, probably with good reason. When pirates still prowled the seas and plagues wiped out whole cities, conditions for maritime and life insurance were anything but stable, and it could be financially ruinous to assume that they were (Daston, 1987). If psychologists today believe that the mind should reason according to the laws of probability, then either the world itself must have become more stable and predictable, or, conversely, probability theory itself has led us to perceive the world as more predictable.

Besides this assumed general stability of base rates, distributions, likelihoods, and means over time and space, there are more specific structural assumptions that are critical for the application of Bayes' theorem to human reasoning. We shall discuss here the assumption that

166 5. THINKING

the element or sample from which the data D has been observed has been randomly drawn from the population H, to which the prior probability refers. For illustration, consider the urn-and-pokerchips example again. There are two urns, one filled with 70% red chips and 30% blue chips, and the other with 30% red chips and 70% blue chips. One of the urns is selected randomly, and six chips are drawn. We have asked a little girl, Nina, who loves the color red, to draw the chips (she can see the chips). The sample drawn consists of five red chips and one blue. What is your probability that the chips have been drawn from the predominantly red one? The Bayesian formula gives .97. Of course, this value means nothing in a situation where the chips may have been selected by color rather than by a random process. Random sampling is a necessary condition for structural isomorphism and, therefore, for the application of Bayes' theorem. Like concept isomorphism, structural isomorphism cannot be decided upon *per se,* but rather the degree to which it obtains must be evaluated case by case. Consider for example, the textbook problem posed to the students and staff at Harvard Medical School: "If a test to detect a disease whose prevalence is 1/1000 has a false positive rate of 5%, what is the chance that a person found to have a positive result actually has the disease, assuming you know nothing about the person's symptoms or signs?" (Tversky & Kahneman, 1982a, p. 154)

The question is, was the person randomly drawn from the population to which the base rate refers to or not? Although it is emphasized that we have no further diagnostic information, nothing is said about how the person was selected. Clinicians, however, know that patients are not usually selected by random sampling—except in large survey studies—but, rather, they visit the doctor for some reason. If this is true, then the patient in the example selected himself by some reason such as pain and possibly also selected a particular kind of clinic or specialist. In this case, the person cannot be compared to a random drawing, and Bayes' theorem is not applicable. Therefore, depending on what the members of Harvard Medical School assume, different answers are possible using the given base rates. If they assume random sampling, perhaps because they anticipate what is expected from them, they may reason according to Bayes' theorem and give an answer around 2% (as about 18% of the subjects did). If they refer, however, to their own experience, they may give any answer up to 95%, which would conform to the principal of indifference and was the modal answer observed.

Lack of isomorphism because of lack of or uncertainty about random sampling is in no way restricted to the example given. For instance, in their famous Tom W. problem, where the graduate specialization area of Tom W. has to be predicted from a personality sketch, Kahneman and Tversky (1973) did not even pretend that the personality sketch was

FUNDAMENTAL ASSUMPTIONS IN THE NORMATIVE PROGRAM 167

randomly chosen. This lack of structural isomorphism, however, could be easily resolved by making the random character of the drawing explicit in the instructions. However, as for concept isomorphism, such carefully worded instructions relegate isomorphism to textbooks, for random selection processes are rare in real world situations and less easily established.

We shall turn now to a deeper issue concerning structural isomorphism, which arises even in textbook problems.

Consider the Engineer-Lawyer problem, in which it is explicitly stated that the personality description is "chosen at random from the 100 available descriptions." However, almost everyone knows this is a lie. The descriptions were in fact deliberately constructed to match the American stereotype of an engineer, or a lawyer, or to appear totally uninformative. If the subjects realize this and don't want to be fooled (particularly if there is a bonus involved), they must disregard the given base rates—if they are good Bayesians. There is no Bayesian answer in the absence of a random process—and such a consideration makes us wonder whether even the experimenters are loyal Bayesians. To summarize the last point: It may not be sufficient to say that the sample was randomly chosen, if in fact it was not. Even for textbook problems, instructions alone may not be sufficient for isomorphism.

The point we wish to make about isomorphism is not that the naive subjects investigated always reason in a sophisticated way about isomorphism; some professional experimenters do not either. The point is that without isomorphism we cannot claim that the value we calculate using Bayes' theorem is "correct." As a consequence, since neglect of base rates is defined relative to the "correct" value, the phenomenon itself disappears. The further conclusion that the man-in-the-street's reasoning is biased and irrational is in turn unwarranted. It may indeed be the case that the subjects' reasoning may be untouched by probability theory—but without isomorphism one cannot show this.

Does Statistics Speak With One Voice?

"Inductive reasoning, to be correct, must satisfy certain statistical principles." (Nisbett, Krantz, Jepson, & Kunda, 1983, p. 339) Regrettably, "people commit serious errors of inference" (p. 340), and "it is disturbing to learn that the heuristics people use in such tasks do not respect the required statistical principles" (p. 339). Conclusions of this kind are unfounded if isomorphism does not hold. But even if it does, a second fundamental assumption is necessary to warrant these pessimistic conclusions: Even if we agree that sound inductive reasoning is synonymous with statistical reasoning, we must assume that all statistical theories give the same answer to a problem. In other words, if the application of Bayes' theorem gives one answer, other statistical theories cannot give a different answer. Note that if this assumption is false, the normative pillars of the program of Kahneman, Tversky and others collapse. Like the isomorphism assumption, this unambiguous answer assumption is taken for granted and has seldom been discussed.

The character of this second assumption is different from that of the first. The isomorphism assumption is, at least in principle, testable for each application; in contrast, the unambigous answer assumption is of the nature of a philosophical tenet: The application of Bayes' theorem gives a single answer, and this answer is the best statistical formulation of inductive inference. We shall show that this assumption is wrong with respect to specific applications: There are other Gods besides Bayes' theorem, even statistical ones.

First, using Birnbaum's (1983) analysis of the familiar Cab Problem as an example, we shall show that at the concrete experimental level statistics does not speak with one voice. Then we shall analyze the general issue at stake.

Neyman and Pearson and Blue Cabs

What would happen if we applied the statistical theory of Neyman and Pearson to the Cab Problem? Figure 5.1 illustrates the representation of the problem by Neyman and Pearson's theory; for convenience we have chosen the more well-known language of signal detection theory, which is equivalent to that of Neyman and Pearson (see chapter 2).

As in Bayes' theorem, there are two hypotheses, "Green" and

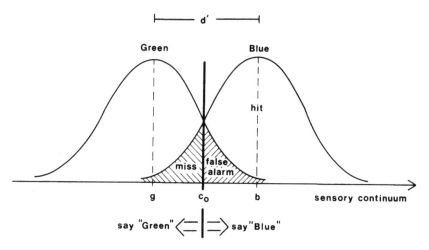

FIGURE 5.1. Representation of the Cab Problem by Neyman and Pearson's theory (signal detection theory).

FUNDAMENTAL ASSUMPTIONS IN THE NORMATIVE PROGRAM   169

"Blue", and two likelihoods $p(``B"|B)$ and $p(``B"|G)$, which are now called the hit rate and the false alarm rate. The first important difference arises with the *criterion* that exists in Neyman and Pearson's theory but not in Bayes'. Recall that the criterion is a point on the abscissa that varies with the cost–benefit analysis of the two possible errors, false alarms and misses. Each criterion corresponds to a pair of hit and false alarm rates, and the locus of all such pairs—following a shift in the criterion—is called the ROC curve (receiver operating characteristic). Thus, the first difference is the following: In Bayes' theory, the eye witness is characterized by a single pair of probabilities, the percentage of correct identifications and errors. In contrast, in signal detection theory the witness is represented by a continuum of such pairs, that is, by the ROC curve.

A second fundamental difference interlocks with the first: No prior probabilities or base rates are specified and revised into posterior probabilities in Neyman and Pearson's theory. But the theory allows for shifting the decision criterion in response to a shift in base rates, and so does signal detection theory. For instance, we have evidence that, for human witnesses, the ratio of the hit rate to the false alarm rate is dependent on the signal probabilities, that is, on the base rates (see Birnbaum, 1983; Luce, 1980; Schum, 1981). Now we can specify the essential difference. The so-called normative answer by Bayes' theorem implies that the ratio of the hit rate to false alarm rate is *independent* of the ratio of the base rates, as can be easily seen from the odds version of Bayes' theorem:

$$\frac{p(B|``B")}{p(G|``B")} = \frac{p(B)}{p(G)} \times \frac{p(``B"|B)}{p(``B"|G)}$$

In contrast, the signal detection view permits the ratio of the hit and false alarm rates to be *dependent* on the base rates. All the influence of the base rates is already contained in the setting of the criterion, and thus in the value of the likelihood ratio itself. This essential difference can be illustrated by Fig. 5.2, where point c_0 represents the reliability of the witness report. According to signal detection theory, an effect of a change in base rates is already contained in the value of the likelihood ratio itself: the ratio varies along the *curved* line known as the ROC curve. According to the Bayesian solution, a change in the base rates does not influence the value of the likelihood ratio itself; rather the change is modeled by multiplying by a constant likelihood ratio. All constant likelihood ratios lie, however, on a *straight* line through c_0, as shown by the dotted line in Fig. 5.2.

Let us now consider again the two pieces of information given (Tversky and Kahneman, 1980):

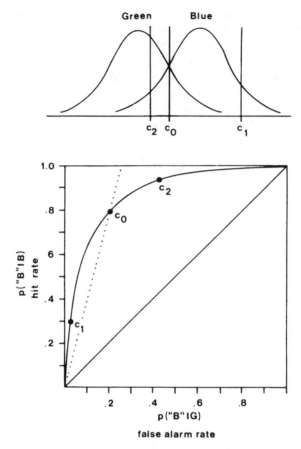

FIGURE 5.2. The performance of the eye witness as characterized by a continuum of ratios between hit and false alarm rates. His hit and false alarm rates depend on the criterion, and the ratio of hits to false alarm *changes,* as shown by the ROC curve, if the criterion is shifted away from c_0 (assuming constant d'). For comparison, the dotted line shows the location of all ratios equal to that obtained with c_0. Two alternative criterion settings are shown: c_1 is implied by the hypothesis that the witness minimizes the sum of all errors, and c_2 is implied by range frequency theory (after Birnbaum, 1983).

(i) 85% of the cabs in the city are Green and 15% are Blue.

(ii) A witness identified the cab as a Blue cab. The court tested his ability to identify cabs under the appropriate visibility conditions. When presented with a sample of cabs (half of which were Blue and half of which were Green) the witness made correct identifications in 80% of the cases and erred in 20% of the cases. (p. 62)

Recall that the median answer of the subjects was 80%, whereas Tversky and Kahneman calculated 41% using Bayes' theorem. Birnbaum

FUNDAMENTAL ASSUMPTIONS IN THE NORMATIVE PROGRAM   171

(1983) has given the following signal detection analysis of the problem. Signal detection theory assumes that each color of the cab produces a normal distribution on a sensory continuum (for convenience, different distributions could be assumed). If a value on the continuum exceeds the criterion, the eye witness reports Blue, otherwise Green, as shown in Fig. 5.1. Assuming equal variances, set to 1.0, the distance d' between the means of the two distributions can be calculated from a false alarm rate of 20% and a hit rate of 80%. For instance, the false alarm rate of 20% determines the distance $(c_o - g)$, that is, the distance between the criterion and the mean value g of Green cabs on the sensory continuum. From the normal curve table we get for this distance a value of .84, and the same value for $(b - c_o)$. Since $d' = b - g$ (the sum of the two values), we get $d' = 1.68$. From d', we can in turn determine the ROC curve in Fig. 5.2: If we move the criterion (in Fig. 5.1) from the extreme left side of the sensory continuum to the extreme right side, we get all pairs of hit and false alarm rates in the ROC curve in Fig. 5.2, from the upper right corner to the lower left corner. This ROC curve contains the point c_o, which represents the criterion of the eye witness in the court's test.

The instructions in the Cab Problem say that the witness was tested under the appropriate visibility conditions. In signal detection terms, this means that the sensitivity d' of the witness was similar in the test *and* the night of the accident. In other words, we can assume that the ROC curve in Fig. 5.2 is the appropriate one for the night of the accident (a different d' would imply a different ROC curve). But can we also assume that the criterion was the same? In fact, the base rates in the court's test were different from those in the city, 50:50 as opposed to 85:15. Thus, the essential question becomes, given a different base rate of cabs, where was the criterion at the time of the accident? Signal detection theory tells us that the criterion must have been located on the ROC curve, but it does not tell us where. This is a consequence of the subjective part in Neyman and Pearson's theory: How a criterion is established in a certain situation depends on extrastatistical considerations. The first conclusion from the Neyman and Pearson analysis of the Cab Problem is: The criterion of the eye witness at the time of the accident was located somewhere on the ROC curve in Fig. 5.2; but if we want to know exactly where, we need in addition a psychological theory of criterion adjustment.

What do we know about criterion switch as a function of changing base rates? There are several psychological hypotheses, of which we shall consider two.

1. *The Witness Minimizes Incorrect Testimony.* This first hypothesis assumes that the witness has a definite (correct or incorrect) idea of the base rate of Blue cabs. The *error minimizing* hypothesis postulates that the witness tries to adjust his criterion in a way that minimizes incorrect

172   5. THINKING

testimony. This may be considered a reasonable strategy in a hit-and-run situation, where incorrect testimony might cause harmful consequences. Let us assume that the witness is aware that there are only 15% Blue cabs in the city. Then he should set the criterion at the far right, because the most probable error is a false alarm, that is, to say Blue although the cab was Green. This is a consequence of the greater number of Green cabs. However, the farther to the right the criterion is moved, the fewer extra false alarms are avoided and the more misses occur. The ideal location of the criterion that minimizes the sum of both errors (see Birnbaum, 1983) is called c_1 in Fig. 5.2. For c_1, the probability of a false alarm is only .012, the miss rate is .698, and the hit rate is .302. Multiplying both error rates by the corresponding base rates, the overall number of errors sum up to 11.5% ($p("B"|G)p(G) + p("G"|B)p(B) = 11.5\%$). In other words, this criterion location achieves 88.5 correct testimonies. We can now calculate the probability that the cab was actually Blue given that the witness said it was Blue (using Bayes' theorem):

$$p(B|"B") = .15 \times .302/(.15 \times .302 + .85 \times .012) = .82(!).$$

This answer, based on a Neyman and Pearsonian analysis and an error-minimizing hypothesis, is quite different from the purely Bayesian answer of .41. However, it happens to be close to the median answer of .80 that the subjects gave. Note that if we were to cast the value of .82 into the Bayesian vocabulary, we would conclude *base rate neglect*. In contrast, this value follows from a Neyman and Pearson analysis *and* the psychological assumption that the witness minimizes errors *bearing in mind base rates*.

2. *Range-frequency Theory.* Let us assume that the witness is ignorant of the base rate of Blue cabs in the city. Therefore the strategy of minimizing incorrect testimony would not be of much use for him. What do we know about the behavior of witnesses in such a situation? Range-frequency theory (Parducci & Sandusky, 1970) assumes that because of this lack of information and lack of feedback a witness tends to use each of his response alternatives equally often. This means that he tends to give the same number of Blue and Green answers in repeated trials. Since there are more Green cabs, this corresponds to shifting the criterion to the left (see Fig. 5.2). The shift increases both the hit and the false alarm rate; the criterion is shifted to a point c_2, where hits and false alarms account for 50% of all responses, where $p("B") = .50$. Numerically, we obtain a hit rate of .933 and a false alarm rate of .28, by the same reasoning as before. From this, we calculate the probability that the cab was Blue given the witness report Blue as

$$p(B|"B") = .28.$$

FUNDAMENTAL ASSUMPTIONS IN THE NORMATIVE PROGRAM   173

If we persisted in seeing the world in Bayesian terms, we might consider such an answer as conservatism, as an overweighting of base rates. In contrast, it follows from a Neyman and Pearsonian analysis *and* the psychological assumption that because the witness *knows nothing about the base rates* he tries to distribute his responses equally.

There are other psychological hypotheses such as probability matching (see Birnbaum, 1983), each one corresponding to a point on the ROC curve. In all cases, the witness is an optimal observer in the sense of signal detection theory, or an "optimal test" in the sense of the statistical theory of Neyman and Pearson. Moreover, these alternative explanations of the observed posterior probability need not cast the phenomenon into the Bayesian language of conservatism or base rate neglect. Furthermore, these alternative explanations show that there is more psychological theory to be applied than is suggested by sole reliance on Bayes' theorem.

Note that the divergent results are not limited to the particular example where the court tested under different base rates than those in the city. Even if the court had tested with the same base rates and even if the subject had perceived the base rates as the same, a Neyman and Pearsonian analysis would not conclude that the criterion is also constant. Any other difference between the situation of the witness at night and the situation being tested for his reliability may influence the cost–benefit analysis that sets the criterion. For instance, even if the court tested under the same base rates, the witness who had previously given the testimony Blue might shift the criterion in the test *depending* on his earlier testimony. Recall that because the witness testified Blue, the testimony— if wrong—can only be a false alarm, not a miss. If the witness wants to avoid giving the impression that his testimony could be wrong, he may shift the criterion in the court's test so as to reduce false alarms at the cost of misses.

In general, the setting of the criterion is influenced by content and context beyond mere base rates. There is no formal way to prescribe to the optimal observer how to select the criterion, just as the mathematical part of Neyman and Pearson's theory does not prescribe to the statistician how to make a cost–benefit analysis to balance the Type I and Type II errors. On the contrary, Neyman and Pearson always emphasized (see chapter 1) that mathematical and subjective aspects are both necessary for a theory of hypothesis testing.

Alternative Statistical Theories

The signal detection analysis of the Cab Problem shows that alternative normative solutions can be found if different statistical models are introduced. Alternative answers are a consequence of alternative statisti-

174   5. THINKING

cal theories, which give different answers to the same question or even phrase the question in different ways. This has been shown in chapter 1 and in various examples throughout subsequent chapters. At a more fundamental level, statistics does not speak with one voice for the same reason that geometry does not speak with one voice: There is Euclidian geometry, but since the 19th century we have known that alternative geometries, such as curved Riemannean spaces, can be constructed. Just as a geometry can be based on axioms other than the Euclidian axioms, probability theories can be based on different assumptions (e.g. Cohen 1980, 1981; Shafer, 1976). The interesting question is whether a particular statistical theory is *descriptive* or not given a particular content and context, not whether humans deviate from the one so-called correct theory or not. Similarly the interesting question in cosmology is which geometry describes real space not whether real space deviates from Euclidean geometry. Finally, the development of probability theory itself shows that alternative assumptions have always been made: for instance, even Jakob Bernoulli did not wholly accept the additivity "law" from which Bayes' theorem is derived (Bernoulli, 1966, pp. 25–31; Daston, 1979).

Psychologists, however, seldom realize that statisticians and philosophers debate the merits of alternative theories of statistics as models of sound inductive reasoning. This blind spot seems to a considerable extent due to the impact of the inference revolution, which leveled different and competing statistical theories into a single truth, anonymously called inferential statistics. Of course, this gave psychologists a consensus about methodology at least, in the absence of any agreed upon unifying theory. However, the price of consensus was a blind spot at the level of statistical inference (see chapter 1), which was soon transported by way of the new metaphor of the mind as a statistician to the level of theory.

THE FISHERIAN MIND: CAUSAL REASONING

David Hume (1739–1740/1955) argued that causal relations cannot be observed. Albert Michotte investigated the conditions under which the mind—ignorant of Hume's dictum—immediately "sees" a causal relationship. Michotte (1946/1963, 1952), strongly influenced by Külpe in Würzburg, observed that certain temporal-spatial relationships between two visual objects, usually moving dots, produced phenomenal causality. For instance, the subjects "saw" that one object launches, pushes, or chases another, or that the objects were attacking or fleeing from another. Fritz Heider (1958), influenced by Gestalt theory and Brunswik's probabilistic functionalism, considered causal schemes as central for the percep-

THE FISHERIAN MIND: CAUSAL REASONING   175

tion of social relations. He suggested that causal reasoning might be analogous to experimental methods and metaphorically talked about an implicit "factor analysis" (p. 297). In 1967, Harold H. Kelley followed Heider's suggestion, but changed the metaphor into "analysis of variance." Kelley claimed that the long sought after laws of causal reasoning are the tools of the behavioral scientist: Fisher's analysis of variance.

Scientists' Tools = Laws of Causal Reasoning

The main idea was that the mind draws causal inferences in the same way as the experimenter draws causal inferences, by calculating F-values for testing null hypotheses about main and interaction effects in analysis of variance (ANOVA).

> The assumption is that the man in the street, the naive psychologist, uses a naive version of the method used in science. Undoubtedly, his naive version is a poor replica of the scientific one—incomplete, subject to bias, ready to proceed on incomplete evidence, and so on. Nevertheless, it has certain properties in common with the analysis of variance as we behavioral scientists use it (Kelley, 1973, p. 109)

This analogy with statistics heightened the interest in causal reasoning or causal attribution, and the topic became the fastest expanding research area within experimental social psychology.[6] Kelley's ANOVA model became, without doubt, the most prominent and influential theory of causal reasoning; the dinosaurian proportions of empirical research in the 1970s and even in the 1980s are well documented (see Fisch & Daniel, 1982; Kelley & Michaela, 1980).

Kelley assumed that the mind calculates an analysis of variance with three independent variables, which he called person, entity, and circumstances (time and modality). These were the potential causes for an observed behavior. Consider for example the following information presented to the subjects in a typical study (McArthur, 1972, quoted in Kelley, 1973): "Paul is enthralled by a painting he sees at the art museum. Hardly anyone who sees the painting is enthralled by it. Paul is also enthralled by almost every other painting. In the past, Paul has almost always been enthralled by the same painting" (p. 110).

The subjects were asked what probably caused the observed behavior (being enthralled by the painting). Has the cause to do with Paul (person),

---

[6]Two kinds of theories have been proposed, depending on whether a person has available multiple observations or only a single observation for making a causal inference. The ANOVA model is the most prominent of the first kind; for models for the single observation case see, for example, Kelley (1967, 1973), Jones (1979), and Reeder and Brewer (1979).

176 5. THINKING

the painting (entity), the particular circumstances (time), or some combination of these factors? In McArthur's study, 85% of her college students inferred from information of this kind that the cause is in the person. The problem is constructed to provide the intuitive Fisherian mind with exactly the three pieces of information considered relevant: the covariation of the three independent variables, person, entity, and circumstances, with the dependent variable, the observed behavior. The data given is that (a) other persons disagree, which is called *low consensus;* (b) Paul hardly ever responds differentially to different entities, which is called *low distinctiveness;* and (c) Paul is consistent over time, which is called *high consistency.*

The assumption is that causal reasoning of the man-in-the-street can be explained by an analysis of variance of this covariation information. Recall that analysis of variance tests null hypotheses about main effects and interaction effects by calculating the ratio of a between-means variance to an error-variance, called the F-ratio (after Fisher). If the value of F is sufficiently high (depending on the level of significance), then the value is called significant; and from this it is often concluded that a causal effect has been "observed." (The latter is of course, in practice only and cannot be justified by statistical theory; see chapter 1). By analogy, the mind calculates F-values to discover the cause of the reported behavior:

> The first criterion (distinctiveness) seems to correspond to the numerator or between-condition term in the usual F ratio and the last three criteria (consistency over time, modality, and persons) correspond to the error or within-condition term. As a measure, then, of a person's state of information regarding a given entity, the theory suggests an analogue of the F ratio in which the degree of differentiation between the various entities is compared with the stability of attribution (based on the consistencies and consensus) with respect to the given entity (Kelley, 1967, p. 198)

In that example, where distinctiveness is low, consensus high, and consistency high, the F-value is low for entity and circumstances, but high for person. Therefore, the subject should perceive the cause in the person. Note that the predictions are always derived from the particular combination of the three kinds of information; the model does not predict any particular main effect, say, of "person" itself. In fact, most of the studies were not constructed to test whether the mind reasons analogously to Fisher's analysis of variance, but rather assumed it did and studied the magnitude of the effects (see Jaspars, Hewstone, & Fincham, 1983). In recent years, the ANOVA model of causal reasoning has been criticized, for example because experiments seemed to show that consensus information has only small impact on causal inferences and that the man-in-the-street is not very good at estimating covariances (see Jaspars,

Hewstone, & Fincham, 1983; Newcombe & Rutter, 1982). We shall not go into a discussion of particular experimental findings but instead analyze how the theory of causal reasoning mirrors the structure of the statistical tool.

The Conceptual Skeleton

It is important to keep in mind that in the following discussion the ANOVA analogy is *not* meant to be restricted to the particular problems posed to the subject but is meant to describe the everyday reasoning of the man-in-the-street, as Kelley (1967) expresses it.

The Mind as an Indefatigable Causal Search Automaton. The research question suggested by the ANOVA analogy is, *what* cause is inferred given a certain combination of information? It is not *whether* the mind searches for a cause at all, or under *which* conditions causal explanations are sought. It is implicitly assumed that the mind is constantly on the lookout for causes in all contexts. Like the typical psychologist armed with ANOVA, the mind is assumed always to pose the causal question, and only the causal question. The neglect of the questions why, when, and for what purpose causal explanations are given is new. Earlier, Michotte's (1952, 1946/1963) work had focused on the conditions under which causal impressions do and do not occur. Similarly, recent research indicates that if the subject is *not* asked for a causal inference, then causal reasoning occurs only for events with particular contents, for example, for unexpected and negative events (Nesdale, 1983; Wong & Weiner, 1981).

A second point is linked to the first. Whereas Michotte's work still reflects the broad Aristotelian conception of four kinds of causes (see Gavin, 1972), the ANOVA-mind knows only the one kind of causal reasoning for which ANOVA is designed. This rules out one of the most common kinds of causal reasoning in everyday life, teleological explanations or reasons (see Kruglanski, 1975). Because the Fisherian mind does not provide teleological answers, the problems are constructed not to elicit them.

It is interesting how the analogy between ANOVA and causal reasoning bears witness to the exaggerated emphasis on null hypotheses testing. The analogy is in fact between the mind and the average experimenter, who believes in the omnipotence of null hypotheses testing, rather than between the mind and the statistical theory, which does not justify causal inferences from F-values.

Analysis of Variance as Rational Reasoning. Just as Kahneman and Tversky identify Bayes' theorem with rationality, Kelley (1973) identifies analysis of variance with correct and complete causal reasoning. Insofar

178 5. THINKING

as it deviates from the normative ANOVA-mind, the mind of the man in the street is considered as a "poor replica of the scientific one," a "naive version" which is "incomplete" and "subject to bias" (p. 109). The institutionalized "causal instrument" of the psychologist is prescribed as the normative causal instrument of the mind. It is ironic that null hypotheses testing itself is far from being accepted as a normative instrument—outside of psychology. For instance, as we pointed out in chapter 1, Jerzy Neyman believed that Fisher's methods of testing are in a mathematically definable sense worse than useless, and as we have shown in chapter 3, a sole reliance on analysis of variance may suggest essentially inappropriate conclusions to the experimenter.

Content-Independence and Context-Independence. As with the research centering on Bayes' theorem, the formal analogy suggests that the supposed laws of causal reasoning operate independently of the particular content and context. But research contradicts these assumptions. For example, causal inferences differ depending on whether the behaviour to be explained is interpreted as a success or as a failure, with successes more often being attributed to the person (Frieze & Weiner, 1971; Hewstone & Jaspars, 1983).

Neglect of Information Search. Statistical theories of inference and hypotheses testing are applied *after* the data has been collected. Consequently, statistical metaphors of reasoning show a blind spot for the process of information search. Like the Bayesian analogy, the Fisherian model is not concerned with the search processes entailed by such questions as What potential causes should I look for? and How can I find information concerning the covariation of the supposed cause and the behaviour in question? The analogy with Fisherian statistics excludes the heuristic process of making relevance judgements about what to look for. And, as a consequence, it excludes errors made in information collection, storage, and retrieval (see Nisbett & Ross, 1980).

Reasoning is Induction. Fisher bets on pure induction, whereas a Bayesian can consider the prior probabilities as expressions of beliefs and expectations. Fisher's dictum that induction is the only way that new knowledge comes into the world (see chapter 1) has its mirror image in Kelley's (1973) conception of causal reasoning. The mind is assumed to be a data-driven inductive statistician, responding only to the raw data given and excluding from consideration his own expectations, beliefs, and prior knowledge. To clarify the analogy, let us imagine that Kelley lived a century and a half earlier. He might have taken the statistical models of the astronomers rather than ANOVA as the model of causal reasoning. As we pointed out in chapter 1, the astronomers used their statistical tests to reject *data,* not hypotheses. They assumed (at least, provisionally) that the theory was correct and mistrusted the data; they used the test to reject observations as outliers. If Kelley had proposed that the mind reasons like these 19th-century statisticians, the mind would have appeared to be expectation driven rather than data driven. Given results such as those reported by Ajzen (1977) and Fiedler (1980), the man-in-the-street is directed in many situations by his implicit theories and beliefs rather than by information. If this is true, the astronomer's statistical tests provide a better descriptive model than the current practice in psychology. The mind may reject the data rather than its hypothesis.

RATIONALITY

Why have experimental psychologists become so involved with how people *should* think, even though prescription is atypical of experimental psychology? What does an empirical science gain by claiming that statistical theory *is* rational thinking? We have repeatedly pointed out that some interesting issues are lost, such as the analysis of information search and of the role of the task, and that the normative view contaminates the descriptive results, in the phenomena reported and in the explanations proposed. Furthermore, we have shown that the supposed normative statistical theory cannot even give a unique answer to very simple textbook problems since isomorphism is notoriously difficult to establish. Finally, alternative statistical theories may even lead to different answers and, in the case of Neyman and Pearson's theory, postulate that informed judgment is as necessary as statistical theory. Why do psychologists of the caliber of Kahneman and Tversky nevertheless adhere to the idea that Bayes' theorem *is* rationality for all contents and contexts?

In most studies that claim to have demonstrated human errors, biases, and shortcomings, no argument is given to explain why the statistical rule applied *is* rational, nor is rationality independently defined. Kelley (1973), for instance, simply seems to assume that analysis of variance is "the method used in a science" (p. 109) and is thus correct and therefore is the correct instrument for the causal reasoning of the man-in-the-street. Notable exceptions are Nisbett and Ross (1980), who indeed raise the question of how one knows that a rule like Bayes' theorem is correct or normatively appropriate and therefore that the subjects' reasoning is wrong: "We follow conventional practice by using the term 'normative' to describe the use of a rule when there is *a consensus among formal scientists* that the rule is appropriate for the particular problem" (p. 13, italics ours).

The common denominators here are two accepted illusions. First, the statistical methods institutionalized are not "the methods used in science." Neither physics, chemistry, nor astronomy ever subscribed to

180   5. THINKING

statistical techniques of inference; in these fields, inference is still guided by informed personal judgment rather than a mechanical rule. Second, among the "formal scientists," presumably mathematicians and statisticians, there exists *no* consensus about a "normative" rule of inductive inference. Even among those statisticians whose ideas were merged into the hybrid technique of inference now used in psychology, Fisher and Neyman and Pearson—and one could as well add Bayes—there was anything but a consensus about a rule of inference.

Mechanization of Inductive Inference

We propose that *one* explanation for the fascination with a single formula of rationality peculiar to this branch of psychology is the fascination with mechanized inductive inference. This ideal has two major sources—the age-old dream of philosophers, to achieve a full formalization of some aspects of knowledge, and the *fait accompli* of the inference revolution. A sterling example among the philosophers is Rudolf Carnap's quantitative inductive logic, which was intended to formalize intuitive inferences, in every-day situations and in science (Carnap & Stegmüller, 1959). This program has been mostly abandoned by philosophers. In contrast, the mechanization of scientific inference, institutionalized through the inference revolution, is still the received truth by psychologists. It seems to us that this ideal of a single mechanical rule is the essence of this old philosophical and new psychological concept of rational thinking.

Elimination of Subjectivity

The prescription that all minds should mechanically apply the same statistical rule to all contents and contexts has two important consequences. First, it eliminates the whole range of subjectivity, from mere spontaneity to personal informed judgment. With this the purposive aspect is excluded from the meaning of rationality: With different goals in mind, different subjects may arrive at different decisions or behaviors, with conflicting goals within an individual there may not even exist a single correct solution (see Einhorn & Hogarth, 1981). Thus, "objective" rationality is thinking by no subject in particular.

A second aspect of this narrowing of what rationality means again bears witness to the philosopher's dream of mechanization. In Karl Popper's (1935/1959) terms, it is the "context of justification", the testing and evaluation of theories given data, which is the target of mechanization. Popper explicitly throws out of the philosophy of science the "context of discovery", how we arrive at the theory and the data in the first place. For him, the search processes and judgments of relevance involved in discovery are too subjective to be formalizable, and should be studied by psychology (p. 31). But the new psychologists of thinking follow the philosopher's model and throw out these subjective processes of information search and relevance judgments. The statistical analogy defines these processes as irrelevant for rational thinking.

This elimination of subjectivity implies that the statistical theory to which rational judgment is equated cannot be Neyman and Pearson's. They require subjective judgment, the setting of the criterion, which may represent individual purposes, cost–benefit analyses, and other subjective considerations. Bayesian theory, known to philosophers and statisticians as subjective probability, ceases to be so among the psychologists, who are always careful to specify the prior probabilities.

In sum, the belief that Bayes' theorem or another theory of statistical inference *is* rational thinking empties rationality of its most interesting aspects: Rationality is without purpose, without weights for conflicting goals, without information search and exploration, without judgments of relevance, without reflection of content, without use of contextual information and cost–benefit considerations. To the disappointment of philosophers like Popper, it also leaves out the context of discovery, the truly psychological problem of creativity explored by the Würzburg and Gestalt schools. And the fascination with such mechanical rationality tends to divorce the psychology of inductive thinking from all these aspects, if only by dismissing them as sources of irrationality. Our view is that the task of a psychology of thinking is to understand how these various sources direct human thought rather than to judge whether thinking is rational or not.

6 Conclusions

Throughout this book we have argued for a striking analogy between the statistical tools used by psychologists and the theories advanced to explain perception, memory, thinking, and other cognitive processes. The time has come to restate our thesis concerning how and why this analogy emerged and flourished when it did, and to reflect upon its wider implications for research.

FROM TOOLS TO THEORIES: IN THEIR OWN IMAGE

Prior to about 1940, psychologists relied on largely informal and nonstandardized methods to evaluate their data: critical ratios, rules of thumb (e.g. three times the probable error), or simply eyeballing the data to determine whether it was "significant" in the everyday sense of the word. There existed no consensus about which methods should be used, and indeed little concern about the issue. Between roughly 1940 and 1955, this situation altered radically. During this period a set of statistical methods took psychology by storm: textbooks taught the new methods, and journals enforced them. Although psychologists may have agreed on little else, they were united in their belief that such methods were the *sine qua non* of rigorous psychological research. We have called this massive and successful institutionalization of statistical methods the *inference revolution*.

What textbook presentations led psychologists to view as a single, monolithic body of statistics was actually an odd hybrid of at least two

FROM TOOLS TO THEORIES: IN THEIR OWN IMAGE **183**

distinct approaches to hypothesis testing, those of Ronald Fisher and of Jerzy Neyman and Egon Pearson, occasionally supplemented by yet a third approach, that of Thomas Bayes and his followers. Statisticians consider these approaches to be mutually incompatible, and heated, sometimes bitter controversies still rage between the rival camps. However, psychologists learned that there was only *one* statistics, despite the contradictory elements their textbook hybrid actually lumped together. This spurious harmony between rival statistical approaches was achieved partly through historical accident and partly through wishful thinking. Fisher's work was the first they encountered, and they later grafted Neyman and Pearson's more consistent theory onto it. Statistics was attractive because it seemed to offer the sort of quantitative rigor and consensus at the level of method which psychology obviously lacked at the level of theory, and psychologists turned a blind eye toward controversies within statistics—they had plenty of controversies of their own.

Moreover, this attempt to do the impossible, to make a single unified theory out of the immiscible approaches within statistics, seemed to offer a great, though illusory benefit. Such forced unifications necessarily introduced confusions and outright errors into the textbooks and into the interpretations, but these confusions and errors all promised what was most wanted: a way of rigorously inferring the validity of research hypotheses from the data. Conversely, the more accurate the textbook from a statistical point of view, the more useless it would have appeared to practicing experimenters. Perhaps this is one reason why repeated attempts since 1960 to expose these errors and confusions in the hybrid statistics have had almost no impact on practice. It was precisely those errors and confusions—that rejecting the null hypothesis informs us about the validity of the research hypothesis, about its probability, about the size of the effect, about the replicability of the effect, or about the quality of the experiment—that had made the hybrid statistics indispensable.

Thus far tools. We have claimed that in psychology tools that are both indispensable and prestigious—most recently, statistics and the computer—are transformed into theories. That is, the scientist's own methods are reinterpreted as models of cognitive processes. A precondition for this transformation is of course a prevailing cognitive approach: one needs a "homunculus" to cast as the statistician. Hence it was the *intersection* of the inference and cognitive revolutions that explained the timing of the wave of theories using the metaphor of the intuitive statistician. One without the other would not have been sufficient, and the history of 20th-century psychology provides evidence to this effect. Thurstone's is a case of the statistics without the homunculus: his model of perception is formally equivalent to signal detection theory, but without a decision

184 6. CONCLUSIONS

maker in the brain, it could not become such. Brunswik's is a case of the homunculus with the wrong kind of statistics: his intuitive statistician used Karl Pearson's correlation statistics and was generally rejected and misunderstood by Brunswik's contemporaries. Pre-inference revolution cognitive theories, like those of the Würzburg or Gestalt schools, are wholly lacking in statistical metaphors.

But the literature of the new style cognitive psychology abounds in examples of the intuitive statistician at work—using Neyman–Pearson theory to detect objects, using Fisher's theory to make causal attributions, using (or, notably, failing to use) Bayes's theory for inductive reasoning. A different brand of statistics reigns in each area, and researchers generally ignore alternative models for intuitive statistical processes, following the example of the textbook writers in thus suggesting that statistics is statistics is statistics. It is extremely rare for researchers to apply an alternative statistical model in these fields—for example, Neyman–Pearson theory to the Bayes-dominated psychology of inductive thinking—although such alternatives enrich the field with competing predictions, new explanations, and even a fresh idea of what the phenomena themselves might be. Equally revealing is the insertion of a new normative element into purportedly empirical studies of cognitive processes: researchers are now concerned with how people should think, as well as how they actually do. Statistical standards are normative for psychologists, and they in turn have made them normative for their hapless subjects. In converting their statistical tools into theories, psychologists have effectively made their subjects over in their own image.

THE INTEGRATIVE PERSPECTIVE

Out of the confusions and illusions of the hybrid statistical methods has arisen a theoretical metaphor rich in new questions, new data, and unifying perspectives. In signal detection theory, for example, researchers now distinguish two aspects previously merged, the "sensitivity" of the observer, and the "criterion-setting"—the latter being the analogue of Neyman and Pearsons' cost–benefit analysis. Carrying the Neyman and Pearson analogy further, signal detection theorists now observe two types of errors of perceptual judgment, as opposed to the single error suggested by the old threshold model—thus new data emerge. As we have pointed out repeatedly, it is the new metaphor that creates the new data, not the other way around. The old psychophysical problem of absolute and differential thresholds, and the equally old memory problem of recognition can now be unified by the same formal language, that of Neyman–Pearson theory. Although the methodological attempts to mechanize experimenters' inference have been on the whole disappointing, the same cannot thus be said of the theoretical approaches they inspired. It is ironic that out of such a dubious usage of a tool should have come such a fertile and promising theoretical metaphor.

BLIND SPOTS

Nonetheless, some of the blind spots in the hybrid statistical methods and their associated illusions have been imported into the theories that employ the metaphor of the intuitive statistician. Three such blind spots emerge from our investigations. First, just as the exaggerated emphasis on statistical analysis in psychological research has pushed the prior problems of measurement into the background, so the new cognitive theories have largely eliminated the processes of information search. Second, just as statistical tools are thought to be mechanically applicable to each and every situation, so the intuitive statistician is thought to apply formal methods (or equally formal heuristics) without regard to content and context. Informed judgment, flexible and sensitive to particular circumstances, no longer plays a role in either psychological research or everyday reasoning, or should not, according to the new tools and the theories they have become. Third, just as psychologists equate respectable research with the application of certain statistical methods, so thinking is judged rational or irrational according to whether it follows certain statistical rules like Bayes' theorem or not.

THE INTUITIVE STATISTICIAN RECONSIDERED

Although the new theories all address some aspect of perception or reasoning under uncertainty, it is not always clear just wherein the uncertainty lies. In general, the uncertainty is located in the information given rather than in the processing of that information. However, different statistical models (or their applications) produce differences in the nature of the processing. The possibility of mechanical application in Fisher's theory is mirrored in the mechanical processes of Harold Kelley's causal attribution theory. In the hands of the current researchers of inductive thinking, Bayes' "subjective" theory is made equally mechanical by specifying the prior probabilities in advance, thereby eliminating the source of subjectivity. Neyman and Pearson-derived theories grant a larger role to the subjective element by distinguishing a mechanical mathematical aspect and an emphatically non-mechanical criterion-setting aspect. All three are uncertain in that they provide only probabilistic

186   6. CONCLUSIONS

solutions to the problems posed, but the first two, by specifying the information in advance as well as the nature of the processing, effectively make both deterministic. Thus, from the standpoint of psychological prediction, the intuitive statistician theories include less uncertainty than, for example, behaviouristic learning theories in which the initial repertoire of responses is assumed random, and their repetition a purely probabilistic function of past reinforcements. Here, behaviour can be predicted only with a certain probability, whereas the decision of the intuitive statistician can in principle be predicted with certainty.

The intuitive statistician is a kind of homunculus, but it is by no means a free agent. Because the homunculus is assumed to calculate (rather than, for example, to restructure), its response is as predictable as the outcome of applying a statistical package. Context-sensitive analyses of conduct under uncertainty seem to give the homunculus back a measure of free agency and therefore to disrupt psychological predictions. Formal calculations might be supplemented or replaced by psychological strategies that vary with the individual and the circumstances, but which nonetheless lead to predictable responses once specified. For example, in Kahneman and Tversky's Cab Problem, the witness might well follow a strategy of minimizing the error of calling a green cab blue, whereas in other situations he might strive to maximize correct identifications overall. The explanations are indeed complicated by taking into account goals and the various strategies they dictate, but predictability is thereby salvaged, and arguably made more accurate.

It seems at first glance paradoxical that theories about conduct and belief under uncertainty should in fact contain so little uncertainty. But in this, too, they resemble the tools from which they are derived. These tools of statistical inference, as applied in psychology, aim to reduce uncertain situations—Is this hypothesis correct? Could these results be replicated?—to certain ones by the applications of rules. We cannot be sure that a given psychological conclusion drawn from data is correct, but we can be sure that it was reached in the one and only correct way. The experimenter who follows these rules is not confronted with a set of alternatives to choose from, any more than the intuitive statistician faces an array of strategies for dealing with an uncertain situation. In the one case, eliminating uncertainty ideally leads to consensus; in the other, to predictability.

Consensus and predictability are admirable scientific goals, but they can be purchased at too high a price. Psychologists are not the first to be dazzled by statistics: as Napoleon's bureaucrats used to say, if you want something from the Emperor, just show him statistics. And practitioners of a discipline still unsure of its scientific status are especially prone to fits of quantiphrenia. However, what we have called the inference revolution reveals an attitude towards statistics that may actually further distance the social sciences from the natural sciences they seek to emulate. Enthusiasm for statistics as mechanized inference is a rather restricted phenomenon. In other disciplines that make use of statistics, like biology, they are used as auxiliary tools, and others, like physics, shun such aids to inference altogether. In psychology, the lack of a theoretical consensus may have added to the attraction of a methodological consensus, however uncritical. If there are lessons to be learned from the history of the intuitive statistician, they would be the importance of a reasoned, rather than blind application of the tools that made the metaphor possible, and a healty caution in theory concerning the blind spots that have become all too evident in the tools.

References

Ach, N. (1905). *Über Willenstätigkeit und das Denken*. Göttingen: Vandenhoeck & Ruprecht.

Acree, M. C. (1978). *Theories of statistical inference in psychological research: A historico-critical study*. Ann Arbor, MI: University Microfilms International, H790H7000.

Ajzen, I. (1977). Intuitive theories of events and the effects of base-rate information on predictions. *Journal of Personality and Social Psychology, 35,* 303-314.

American Psychological Association (1974). *Publication Manual* (2nd ed.), Washington, DC: Author.

Anderson, J. A. (1973). A theory for the recognition of items from short memorized lists. *Psychological Review, 80,* 417-438.

Anderson, J. R., & Bower, G. H. (1973). *Human associative memory*. Washington, DC: Winston.

Anderson, N. H. (1970). Functional measurement and psychophysical judgement. *Psychological Review, 77,* 153-170.

Anderson, N. H. (1980). Information integration theory in developmental psychology. In F. Wilkening, J. Becker, & T. Trabasso (Eds.), *Information integration by children*. Hillsdale, NJ: Lawrence Erlbaum Associates.

Anderson, N. H. (1981). *Foundations of information integration theory*. New York: Academic Press.

Anderson, N. H. (1982). *Methods of information integration theory*. New York: Academic Press.

Anderson, N. H. & Cuneo, D. O. (1978). The height + width rule in children's judgments of quantity. *Journal of Experimental Psychology: General, 107,* 335-378.

Anderson, N. H., & Shanteau, J. (1977). Weak inference with linear models. *Psychological Bulletin, 84,* 1155-1170.

Anderson, R. L. & Bancroft, T. A. (1952). *Statistical theory in research*. New York: McGraw-Hill.

Arbuthnot, J. (1710). An argument for Divine Providence, taken from the constant Regularity observed in the Births of both Sexes. *Philosophical Transactions of the Royal Society of London, 27,* 186-190.

190 REFERENCES

Aristotle (1941). *De Anima* and *De Memoria*. In *The Basic Works of Aristotle* (Ed. R. McKeon). New York: Random House. (Original work appeared in 4th century B.C.)

Ash, M. G. (1980). Wilhelm Wundt and Oswald Külpe on the institutional status of psychology: An academic controversy in historical context. In W. G. Bringmann & R. D. Tweney (Eds.), *Wundt Studies*. Toronto: Hogrefe.

Atkinson, R. C., & Crothers, E. J. (1964). A comparison of paired-associate learning models having different acquisition and retention axioms. *Journal of Mathematical Psychology, 1*, 285-315.

Atkinson, R. C., & Juola, J. E. (1974). Search and decision processes in recognition memory. In D. H. Krantz, R. C. Atkinson, R. D. Luce, & P. Suppes (Eds.), *Contemporary developments in mathematical psychology. Vol. 1. Learning, memory and thinking.* San Francisco: W. H. Freeman.

Atkinson, R. C., & Shiffrin, R. M. (1968). Human memory: A proposed system and its control processes. In K. W. Spence & J. T. Spence (Eds.), *The psychology of learning and motivation*, Vol. 2. New York: Academic Press.

Attneave, F. (1959). *Applications of information theory to psychology.* New York: Holt, Rinehart & Winston.

Baddeley, A. D., & Hitch, G. (1974). Working memory. In G. H. Bower (Ed.), *The psychology of learning and motivation*, Vol. 8. New York: Academic Press.

Baird, J. C., Green, D. M., & Luce, R. D. (1980). Variability and sequential effects in cross-modality matching of area and loudness. *Journal of Experimental Psychology: Human Perception and Performance, 6*, 277-289.

Bakan, D. (1966). The test of significance in psychological research. *Psychological Bulletin, 66*, 423-437.

Bartlett, F. C. (1932). *Remembering: A study in experimental and social psychology.* Cambridge: Cambridge University Press.

Bayes, T. (1763). An essay towards solving a problem in the doctrine of chances. *Philosophical Transactions of the Royal Society of London, 53*, 370-418.

Beardsley, M. C. (1972). Metaphor. In P. Edwards (Ed.) *The Encyclopedia of Philosophy*, Vol. V, New York: Macmillan.

Berkeley, D., & Humphreys, P. (1982). Structuring decision problems and the 'bias heuristic'. *Acta Psychologica, 50*, 201-252.

Bernoulli, J. (1966, 12 February). Translations from James Bernoulli (Bing Sung, Trans.). (Tech. Rep. No. 2). Harvard University, Department of Statistics.

Birnbaum, A. (1977). The Neyman-Pearson theory as decision theory, and as inference theory; with a criticism of the Lindley–Savage argument for Bayesian theory. *Synthese, 36*, 19-49.

Birnbaum, M. H. (1982). Controversies in psychological measurement. In B. Wegener (Ed.), *Social attitudes and psychophysics*. Hillsdale, NJ: Lawrence Erlbaum Associates.

Birnbaum, M. H. (1983). Base rates in Bayesian inference: Signal detection analysis of the cab problem. *American Journal of Psychology, 96*, 85-94.

Blavais, A. S. (1975). Visual analysis: theory of Lie group representations. *Mathematical Biosciences, 28*, 45-67.

Boole, G. (1958). *An investigation of the laws of thought.* New York: Dover. (Original work published 1854)

Boring, E. G. (1920). The logic of the normal law of error in mental measurement. *American Journal of Psychology, 31*, 1-33.

Boring, E. G. (1942). *Sensation and perception in the history of experimental psychology.* New York: Appleton-Century.

Boring, E. G. (1957). *A history of experimental psychology. 2nd ed.* New York: Appleton-Century.

REFERENCES   191

Boring, E. G. (1963). Eponym as placebo. In E. G. Boring (Ed.) *History, Psychology and Science: Selected Papers.* New York: Wiley.

Bower, G. H. (1961). Application of a model to paired-associated learning. *Psychometrika,* 26, 255-280.

Bower, G. H., & Trabasso, T. (1964). Concept Identification. In R. C. Atkinson (Ed.), hpl. Studies in mathematical psychology. Stanford, CA: Stanford University Press.

Bredenkamp, J. (1972). *Der Signifikanztest in der psychologischen Forschung.* Frankfurt/Main: Akademische Verlagsgesellschaft.

Brehmer, B. (1979). Preliminaries to a psychology of inference. *Scandinavian Journal of Psychology,* 20, 193-210.

Brehmer, B. Brunswikian psychology for the 1990s. In K. M. J. Lagerspetz & P. Niemi (Eds.) *Psychology in the 1990s.* North Holland: Elsevier, 1984.

Broadbent, D. E. (1958). *Perception and communication.* New York: Pergamon Press.

Broadbent, D. E. (1984). The Maltese cross: A new simplistic model for memory. *The Behavioral and Brain Sciences,* 7, 55-94.

Brown, F. L. Introduction to statistical methods in psychology. Appendix in G. A. Miller & R. Buckhout, *Psychology: The science of mental life.* New York: Harper & Row, 1973.

Brown, W., & Thomson, G. H. (1921). *The essentials of mental measurement.* Cambridge: Cambridge University Press.

Bruner, J. S. (1973). *Beyond the information given.* New York: Norton.

Brunswik, E. (1933). Die Zugänglichkeit von Gegenständen für die Wahrnehmung und deren quantitative Bestimmung. *Archiv für die gesamte Psychologie,* 88, 377-418.

Brunswik, E. (1934). *Wahrnehmung und Gegenstandswelt: Grundlegung einer Psychologie vom Gegenstand her.* Leipzig: Deuticke.

Brunswik, E. (1937). Psychology as a science of objective relations. *Philosophy of Science,* 4, 227-260.

Brunswik, E. (1939a). Probability as a determiner of rat behavior. *Journal of Experimental Psychology,* 25, 175-197.

Brunswik, W. (1939b). Perceptual characteristics of schematized human figures. *Psychological Bulletin,* 36, 553.

Brunswik, E. (1945). Social perception of traits from photographs. *Psychological Bulletin,* 42, 535-536.

Brunswik, E. (1950). *The conceptual framework of psychology.* Chicago: University of Chicago Press.

Brunswik, E. (1955a). Representative design and probabilistic theory in a functional psychology. *Psychological Review,* 62, 193-217.

Brunswik, E. (1955b). In defense of probabilistic functionalism: A reply. *Psychological Review,* 62, 236-242.

Brunswik, E. (1956). *Perception and the representative design of psychological experiments.* Los Angeles: University of California Press.

Brunswik, E., & Kamiya, J. (1953). Ecological cue-validity of "proximity" and of other Gestalt factors. *American Journal of Psychology,* 66, 20-32.

Bühler, K. (1907). Tatsachen und Probleme zu einer Psychologie der Denkvorgänge: I. Über Gedanken. *Archiv für die gesamte Psychologie,* 9, 297-365.

Bühler, K. (1913). *Die Gestaltwahrnehmungen.* Stuttgart: Spemann.

Bush, R. R., & Mosteller, F. (1951). A mathematical model for simple learning. *Psychological Review,* 58, 313-323.

Bush, R. R., & Mosteller, F. (1959). A comparison of eight models. In R. R. Bush & W. K. Estes (Eds.), *Studies in mathematical learning theory.* Stanford, CA: Stanford University Press.

Calfee, R. C., & Atkinson, R. C. (1965). Paired-associate models and the effects of list length. *Journal of Mathematical Psychology,* 2, 254-265.

192 REFERENCES

Carnap, R., & Stegmüller, W. (1959). *Induktive Logik und Wahrscheinlichkeit.* Wien: Springer.

Cartwright, N. (1987). Max Born and the reality of quantum probabilities. In L. Krüger, G. Gigerenzer, & M. S. Morgan (Eds.), *The Probabilistic Revolution. Vol. II: Ideas in the Sciences.* Cambridge, MA: MIT Press.

Carver, R. P. (1978). The case against statistical significance testing. *Harvard Educational Review, 48,* 378-399.

Cason, H. & Cason, E. B. (1925). Association tendencies and learning ability. *Journal of Experimental Psychology, 8,* 167-189.

Cohen, I. B. (1987). Scientific revolutions, revolutions in science, and a probabilistic revolution 1800-1930. In L. Krüger, L. J. Daston, & M. Heidelberger, (Eds.), *The Probabilistic Revolution Vol. I: Ideas in History.* Cambridge, MA: MIT Press.

Cohen, J. (1962). The statistical power of abnormal-social psychological research: A review. *Journal of Abnormal and Social Psychology, 65,* 145-153.

Cohen, L. J. Bayesianism versus Baconianism in the evaluation of medical diagnosis. *British Journal for Philosophy of Science,* 1980, *31,* 45-62.

Cohen, L. J. Can human irrationality be experimentally demonstrated? *The Behavioral and Brain Sciences,* 1981, *4,* 317-370.

Coombs, C. H., Dawes, R. M., & Tversky, A. (1970). *Mathematical psychology: an elementary introduction.* Englewood Cliffs, NJ: Prentice-Hall.

Coon, D. B. (1982). Eponymy, obscurity, Twitmyer and Pavlov. *Journal of the History of the Behavioral Sciences, 18,* 255-262.

Crocker, J. (1981). Judgment of covariation by social perceivers. *Psychological Bulletin, 90,* 272-292.

Cronbach, L. J. (1957). The two disciplines of scientific psychology. *American Psychologist, 12,* 671-684.

Cuneo, D. O. (1980). A general strategy for judgments of quality: The height & width rule. *Child Development, 51,* 299-301.

Danziger, K. (1980). The history of introspection reconsidered. *Journal of the History of the Behavioral Sciences, 16,* 241-262.

Danziger, K. (1985). The origins of the psychological experiment as a social institution. *American Psychologist, 40,* 133-140.

Danziger, K. (1987). Statistical method and the historical development of research practice in American psychology. In L. Krüger, G. Gigerenzer, & M. S. Morgan (Eds.), *The Probabilistic Revolution, Vol. II: Ideas in the Sciences.* Cambridge, MA: MIT Press.

Dashiell, J. F. (1939). Some reapprochements in contemporary psychology. *Psychological Bulletin, 36,* 1-24.

Daston, L. J. (1979). D'Alembert's critique of probability theory. *Historia Mathematica, 6,* 259-279.

Daston, L. J. (1980). Probabilistic expectation and rationality in classical probability theory. *Historia Mathematica, 7,* 234-260.

Daston, L. J. (1987). The domestication of risk: Mathematical probability and insurance, 1650-1830. In L. Krüger, L. J. Daston, M. Heidelberger, (Eds.), *The Probabilistic Revolution Vol. I: Ideas in History.* Cambridge, MA: MIT Press.

Delboeuf, J. R. L. (1873). Etude psychophysique—Recherches théoriques et expérimentales sur la mesure des sensations et specialement des sensations de la lumière et de fatigue. *Memoires couronnés et autre memoires . . . de l'Académie Royale de Belgique, 23.*

Diamond, S. (1969). Seventeenth century French "connectionism": La Forge, Dilly and Regis. *Journal of the History of the Behavioral Sciences, 5,* 3-9.

Dörner, D. (1983). Heuristic and cognition in complex systems. In R. Groner, M. Groner, & W. F. Bischof (Eds.), *Methods of heuristics.* Hillsdale, NJ: Lawrence Erlbaum Associates.

REFERENCES 193

Duncker, K. (1926). A qualitative study of productive thinking. *Pedagogical Seminary, 33,* 642-708.

Duncker, K. (1945). On problem solving (L. S. Lees, Trans.) *Psychological Monographs,* 1945, *58,* (5, Whole No. 270). (Original work published 1935)

Edgington, E. S. (1974). A new tabulation of statistical procedures used in APA journals. *American Psychologist, 29,* 25-26.

Edwards, W. (1966, December). *Nonconservative probabilistic information processing systems.* ESD-TR-66-404, University of Michigan, Institute of Science and Technology Report 5893-22-F.

Edwards, W. (1968). Conservatism in human information processing. In B. Kleinmuntz (Ed.) *Formal representation of human judgment.* New York: Wiley.

Edwards, W. Lindman, H., & Phillips, L. D. (1965). Emerging technologies for making decisions. *New directions in psychology. II.* New York: Holt, Rinehart & Winston.

Egan, J. P. (1975). *Signal detection theory and ROC analysis.* New York: Academic Press.

Einhorn, H. J. (1980). Learning from experience and suboptimal rules in decision making. In T. S. Wallsten (Ed.), *Cognitive processes in choice and decision behavior.* Hillsdale, NJ: Lawrence Erlbaum Associates.

Einhorn, H. J., & Hogarth, R. M. (1981). Behavioral decision theory: Processes of judgment and choice. *Annual Review of Psychology, 32,* 53-88.

Elkin, A. J., & Murray, D. J. (1974). The effects of sleep loss on short-term recognition memory. *Canadian Journal of Psychology, 28,* 192-198.

Evans, J. St B. T. (1984). Heuristic and analytic processes in reasoning. *British Journal of Psychology, 75,* 451-468.

Fechner, G. T. (1860). *Elemente der Psychophysik* (2 vols). Leipzig: Breitkopf & Härtel. English translation of Vol. 1 only: G. T. Fechner, *Elements of psychophysics* (H. E. Adler, trans.). New York: Holt, Rinehart & Winston, 1966.

Fechner, G. T. (1877). *In Sachen der Psychophysik.* Leipzig: Breitkopf & Härtel.

Fechner, G. T. (1897). *Kollektivmasslehre.* (Ed. G. F. Lipps) Leipzig: W. Engelmann.

Fiedler, K. (1980). Kognitive Verarbeitung statistischer Information: Der "vergebliche Konsensus-Effekt". *Zeitschrift für Sozialpsychologie, 11,* 25-37.

Fisch, R., & Daniel, H. D. (1982). Research and publication trends in experimental social psychology: 1971–1980. A thematic analysis of the Journal of Experimental Social Psychology, and the Zeitschrift für Sozialpsychologie. *European Journal of Social Psychology, 12,* 335-412.

Fischhoff, B., Slovic, P., & Lichtenstein, S. (1979). Subjective sensitivity analysis. *Organizational Behavior and Human Performance, 23,* 339-359.

Fisher, R. A. (1922). On the mathematical foundations of theoretical statistics. *Philosophical Transactions of the Royal Society of London, 222A,* 309-368.

Fisher, R. A. (1925). *Statistical methods for research workers.* Edinburgh: Oliver & Boyd.

Fisher, R. A. (1933). The contributions of Rothamsted to the development of the science of statistics. *Annual Report of the Rothamsted Experimental Station,* 43-50. (Reprinted in *Collected Papers,* Vol. 3, pp. 84-91)

Fisher, R. A. (1935). *The design of experiments.* Edinburgh: Oliver & Boyd, (8th ed. 1966).

Fisher, R. A. (1955). Statistical methods and scientific induction. *Journal of the Royal Statistical Society (B), 17,* 69-78.

Flanagan, M. F., & Dipboyle, R. L. (1980). Representativeness does have implications for the generalizability of laboratory and field research findings. *American Psychologist, 35,* 464-467.

Frenkel-Brunswik, E. (1942). Motivation and behavior. *Genetic Psychology Monographs, 26,* 121-265.

Frieze, I. H., & Weiner, B. (1971). Cue utilization and attributional judgments for success and failure. *Journal of Personality, 39,* 591-605.

194   REFERENCES

Gal, S. (1980). *Search games*. New York: Academic Press.

Galanter, E. (1974). Stanley Smith Stevens (1906-1973). *Psychometrika, 39,* 1-2.

Galanter, E., & Luce, R. D. (1974). Robert R. Bush: Later career. *Journal of Mathematical Psychology, 11,* 179-189.

Gardner, H. (1985). *The mind's new science: A history of the cognitive revolution.* New York: Basic Books.

Gavarret, J. (1840). *Principes généraux de statistique medicale.* Paris.

Gavin, E. A. (1972). The causal issue in empirical psychology from Hume to the present with emphasis upon the work of Michotte. *Journal of the History of the Behavioral Sciences, 8,* 302-320.

Gescheider, G. A., Wright, J. H., Weber, B. J., & Barton, W. G. (1971). Absolute thresholds in vibrotactile signal detection. *Perception and Psychophysics, 10,* 413-417.

Geuter, U. (1984). *Die Professionalisierung der deutschen Psychologie im Nationalsozialismus.* Frankfurt/Main: Suhrkamp.

Gibson, J. J. (1950). *The perception of the visual world.* Boston: Houghton Mifflin.

Gibson, J. J. (1959). Perception as a function of stimulation. In S. Koch (Ed.) *Psychology: a study of a science.* Vol. 1. New York: McGraw-Hill.

Gibson, J. J. (1966). *The senses considered as perceptual systems.* Boston: Houghton Mifflin.

Gibson, J. J. (1979). *The ecological approach to visual perception.* Boston: Houghton Mifflin.

Gibson, J. J., Kaplan, G. A., Reynolds, H. N., & Wheeler, K. (1969). The change from visible to invisible: A study of optical transitions. *Perception and Psychophysics, 5,* 113-116.

Gigerenzer, G. (1981) *Messung und Modellbildung in der Psychologie.* Munich: Ernst Reinhardt (UTB).

Gigerenzer, G. (1983a). Interpretations of variability in the history of psychology. In M. Heidelberger, L. Krüger, & E. R. Rheinwald (Eds.), *Probability since 1800.* Bielefeld: B. Kleine.

Gigerenzer, G. (1983b). Über die Anwendung der Informations-Integrations-Theorie auf entwicklungspsychologische Problemstellungen: Eine Kritik. *Zeitschrift für Entwicklungspsychologie und Pädagogische Psychologie, 15,* 101-120.

Gigerenzer, G. (1983c). Informationsintegration bei Kindern: Eine Erwiderung auf Wilkening. *Zeitschrift für Entwicklungspsychologie und Pädagogische Psychologie, 15,* 216-221.

Gigerenzer, G. (1984a). External validity of laboratory experiments: The frequency-validity relationship. *American Journal of Psychology, 97,* 185-195.

Gigerenzer, G. (1984b). Lässt sich die Flächenwahrnehmung als "kognitive Algebra" beschreiben? *Psychologische Beiträge, 26,* 113-119.

Gigerenzer, G. (1987a). Probabilistic thinking and the fight against subjectivity. In L. Krüger, G. Gigerenzer, & M. S. Morgan (Eds.), *The probabilistic revolution. Vol. II: Ideas in the Sciences.* Cambridge, MA: MIT Press.

Gigerenzer, G. (1987b). Survival of the fittest probabilist: Brunswik, Thurstone, and the two disciplines of psychology. In L. Krüger, G. Gigerenzer, & M. S. Morgan (Eds.): *The probabilistic revolution: Vol. II: Ideas in the sciences.* Cambridge, MA: MIT Press.

Gillund, G., & Shiffrin, R. M. (1984). A retrieval model for both recognition and recall. *Psychological Review, 91,* 1-67.

Ginosar, Z., & Trope, Y. (1980). The effects of base rates and individuating information on judgments about another person. *Journal of Experimental Social Psychology, 16,* 228-242.

Green, D. M., & Swets, J. A. (1966). *Signal detection theory and psychophysics.* New York: Wiley.

REFERENCES 195

Greenough, M. (1985, October). *Synapses on demand: A basis for long-term memory.* Talk given at the University of Toronto.

Gregory, R. L. (1970). *The intelligent eye.* London: Weidenfeld & Nicolson.

Gregory. R. L. (1974a). *Concepts and mechanisms of perception.* New York: Scribner.

Gregory, R. L. (1974b). Choosing a paradigm for perception. In E. C. Carterette & M. P. Friedman (Eds.), *Handbook of perception, Vol. 1. Historical and philosophical roots of perception.* New York: Academic Press.

Gregory, R. L. (1980). The confounded eye. In R. L. Gregory & E. H. Gombrich (Eds.), *Illusion in nature and art.* New York: Scribner.

Griggs, R. A. (1983). The role of problem content in the selection task and THOG problem. In J. St B. T. Evans (Ed.), *Thinking and reasoning: Psychological approaches.* London: Routledge & Kegan Paul.

Gruber, H. E. (1977). The fortunes of a basic Darwinian idea: Chance. In R. W. Rieber & K. Salzinger (Eds.), *The roots of American psychology: Historical influences and implications for the future.* New York: New York Academy of Sciences.

Guilford, J. P. (1936). *Psychometric methods.* New York: McGraw-Hill.

Guilford, J. P. (1954). *Psychometric methods.* 2nd edition. New York: McGraw-Hill.

Haber, R. N. (1979, September). *Perception—A 100-year perspective.* Invited address presented at the American Psychological Association Convention, New York.

Hacking, I. (1965). *Logic of statistical inference.* Cambridge: Cambridge University Press.

Hacking, I. (1975). *The emergence of probability.* Cambridge: Cambridge University Press.

Hacking, I. (1987). Was there a probabilistic revolution, 1800-1930? In L. Krüger, L. J. Daston, & M. Heidelberger (Eds.) *The probabilistic revolution. Vol. I, Ideas in history.* Cambridge, MA: MIT Press.

Hammond, K. R., Stewart, T. R., Brehmer, B., & Steinmann, D. O. (1975). Social judgment theory. In M. F. Kaplan & S. Schwartz (Eds.), *Human judgment and decision processes.* New York: Academic Press.

Hammond, K. R. & Wascow, N. E. (Eds.) (1980). *Realizations of Brunswik's representative design.* San Francisco: Jossey-Bass.

Hartley, D. (1970). Observations on man. In R. Brown (Ed.), *Between Hume and Mill: An anthology of British philosophy: 1749-1843.* New York: Random House. (Original work published 1749)

Hartmann, G. W. (1931). The concept and criteria of insight. *Psychological Review, 38,* 243-253.

Hays, W. L. (1963). *Statistics for psychologists.* New York: Holt, Rinehart & Winston.

Hebb, D. O. (1949). *The organization of behavior.* New York: Wiley.

Hegelmaier, F. (1852). Ueber das Gedächtniss für Linearanschauungen. *Archiv für psychologische Heilkunde, 11,* 844-853. (Fechner refers to this journal as *Vierordts Archiv.*)

Heidelberger, M. (1987). Fechner's indeterminism: from freedom to laws of chance. In L. Krüger, L. J. Daston, & M. Heidelberger (Eds.), *The probabilistic revolution. Vol. I. Ideas in history.* Cambridge, MA: MIT Press (Bradford Books).

Heider, F. (1958). *The psychology of interpersonal relations.* New York: Wiley.

Heisenberg, W. (1927). Über den anschaulichen Inhalt der quantentheoretischen Kinematik und Mechanik. *Zeitschrift für Physik, 43,* 172-198.

Helmholtz, H. von (1962). *Treatise on psychological optics* (3 vols.). New York: Dover. (Original work published 1856-1866)

Helmholtz, H. von (1968). The facts of perception. Translation of Founder's Day address at the University of Berlin, 1879. Reprinted in R. M. Warren and R. P. Warren, *Helmholtz on perception: its physiology and development.* New York: Wiley, 1968.

Herbart, J. F. (1816). *Lehrbuch zur Psychologie.* Hamburg and Leipzig: G. Hartenstein. (2nd ed., 1834), translated by M. K. Smith, as J. F. Herbart, *A text-book in psychology.* New York: Appleton.

196 REFERENCES

Hering, K. E. K. (1977). *The theory of binocular vision* (B. Bridgeman & L. Stark, Ed. & Trans.). New York: Plenum Press. (Original work published 1868)

Hewstone, M., & Jaspars, J. (1983). A re-examination of the role of consensus, consistency and distinctiveness: Kelley's cube revisited. *British Journal of Social Psychology, 22,* 41-50.

Hilgard, E. R. (1955). Discussion of probabilistic functionalism. *Psychological Review, 62,* 226-228.

Hochberg, J. (1979). Sensation and perception. In E. Hearst (Ed.), *The first century of experimental psychology.* Hillsdale, NJ: Lawrence Erlbaum Associates.

Hoffman, W. C. (1966). The Lie-algebra of visual perception. *Journal of Mathematical Psychology, 3,* 65-98.

Hogben, L. (1957). *Statistical theory.* New York: Norton.

Hogben, L. (1970). Significance as interpreted by the school of R. A. Fisher. In D. E. Morrison & R. E. Henkel (Eds.), *The significance test controversy—A reader.* Chicago: Aldine.

Hull, C. L. (1943a). *Principles of Behavior.* New York: Appleton-Century-Crofts.

Hull, C. L. (1943b). The problem of intervening variables in molar behavior theory. *Psychological Review, 50,* 273-291.

Hull, C. L., Hovland, C. I., Ross, R. T., Hall, M., Perkins, D. T., & Fitch, F. B. (1940). *Mathematico-deductive theory of rote learning.* New Haven: Yale University Press.

Hume, D. (1955). *A treatise on human nature* (L. A. Selby-Bigge, Ed.) Oxford: Clarendon Press (Original work published) 1739-1740)

Humphrey, G. (1963). *Thinking: An introduction to its experimental psychology.* New York: Wiley.

Ittelson, W. H. (1962). Perception and transactional psychology. In S. Koch (Ed.), *Psychology: A study of a science* (Vol. 4). New York: McGraw-Hill.

James, W. (1950). *The principles of psychology* (2 vols.). New York: Dover. (Original work published 1890, Henry Holt)

Jaspars, J., Hewstone, M., & Fincham, F. D. (1983). Attribution theory and research. The state of the art. In J. Jaspars, F. D. Fincham, & M. Hewstone, (Eds.), *Attribution theory and research: Conceptual, developmental and social dimensions.* London: Academic Press.

Johnson-Laird, P. N. (1983). *Mental models.* Cambridge: Cambridge University Press.

Jones, E. E. (1979). The rocky road from acts to dispositions. *American Psychologist, 34,* 104-117.

Kahneman, D., Slovic P., & Tversky, A. (Eds.) (1982). *Judgments under uncertainty: Heuristics and biases.* Cambridge: Cambridge University Press.

Kahneman, D. & Tversky, A. (1972). Subjective probability: A judgment of representativeness. *Cognitive Psychology, 3,* 430-454.

Kahneman, D., & Tversky, A. (1973). On the psychology of prediction. *Psychological Review, 80,* 237-251.

Kahneman, D., & Tversky, A. (1982). On the study of statistical intuitions. In D. Kahneman, P. Slovic, & A. Tversky (Eds.), *Judgments under uncertainty: Heuristics and biases.* Cambridge: Cambridge University Press.

Kelley, H. H. (1967). Attribution theory in social psychology. In D. Levine (Ed.), *Nebraska symposium on motivation.* Vol. 15. Lincoln: University of Nebraska Press.

Kelley, H. H. (1973). The process of causal attribution. *American Psychologist, 28,* 107-128.

Kelley, H. H., & Michaela, I. L. (1980). Attribution theory and research. *Annual Review of Psychology, 31,* 457-501.

Kelly, G. A. (1955). *The psychology of personal constructs.* 2 vols. New York: Norton.

Kempthorne, O. (1972). Theories of inference and data analysis. In T. A. Bancroft (Ed.), *Statistical papers in honor of George W. Snedecor.* Ames: Iowa State University Press.

REFERENCES 197

Kendall, M. G. (1942). On the future of statistics. *Journal of the Royal Statistical Society*, *105*, 69-80.

Kendall, M. G. (1943). *The advanced theory of statistics*. Vol. I. New York: Lippincott.

Keynes, J. M. (1943). *A treatise on probability*. London: Macmillan. (Original work published 1921)

Köhler, W. (1917). Intelligenzprüfungen an Anthropoiden. *Abhandlungen der Königlich Preussischen Akademie der Wissenschaften* (Berlin), physikalisch-mathematische Klasse (whole No. 1).

Krantz, D. H. (1969). Threshold theories of signal detection. *Psychological Review*, *76*, 308-324.

Krüger, L., Daston, L. J., & Heidelberger, M. (Eds.) (1987). *The probabilistic revolution Vol. I: Ideas in history*. Cambridge, MA: MIT Press.

Krüger, L., Gigerenzer, G., & Morgan, M. S. (Eds.) (1987). *The probabilistic revolution Vol. II: Ideas in history*. Cambridge, MA: MIT Press.

Kruglanski, A. W. (1975). The endogenous-exogenous partition on attribution theory. *Psychological Review*, *85*, 387-406.

Kuhn, T. S. (1970). *The structure of scientific revolutions*. 2nd ed. Chicago: University of Chicago Press.

Kuhn, T. S. (1977). *The essential tension*. Chicago: University of Chicago Press.

Külpe, O. (1912). Über die moderne Psychologie des Denkens. *Internationale Monatsschrift für Wissenschaft, Kunst und Technik*, June, 1912, pp. 1070ff. Published later as appendix in O. Külpe, *Vorlesungen über Psychologie*, K. Bühler (Ed.). Leipzig: Hirzel, 1922. (Excerpts in J. M. Mandler & G. Mandler, *Thinking: From association to Gestalt*. New York: Wiley, 1964.)

Laming, D. (1973). *Mathematical psychology*. New York: Academic Press.

Laming, D. (1985). Some principles of sensory analysis. *Psychological Review*, *92*, 462-485.

Laplace, P. S. (1878-1912). Mémoire sur la probabilité des causes par les événements. *Oeuvres complètes*. (Vol. 8). (J. Bertrand & J. B. Dumas, Eds.). 14 vols. Paris: Gauthier-Villars. (Original work published 1774)

Laplace, P. S. (1951). *A philosophical essay on probabilities*. F. W. Truscott & F. L. Emory, Trans.). New York: Dover. (Original work published 1814)

Lindsay, P. H., & Norman, D. A. (1972). *Human information processing*. New York: Academic Press.

Locke, J. (1959). *An essay concerning human understanding*. 1690. (A. C. Fraser, Ed.). New York: Dover. (Original work published 1690)

Lohaus, A. (in press). Der Einsatz von Antwortskalen in der Datenerhebung bei Kindern und Jugendlichen. *Zeitschrift für Entwicklungspsychologie und Pädagogische Psychologie*.

Lotze, R. H. (1852). *Medicinische Psychologie oder Physiologie der Seele*. Leipzig: Weidmann.

Lovie, A. D. (1979). The analysis of variance in experimental psychology: 1934-1945. *British Journal of Mathematical and Statistical Psychology*, *32*, 151-178.

Luce, R. D. (1959). *Individual choice behavior*. New York: Wiley.

Luce, R. D. (1963). A threshold theory for simple detection experiments. *Psychological Review*, *70*, 61-79.

Luce, R. D. (1977a). Thurstone's discriminal processes fifty years later. *Psychometrika*, *42*, 461-489 (a).

Luce, R. D. (1977b). The choice axiom after twenty years. *Journal of Mathematical Psychology*, *15*, 215-233.

Luce, R. D. (1980). Comments on the chapters by MacCrimmon, Stanbury and Wehrung, and Schum. In T. S. Wallsten (Ed.), *Cognitive processes in choice and decision making*. Hillsdale, NJ: Lawrence Erlbaum Associates.

198 REFERENCES

Luce, R. D. & Green, D. M. (1972). A neural timing theory for response times and the psychophysics of intensity. *Psychological Review, 79,* 14-57.

Luce, R. D. & Green, D. M. (1974). Neural coding and psychophysical discrimination data. *Journal of the Acoustical Society of America, 56,* 1554-1564.

Lykken, D. T. (1968). Statistical significance in psychological research. *Psychological Bulletin, 70,* 151-159.

Mandler, J. M., & Mandler, G. (Eds.) (1964). *Thinking: From association to Gestalt.* New York: Wiley.

Mandler, J. M., & Mandler, G. (1969). The diaspora of experimental psychologists: The Gestaltists and others. In D. Fleming & B. Bailin (Eds.) *The intellectual migration, Europe and America, 1930-1960.* Cambridge, MA: Harvard University Press.

Manz, W. (1970). Experiments on probabilistic information processing. *Acta Psychologica, 34,* 184-200.

Marbe, K. (1901). *Experimentell-psychologische Untersuchungen über das Urteil.* Leipzig: Englemann.

Markowitz, J., & Swets, J. A. (1967). Factors affecting the slope of empirical ROC curves: comparison of binary and rating responses. *Perception and Psychophysics, 2,* 91-100.

Massaro, D. W. (1969). The role of the decision system in sensory and memory experiments using confidence judgments. *Perception and Psychophysics, 1969, 5,* 270-272.

Massaro, D. W. (1984). Information-processing theory and strong inference: *A paradigm for psychological inquiry.* Report No. 10. Research group on perception and action at the Center for Interdisciplinary Research (ZiF), University of Bielefeld.

Mayer, A., & Orth, J. (1901). Zur qualitativen Untersuchung der Assoziation. *Zeitschrift für Psychologie, 26,* 1-13.

Mayer, R. E. (1977). *Thinking and problem solving.* Glenview, ILL: Scott, Forseman.

McFadden, D. (1974). Conditional logit analysis of quantitative choice behavior. In P. Zarembka (Ed.), *Frontiers in econometrics.* New York: Academic Press.

McGill, W. J. (1963). Stochastic latency mechanisms. In R. D. Luce, R. R. Bush, & E. Galanter (Eds.), *Handbook of mathematical psychology.* Vol. 1. New York: Wiley.

McGill, W. J. (1967). Neural counting mechanisms and energy detection in audition. *Journal of Mathematical Psychology, 4,* 351-376.

McNicol, D. *A primer of signal detection theory.* London: George Allen & Unwin, 1972.

Meehl, P. E. (1978). Theoretical risks and tabular asterisks: Sir Karl, Sir Ronald and the slow progress of soft psychology. *Journal of Consulting and Clinical Psychology, 46,* 806-834.

Melton, A. W. (1962). Editorial. *Journal of Experimental Psychology, 64,* 553-557.

Messer, A. (1906). Experimental-psychologische Untersuchungen uber das Denken. *Archiv für die gesamte Psychologie, 8,* 1-224.

Meyer, D. E. (1970). On the representation and retrieval of stored semantic information. *Cognitive Psychology, 1,* 242-300.

Meyer, D. E. (1973). Correlated operations in searching stored semantic categories. *Journal of Experimental Psychology, 99,* 124-133.

Michotte, A. (1952). Albert Michotte van den Berck (Autobiography). In E. G. Boring, H. S. Langfeld, H. Werner & R. M. Yerkes (Eds.) *A history of psychology in autobiography.* Vol. *IV.* Worcester, MA: Clark University Press, 1952, *4,* 213-236.

Michotte, A. (1963). *The perception of causality.* New York, Basic Books. (Original work published 1946)

Mikesell, W. H., & Bentley, M. (1930). Configuration and brightness contrast. *Journal of Experimental Psychology, 13,* 1-23.

Mill, J. S. (1846). *A system of logic, ratiocinative and inductive.* New York: Harper.

REFERENCES   199

Miller, G. A., & Buckhout, R. (1973). *Psychology: The science of mental life* (Appendix: Introduction to statistical methods in psychology by F. L. Brown). New York: Harper & Row.

Mises, R. von (1957). *Probability, statistics and truth.* London: Allen & Unwin. (Original work published in German by J. Springer, 1928)

Murdock, B. B. Jr. (1962). The serial position effect of free recall. *Journal of Experimental Psychology, 64,* 482-488.

Murdock, B. B. Jr. (1966). The criterion problem in short-term memory. *Journal of Experimental Psychology, 72,* 317-324.

Murdock, B. B. Jr. (1974). *Human memory: Theory and data.* Potomac, MD: Lawrence Erlbaum Associates.

Murdock, B. B. Jr. (1982). A theory for the storage and retrieval of item and associative information. *Psychological Review, 89,* 609-626.

Murdock, B. B. Jr. (1983). A distributed memory model for serial-order information. *Psychological Review, 90,* 316-338.

Murdock, B. B. Jr. (1985a). An analysis of the strength-latency relationship. *Memory and Cognition, 13,* 511-521.

Murdock, B. B. Jr. (1985b). Convolution and matrix systems: A reply to Pike. *Psychological Review, 92,* 130-132.

Murdock, B. B. Jr., & Duffy, P. O. (1972). Strength theory and recognition memory. *Journal of Experimental Psychology, 94,* 284-290.

Murray, D. J. (1966). Intralist interference and rehearsal time in short-term memory. *Canadian Journal of Psychology, 20,* 413-426.

Murray, D. J. (1980). Analysis of search times in paired associate learning. *Bulletin of the Psychonomic Society, 16,* 465-468.

Murray, D. J. (1982). Rated associability and episodic memory. *Canadian Journal of Psychology, 36,* 420-434.

Murray, D. J. (1987). A perspective for viewing the integration of probability theory into psychology. In L. Krüger, G. Gigerenzer, & M. S. Morgan (Eds.), *The probabilistic revolution. Vol. II: Ideas in the sciences.* Cambridge, MA: MIT Press.

Murray, D. J., & Hitchcock, C. H. (1974). The nature of the memory deficit in Korsakoff's psychosis. *Canadian Journal of Psychology, 27,* 414-421.

Murray, D. J., & Smith, K. H. (in preparation). Articulatory suppression, cognitive suppression, and short-term memory.

Neisser, U. (1967). *Cognitive psychology.* New York: Appleton-Century-Crofts.

Nesdale, A. R. (1983). Effects of person and situation expectations on explanation seeking and causal attributions. *British Journal of Social Psychology, 22,* 93-99.

Neville, H. (1985, September). *Effects of early sensory and early language experience on the development of cerebral organization.* Talk given at Queen's University at Kingston, Ontario, Canada.

Newcombe, R. D., & Rutter, D. R. (1982). Ten reasons why ANOVA theory and research fail to explain attribution processes: 1. Conceptual problems. *Current Psychological Reviews, 2,* 95-108.

Newell, A. & Simon, H. (1972). *Human problem solving.* Englewood Cliffs, NJ: Prentice-Hall.

Neyman, J. (1938). L'estimation statistique traitée comme un problème classique de probabilité. *Actualités Scientifiques et Industrielles, 739,* 25-57.

Neyman, J. (1967a). *A selection of early statistical papers of J. Neyman.* Cambridge: Cambridge University Press.

Neyman, J. (1967b). R. A. Fisher (1890-1962): An appreciation. *Science, 156,* 1456-1460.

200 REFERENCES

Neyman, J. (1976). The emergence of mathematical statistics. In D. B. Owen (Ed.), *On the history of statistics and probability*. New York: Dekker, pp. 149-193.

Neyman, J., & Pearson, E. S. On the use and interpretation of certain test criteria for purposes of statistical inference. Part I. *Biometrika*, 1928a, *20A*, 175-240.

Neyman, J, & Pearson, E. S. On the use and interpretation of certain test criteria for purposes of statistical inference. Part II. *Biometrika*, 1928b, *20A*, 263-294.

Nisbett, R. E., Krantz, D. H., Jepson, C., & Kunda, Z., (1983). The use of statistical heuristics in everyday inductive reasoning. *Psychological Review*, *90*, 339-363.

Nisbett, R., & Ross, L. (1980). *Human inference: Strategies and shortcomings of social judgment*. Englewood Cliffs, NJ: Prentice-Hall.

Norman, D. A. (1966a). Memory and decisions. Paper presented at the XVIIIth International Congress of Psychology, Moscow, U.S.S.R.

Norman, D. A. (1966b). Acquisition and retention in short-term memory. *Journal of Experimental Psychology*, *72*, 369-381.

Norman, D. A., Rumelhart, D. E., & the LNR Research Group (1975). *Explorations in cognition*. San Francisco: Freeman.

Norman, D. A., & Wickelgren, W. A. (1969). Strength theory of decision rules and latency in retrieval from short-term memory. *Journal of Experimental Psychology*, *72*, 369-381.

Nunally, J. C. (1975). *Introduction to statistics for psychology and education*. New York: McGraw-Hill.

Parducci, A., & Sandusky, A. J. (1970). Limits on the applicability of signal detection theories. *Perception and Psychophysics*, *7*, 63-64.

Pearson, E. S. (1939). "Student" as statistician. *Biometrika*, *30*, 210-250.

Pearson, E. S. (1962). Some thoughts on statistical inference. *Annals of Mathematical Statistics*, *33*, 394-403.

Pearson, K. (1900). On the criterion that a given system of deviations from the probable in the case of a correlated system of variables is such that it can be reasonably supposed to have arisen from random sampling. *The London, Edinburgh, and Dublin Philosophical Magazine and Journal of Science*, *50*, 157-175.

Pearson, K. (1920). Notes on the history of correlation. *Biometrika*, *13*, 25-45.

Peirce, C. S. (1931-1958). Collected papers. Vol. 7 Science and philosophy. (1975). (Ed. C. Hartshorne and P. Weiss). Cambridge, Mass.: Harvard University Press.

Peters, W. (1933). Versuche über den Einfluss der Form auf die Wahrnehmung der Flächengrösse. *Zeitschrift für Psychologie*, *129*, 323-337.

Peterson, C. R., & Beach, L. R. (1967). Man as an intuitive statistician. *Psychological Bulletin*, *68*, 29-46.

Peterson, C. R., & DuCharme, W. M. (1967). A primacy effect in subjective probability revision. *Journal of Experimental Psychology*, *73*, 61-65.

Peterson, W. W. & Birdsall, T. G. L. (1953) The theory of signal detectability. Electronic Defense Group, University of Michigan, *Technical Report* No. 13 (Sept.)

Phillips, L. D., & Edwards, W. (1966). Conservatism in a simple probability inference task. *Journal of Experimental Psychology*, *72*, 346-354.

Piaget, J. (1969). *The mechanisms of perception*. London: Routledge & Kegan Paul.

Pike, R. (1984). Comparison of convolution and matrix distributed memory systems for associative recall and recognition. *Psychological Review*, *91*, 281-294.

Pollard, P. (1982). Human reasoning: Some possible effects of availability. *Cognition*, *12*, 65-96.

Plateau, J. A. F. (1872). Sur la mesure des sensations physiques et sur la loi qui lie l'intensité de ces sensations à l'intensité de la cause excitante. *Bulletins de l'Académie Royale de Belgique*, 2nd series, *33*, 376-388.

Plato (1937). *Meno*. In B. Jowett, *The dialogues of Plato translated into English*, (2 vols.) New York: Random House.

REFERENCES 201

Plato (1937). *Theaetetus*. In B. Jowett, *The dialogues of Plato translated into English*, (2 vols.). New York: Random House.

Popper, K. R. (1959). The logic of scientific discovery. New York: Basic Books, (Original work published, 1935).

Pylyshyn, Z. W. (1984). *Computation and cognition: Toward a foundation for cognitive science*. Cambridge, MA: MIT Press (Bradford Books).

Raaijmakers, J. G. W., & Shiffrin, R. M. (1980). SAM: A theory of probabilistic search of associative memory. In G. Bower (Ed.), *The psychology of learning and motivation*, Vol. 14. New York: Academic Press.

Raaijmakers, J. G. W., & Shiffrin, R. M. (1981). Search of associative memory. *Psychological Review, 88*, 93-134.

Ratcliff, R. (1978). A theory of memory retrieval. *Psychological Review, 85*, 59-108.

Reeder, G. D., & Brewer, M. B. (1979). A schematic model of dispositional attribution in interpersonal perception. *Psychological Review, 86*, 61-79.

Restle, F., & Greeno, J. G. (1970). *Introduction to mathematical psychology*. Menlo Park, CA: Addison-Wesley.

Richter, H. R., & Gigerenzer, G. (1984). Erste Ergebnisse einer Längsschnittstudie zur Entwicklung der Flächenwahrnehmung. *Psychologische Beiträge, 26*, 654-658.

Rock, I. (1957). The role of repetition in associative learning. *American Journal of Psychology, 70*, 186-193.

Rock, I. (1977). In defense of unconscious inference. In W. Epstein (Ed.), *Stability and constancy in visual perception: Mechanisms and processes*, New York: Wiley.

Rock, I. (1980). Difficulties with a direct theory of perception. *The Behavioral and Brain Sciences, 3*, 398-399.

Rock, I. (1983). *The logic of perception*. Cambridge, MA: MIT Press.

Roediger, H. L. III (1980). Memory metaphors in cognitive psychology. *Memory and Cognition, 8*, 231-246.

Rose, J. E., Brugge, J. F., Anderson, D. J., & Hind, J. E. (1967). Phase-locked response to low-frequency tones in single auditory nerve fibers of the squirrel monkey. *Journal of Neurophysiology, 30*, 769-793.

Rosinsky, R. (1977). *The development of visual perception*. Santa Monica, CA: Goodyear.

Roseboom, W. W. (1960). The fallacy of the null-hypothesis significance test. *Psychological Bulletin, 57*, 416-428.

Rucci, A. J., & Tweney, R. D. (1980). Analysis of variance and the "second discipline" of scientific psychology: A historical account. *Psychological Bulletin, 87*, 166-184.

Schacter, D. L. (1982). *Stranger behind the engram: theories of memory and the psychology of science*. Hillsdale, N.J.: Lawrence Erlbaum Associates.

Schopenhauer, A. (1966). *The world as will and idea* (Trans. E. F. J. Payne). New York: Dover. (Original work published, 1819).

Schum, D. (1981). Shorting out the effects of witness sensitivity and response-criterion placement upon the influential value of testimonial evidence. *Organizational Behavior and Human Performance*. (1982). *27*, 153-196.

Schwartz, S., & Dalgleish, L. (1982). Statistical inference in personality research. *Journal of Research in Personality, 16*, 290-302.

Selz, O. (1913). *Über die Gesetze des geordneten Denkverlaufs. Eine experimentelle Untersuchung*. Stuttgart: Spemann.

Selz, O. (1922). *Zur Psychologie des produktiven Denkens und des Irrtums*. Bonn: F. Cohen.

Semon, R. (1921). *The mneme*. London: George Allen & Unwin. (Original work published 1904)

Semon, R. (1923). *Mnemic Psychology*. London: George Allen & Unwin. (Original work published 1909)

202 REFERENCES

Shafer, G. *A mathematical theory of evidence*. Princeton: Princeton University Press, 1976.

Shaw, R., & Todd, J. (1980). Abstract machine theory and direct perception. *The Behavioral and Brain Sciences, 3*, 400-401.

Shepard, R. N., & Cooper L. A. (1982). *Mental images and their transformations*. Cambridge, MA: MIT Press, 1982.

Siebert, W. M. Frequency discrimination in the auditory system: Place or periodicity mechanisms? *Proceedings of the IEEE*, 1970, *58*, 723-730.

Simon, H. A. (1979). *Models of thought*. New Haven: Yale University Press.

Snedecor, G. W. (1937). *Statistical methods, 1st ed.*. Ames, IA: Collegiate Press.

Solomons, L. M. (1900). A new explanation of Weber's law. *Psychological Review, 7*, 234-240.

Spalding, D. A. (1872). On instinct. *Nature, 6*, 485-486.

Spearman, C. (1908). The method of 'right and wrong cases' without Gauss' formulae. *British Journal of Psychology, 2*, 227-242.

Sperling, G. (1960). The information available in brief visual presentations. *Psychological Monographs, 74*, (11, Whole No. 498).

Stegmüller, W. (1973). *"Jenseits von Popper und Carnap": Die logischen Grundlagen des statistischen Schliessens*. Berlin: Springer.

Sterling, T. D. (1959). Publication decisions and their possible effects on inferences drawn from tests of significance—or vice versa. *Journal of the American Statistical Association, 54*, 30-34.

Sternberg, S. (1966). High-speed scanning in human memory. *Science, 153*, 652-654.

Stevens, S. S. (1951). Mathematics, measurement and psychophysics. In S. S. Stevens (Ed.), *Handbook of experimental psychology*. New York: Wiley.

Stevens, S. S. (1957). On the psychophysical law. *Psychological Review, 64*, 153-181.

Stevens, S. S. A metric for social consensus. *Science*, 1966, *151*, 530-541.

Stone, L. D. (1975). *Theory of optimal search*. New York: Academic Press.

Suppes, P., & Ginsberg, R. (1963). A fundamental property of all-or-none models, binomial distribution of responses prior to conditioning, with application to concept formation in children. *Psychological Review, 70*, 139-161.

Swets, J. A. (1964). Is there a sensory threshold? In J.A. Swets (Ed.) *Signal detection and recognition by human observers*. New York: Wiley.

Swets, J. A. (1986). Indices of discrimination or diagnostic accuracy: Their ROCs and implied models. *Psychological Bulletin, 99*, 100-117.

Swets, J. A., Tanner, W. D., & Birdsall, T. G. (1964). Decision processes in perception. In J. A. Swets (Ed.) *Signal detection and recognition by human observers*. New York: Wiley.

Swijtink, Z. G. (1987). The objectification of observation: Measurement and statistical methods in the nineteenth century. In L. Krüger, L. J. Daston, & M. Heidelberger (Eds.), *The probabilistic revolution. Vol. I: Ideas in history*. Cambridge, MA: MIT Press.

Tanner, W. P. Jr. (1965). *Statistical decision processes in detection and recognition*. Technical Report from the Sensory Intelligence Laboratory, Department of Psychology, University of Michigan.

Tanner, W. P. Jr., & Swets, J. A. (1954). A decision-making theory of visual detection. *Psychological Review, 61*, 401-409.

Thomas, E. A. C., & Legge, D. (1970). Probability matching is a basis for detection and recognition decisions. *Psychological Review, 77*, 65-72.

Thomson, D. M., & Tulving, E. (1970). Associative encoding and retrieval: Weak and strong cues. *Journal of Experimental Psychology, 86*, 255-262.

Thorndike, E. L. (1910). Handwriting. *Teachers' College Record*, 1910, *11* (2).

Thorndike, E. L. (1919). *Mental and social measurement. 2nd ed*. New York: Teacher's College, Columbia University.

REFERENCES   203

Thurstone, L. L. (1927a). Psychophysical analysis. *American Journal of Psychology, 38,* 368-389.

Thurstone, L. L. (1927b). A law of comparative judgment. *Psychological Review, 34,* 273-286.

Thurstone, L. L. (1927c). A mental unit of measurement. *Psychological Review, 34,* 415-423.

Thurstone, L. L. (1927d). Three psychophysical laws. *Psychological Review, 34,* 424-432.

Titchener, E. B. (1905). *Experimental psychology: A manual of laboratory practice.* Vol. 2, Part 2. New York: Macmillan.

Tolhurst, D. J., Movshon, J. A., & Dean, A. F. (1983). The statistical reliability of signals in single neurons in cat and monkey visual cortex. *Vision Research, 23,* 775-785.

Tolman, E. C. (1932). *Purposive behavior in animals and men.* New York: Century.

Tolman, E. C. & Honzik, C. H. "Insight" in rats. *University of California Publications in Psychology,* 1930, *4,* 215-232.

Townsend, J. T., & Ashby, F. G. (1983). *The stochastic modeling of elementary psychological processes.* New York: Cambridge University Press.

Tukey, J. W. (1962). The future of data analysis. *Annals of Mathematical Statistics, 33,* 1-67.

Tulving, E. (1983). *Elements of episodic memory.* New York: Oxford University Press.

Tulving, E., & Thomson, D. M. (1973). Encoding specificity and retrieval processes in episodic memory. *Psychological Review, 80,* 352-373.

Tversky, A. & Kahneman, D. (1971). Belief in the law of small numbers. *Psychological Bulletin, 76,* 105-110.

Tversky, A. & Kahneman, D. (1974). Judgment under uncertainty: Heuristics and biases. *Science, 185,* 1124-1131.

Tversky, A., & Kahneman, D. (1980). Causal schemata in judgments under uncertainty. In M. Fishbein (Ed.), *Progress in social psychology.* Vol. 1. Hillsdale, NJ: Lawrence Erlbaum Associates.

Tversky, A., & Kahneman, D. (1982a). Evidential impact of base rates. In D. Kahneman, P. Slovic, & A. Tversky (Eds.), *Judgements under uncertainty: Heuristics and biases.* Cambridge: Cambridge University Press.

Tversky, A., & Kahneman, D. (1982b). Judgments of and by representativeness. In D. Kahneman, P. Slovic, & A. Tversky (Eds.), *Judgments under uncertainty: Heuristics and biases.* Cambridge: Cambridge University Press.

Ullman, S. (1980). Against direct perception. *The Behavioral and Brain Sciences, 3,* 373-415.

Venn, J. (1888). *The logic of chance.* 3rd ed. London: Macmillan & Co.

Wald, A. (1950). *Statistical decision functions.* New York: Wiley.

Wallach, H. (1976). *On perception.* New York: Quadrangle.

Wason, P. C. (1983). Realism and rationality in the selection task. In J. St B. T. Evans (Ed.), *Thinking and reasoning: Psychological approaches.* London: Routledge & Kegan Paul.

Wason, P. C., & Johnson-Laird, P. N. (1972). *Psychology of reasoning: Structure and content.* Cambridge, MA: Harvard University Press.

Watkins, M. J., & Tulving, E. (1975). Episodic memory: When recognition fails. *Journal of Experimental Psychology: General, 104,* 5-29.

Watson, J. B. (1913). Psychology as the behaviorist views it. *Psychological Review, 20,* 158-177.

Watson, J. B. (1919). *Psychology from the standpoint of a behaviorist.* Philadelphia: Lippincott.

Watson, J. B. (1924). *Behaviorism.* Chicago: University of Chicago Press.

Waugh, N. C. & Norman, D. A. (1965). Primary memory. *Psychological Review, 72,* 89-104.

Weber, E. H. (1978). *The sense of touch.* Contains *De Tactu* (1834), H. E. Ross, Trans., and

204 REFERENCES

Der Tastsinn und das Gemeingefühl, (1846), D. J. Murray Trans. New York: Academic Press.

Wellek, A. (1968). The impact of the German immigration on the development of American psychology. *Journal of the History of the Behavioral Sciences, 4*, 207-229.

Wellek, A. N., & E. Brunswik (1956). *Psychologische Rundschau, 7*, 155-156.

Wertheimer, M. (1912). Experimentelle Studien über das Sehen von Bewegung. *Zeitschrift für Psychologie, 61*, 161-265.

Wertheimer, M. (1945). *Productive thinking*. New York: Harper.

Whiting, H. F., & English, H. B. (1925). Fatigue tests and incentives. *Journal of Experimental Psychology, 8*, 33-49.

Wickelgren, W. A. (1970). Time, interference and rate of presentation in short-term recognition memory for items. *Journal of Mathematical Psychology, 7*, 219-235.

Wickelgren, W. A., & Berian, K. M. (1971). Dual trace theory and the consolidation of long-term memory. *Journal of Mathematical Psychology, 8*, 404-417.

Wickelgren, W. A., & Norman, D. A. (1966). Strength models and serial position in short-term recognition memory. *Journal of Mathematical Psychology, 3*, 316-347.

Wilkening, F. (1979). Combining of stimulus dimensions in children's and adult's judgment of area: An information integration analysis. *Developmental Psychology, 15*, 25-33.

Wilkening, F. (1980). Development of dimensional integration in children's perceptual judgement: Experiments with area, volume and velocity. In F. Wilkening, J. Becker, & T. Trabasso (Eds.), *Information integration by children*. Hillsdale, NJ: Lawrence Erlbaum Associates.

Willis, T. (1971). *Two discourses concerning the soul of brutes*. Gainesville, FL: Scholars' Facsimiles and Reprints. (Original work published 1672)

Wilson, K. V. (1961). Subjectivist statistics for the current crisis. *Contemporary Psychology, 6*, 229-231.

Wong, P. T. P., & Weiner, B. (1981). When people ask "why" questions, and the heuristics of attributional search. *Journal of Personality and Social Psychology, 40*, 650-663.

Woodworth, R. S. (1938). *Experimental psychology*. New York: Holt.

Wundt, W. (1897). *Grundriss der Psychologie*. [Outlines of psychology, by C. H. Judd, trans.] Leipzig: Engelmann.

Wundt, W. (1907). Über Ausfrageexperimente und über die Methoden psychologischen Denkens. *Psychologische Studien, 3*, 301-360.

Yellott, J. J. (1977). The relationship between Luce's choice axiom, Thurstone's theory of comparative judgment, and the double exponential distribution. *Journal of Mathematical Psychology, 15*, 109-144.

Yerkes, R. M. (1929). *The great apes*. New Haven: Yale University Press.

Author Index

A

Ach, N. 138, 140, *189*
Acree, M. C. 8, 21, 22, 23, *189*
Ajzen, I. 179, *189*
American Psychological Association 23, *189*
Anderson, D. J. 54, *201*
Anderson, J. A. 121, *189*
Anderson, J. R. 133, *189*
Anderson, N. H. 62, 67, 92, 94–97, 99–102, *189*
Anderson, R. L. 21
Arbuthnot, J. 4, 5, *189*
Aristotle, 138–139, *190*
Ash, M. G. 146, *190*
Ashby, F. G. 118, *203*
Atkinson, R. C. 115, 126, 131–132, *190, 191*
Attneave, F. 2, *190*

B

Baddeley, A. D. 124, *190*
Baird, J. C. 48, *190*
Bakan, D. 23, 24, 26, *190*
Bancroft, T. A. 21, *189*
Bartlett, F. C. 26, 86, 110–114, 132–133, *190*
Barton, W. G. 60, *194*

Bayes, T. 5, 7, 11, 17, 22, 91, 147–155, 159, 161–163, 165–170, 172–174, 177–181, 183–185, *190*
Beach, L. R. 80, 104, 148–149, *200*
Beardsley, M. C. 1, *190*
Bentley, M. 18, *199*
Berian, K. M. 116–117, *204*
Berkeley, D. 156, *190*
Bernoulli, J. 165, 174, *190*
Birdsall, T. G. L. 42, 43, 44, 45, *200, 202*
Birubaum, A. 12, 16, *190*
Birnbaum, M. H. 98, 157, 168–170, 172–173, *190*
Blavais, A. S. 83, *190*
Boole, G. 137, *190*
Boring, E. G. 9, 40, 65, *190, 191*
Bower, G. H. 125–126, 133, 135, *189, 191*
Bredenkamp, J. 23, 24, 26, *191*
Brehmer, B. 80, 92, 97, *191*, 195
Brewer, M. B. 175, *201*
Broadbent, D. E. 2, 113, 124, *191*
Brown, F. L. 24, *191*
Brown, W. 31, 32, *191*
Brugge, J. F. 54
Bruner, J. S. 104, *191*
Brunswik, E. 17, 61, 62, 65–70, 72, 74–87, 89, 92–95, 97, 103–105, 174, 184, *191, 204*
Buckhout, R. 24, *199*

206 AUTHOR INDEX

Bühler, K. 66, 69, 70, 75, 138–139, 141, 145, 148, *191*
Bush, R. R. 125–126, *191*

C

Calfee, R. C. 126, *191*
Carnap, R. 180, *192*
Cartwright, N. xii, 74, *192*
Carver, R. P. 23, *192*
Cason, E. D. 18, *192*
Cason, H. 18, *192*
Cohen, I. B. 19, *192*
Cohen, J. 26, 27, *192*
Cohen, L. J. 174, *192*
Coombs, C. H. 126, *192*
Coon, D. B. 107, *192*
Cooper, L. A. xi, *202*
Crocker, J. 156, *192*
Cronbach, L. J. 104, *192*
Crothers, E. J. 126, *190*
Cuneo, D. O. 94, 96, 99–101, *189, 192*

D

Dalgleish, L. 24, *201*
Daniel, H. D. 175, *193*
Danziger, K. 27, 140, 146, *192*
Dashiell, J. F. 104, *192*
Daston, L. J. xi, 20, 137, 165, 174, *192, 197*
Dawes, R. M. 126, *192*
Dean, A. F. 48, *203*
Delboeuf, J. R. L. 34, *192*
Diamond, S. 107, *192*
Dipboyle, R. L. 80, *193*
Dorner, D. 147, *192*
Ducharme, W. M. 149, *200*
Duffy, P. O. 119, *199*
Duncker, K. 141–148, 157, *193*

E

Edgington, E. S. 22, *193*
Edwards, W. 147, 149–50, *193, 200*
Egan, J. P. 57, *193*
Einhorn, H. J. 156, 180, *193*
Elkin, A. J. 117, *193*
English, H. B. 18, *204*
Evans, J. St. B. T. 156–157, *193*

F

Fechner, G. T. 29, 30, 32–34, 38, 45, 46, 59, 66, 79, *193*
Fiedler, K. 179, *193*
Fincham, F. D. 176–177, *196*
Fisch, R. 175, *193*
Fisher, R. A. 2, 3, 5, 8–23, 25, 26, 28, 49, 59, 80, 89, 91–92, 96, 98–102, 104, 175, 178, 180, 183–185, *193*
Fischhoff, B. 152, *193*
Fitch, F. B. 108, *196*
Flanagan, M. F. 80, *193*
Frenkel-Brunswik, E. 76, *193*
Frieze, I. H. 178, *193*

G

Gal, S. 128, *194*
Galanter, E. 38, 126, *194*
Gardner, H. xi, 113, 124, *194*
Gavarret, J. 18, *194*
Gavin, E. A. 177, *194*
Gescheider, G. A. 60, *194*
Geuter, U. 146, *194*
Gibson, J. J. 62, 69, 79, 80–86, 89, 92–93, 104, *194*
Gigerenzer, G. xi, xiii, 20, 22, 26, 27, 38, 74, 76, 80, 98, 102, *194, 197, 201*
Gillund, G. 128, 131–133, *194*
Ginsberg, R. 126, *202*
Ginosar, Z. 152, *194*
Green, D. M. 44, 46, 48, 49, 53, 54, 55, 57, *190, 195, 198*
Greeno, J. G. 126, *201*
Greenough, M. 52, *195*
Gregory, R. L. 61, 62, 86–92, 103–105, *195*
Griggs, R. A. 156, *195*
Gruber, H. E. 1, *195*
Guilford, J. P. 31, 32, *195*

H

Haber, R. N. 84, 86, *195*
Hacking, I. 6, 20, *195*
Hall, M. 108, *196*
Hammond, K. R. 80, 97, *195*
Hartley, D. 7, 138, *195*
Hartmann, G. W. 144, *195*
Hays, W. L. 22, *195*

AUTHOR INDEX   207

Hebb, D. O. 86, *195*
Hegelmaier, F. 50, *195*
Heidelberger, M. xi, 20, 32, *195, 197*
Heider, F. 174–175, *195*
Heisenberg, W. xii, 74, *195*
Helmholtz, H. von 34, 61–65, 68, 74–76,
  81–82, 84, 86, 87, 92, 103, 105, *195*
Herbart, J. F. 29, *195*
Hering, K. E. K. 63, 64, 81, 82, *196*
Hewstone, M. 176–178, *196*
Hilgard, E. R. 80, *196*
Hind, J. E. 54, *201*
Hitch, G. 124, *190*
Hitchcock, C. H. 117, *199*
Hochberg, J. 84–85, 92, *196*
Hoffman, W. C. 83, *196*
Hogarth, R. M. 180, *193*
Hogben, L. 12, 15, 23, 24, 26, *196*
Honzik, C. H. 109, *203*
Hovland, C. I. 108, *196*
Hull, C. L. 76, 80, 107–108, 110, 133, *196*
Hume, D. 138, 174, *196*
Humphrey, G. 140–141, 143, *196*
Humphreys, P. 156, *190*

I

Ittelson, W. H. 84, *196*

J

James, W. 60, 107, 124, *196*
Jaspars, J. 176, 178, *196*
Jepson, C. 167, *200*
Johnson-Laird, P. N. 147, 156, *196, 203*
Jones, E. E. 175, *196*
Juola, J. E. 115, *190*

K

Kahneman, D. 7, 67, 137, 150–166,
  168–170, 177, 179, 186, *196, 203*
Kamiya, J. 79, *191*
Kaplan, G. A. 82, *194*
Kelley, H. H. 175–179, 185, *196*
Kelly, G. A. xi, *197*
Kempthorne, O. 21, *197*
Kendall, M. G. 15, 20, *197*
Keynes, J. M. 6, 7, *197*

Köhler, W. 26, 109, 141, 143–146, *197*
Krantz, D. H. 60, 167, *197, 200*
Krüger, L. xi, xiii, 20, *197*
Kruglanski, A. W. 177, *197*
Kuhn, T. S. 19, 20, 146, *197*
Külpe, O. 138–140, 174, *197*
Kunda, Z. 167, *200*

L

Laming, D. 57, 126, *197*
Laplace, P. S. 3, 4, 6, 7, 91, 137, 147, *197*
Legee, D. 57, *202*
Lichtenstein, S. 152, *193*
Lindman, H. 147, *193*
Lindsay, P. H. 128, *197*
Locke, J. 137–138, *197*
Lohaus, A. 102, *197*
Lotze, R. H. 64, *197*
Lovie, A. D. 17, 22, 26, *197*
Luce, R. D. 37, 40, 41, 48, 53, 54, 55, 56,
  57, 60, 115, 126, 169, *190, 194, 197, 198*
Lykken, D. T. 24, *198*

M

Mandler, G. 140, 146, *198*
Mandler, J. M. 140, 146, *198*
Manz, W. 149, *198*
Marbe, K. 138, 145, *198*
Markowitz, J. 48, *198*
Massaro, D. W. 57, 92, *198*
Mayer, A. 140, *198*
Mayer, R. E. 146, *198*
McFadden, D. 55, *198*
McGill, W. J. 53, 54, 55, *198*
McNicol, D. 48, *198*
Meehl, P. E. 27, *198*
Melton, A. W. 23, *198*
Messer, A. 138, 140, 145, *198*
Meyer, D. E. 128–129, *198*
Michaela, I. L. 175, *196*
Michotte, A. 174, 177, *198*
Mikesell, W. H. 18, *199*
Mill, J. S. 64, 138, *199*
Miller, G. A. 24, *199*
Mises, R. von 7, 8, *199*
Morgan, M. S. xi, xiii, 20, *197*
Mosteller, F. 125–126, *191*

208 AUTHOR INDEX

Movshon, J. A. 48, *203*
Murdock, B. B. Jr. 119, 121–123, 132–133, 135, *199*
Murray, D. J. 38, 118, 125, 130, 132, *193, 199*

N

Neisser, U. 120, *199*
Nesdale, A. R. 177, *199*
Neville, H. 52, *199*
Newcombe, R. D. 177, *199*
Newell, A. 3, 147, *199*
Neyman, J. 2, 3, 5, 11, 12, 14–17, 21–24, 26–28, 40, 42, 44–46, 48, 49, 52, 58, 59, 60, 91, 97, 101–102, 114, 123, 133, 136, 151, 168–169, 171–173, 178–181, 183–185, *199, 200*
Nisbett, R. E. 7, 80, 157, 167, 178–179, *200*
Norman, D. A. 115–119, 122, 128, 135, *197, 200, 203, 204*
Nunally, J. C. 24, *200*

O

Orth, J. 140, *198*

P

Parducci, A. 57, 172, *200*
Pearson, E. S. 2, 5, 11, 12, 14–17, 21–24, 26–28, 40, 42, 44–46, 48, 49, 52, 58, 59, 60, 91, 97, 101–102, 114, 123, 133, 135, 151, 168–169, 171–173, 179–181, 183–185, *200*
Pearson, K. 5, 7, 9, 32, 62, 76, 77, 79, 87, 97, 103, 184, *200*
Peirce, C. S. 32, *200*
Perkins, D. T. 108, *196*
Peters, W. 70, *200*
Peterson, C. R. 80, 104, 148–149, *200*
Peterson, W. W. 44, *200*
Phillips, L. D. 147, 149, *193, 200*
Piaget, J. 26, 96, *200*
Pike, R. 121, *200*
Plateau, J. A. F. 33, 34, 38, *200*
Plato 1, *200, 201*
Pollard, P. 156, *200*

Popper, K. R. 12, 180–181, *201*
Pylyshyn, Z, W. 84, *201*

R

Raaijmakers, J. G. W. 127, 130, *201*
Ratcliff, R. 119–120, 122, 130, 133, 135, *201*
Reeder, G. D. 175, *201*
Restle, F. 126, *201*
Reynolds, H. N. 82, *194*
Richter, H. R. 102, *201*
Rock, I. 81, 84, 92, 125, *201*
Roediger, H. L. III, *201*
Rose, J. E. 7, 54, *201*
Roseboom, W. W. 24, *201*
Rosinsky, R. 84, *201*
Ross, L. 80, 157, 178–179, *200*
Ross, R. T. 108, *196*
Rucci, A. J. 20, 22, 23, *201*
Rumelhart, D. E. 128, *200*
Rutter, D. R. 177, *199*

S

Sandusky, A. 57, 172, *200*
Schacter, D. L. 110, *201*
Schopenhauer, A. 64, *201*
Schum, D. 169, *201*
Schwartz, S. 24, *201*
Selz, O. 140–141, 143, 146, *201*
Semon, R. 110–113, 129–130, 132–133, *201*
Shafer, G. 174, *202*
Shanteau, J. 97, *189*
Shaw, R. 82, *202*
Shepard, R. N. xi, *202*
Siebert, W. M. 54, *202*
Shiffrin, R. M. 126–128, 131–133, *190, 194, 201*
Simon, H. A. 3, 146–147, *199*
Slovic, P. 7, 67, 152, *193, 196*
Smith, K. H. 118, *199*
Snedecor, G. W. 10, 21, *202*
Solomons, L. M. 34, 35, 36, 37, *202*
Spalding, D. A. 84, *202*
Spearman, C. 31, *202*
Sperling, G. 124, *202*
Stegmüller, W. 17, 20, 180, *192, 202*
Steinmann, D. O. 97, *195*
Sterling, T. D. 22, 26, *202*

AUTHOR INDEX 209

Sternberg, S. 120, *202*
Stevens, S. S. 26, 30, 34, 38, 39, 40, 41, 42, 49, 67, 68, 94, *202*
Stewart, T. R. 97, *195*
Stone, L. D. 128, *202*
Suppes, P. 126, *202*
Swets, J. A. 42–46, 48, 49, 53, 59, *195, 198, 202*
Swijtink, Z. G. 4, *202*

T

Tanner, W. D. 42, 43, 45, *202*
Tanner, W. P. Jr. 42–44, 48, 50–54, *202*
Thomas, E. A. C. 57, *202*
Thomson, D. M. 130, 133–134, *202, 203*
Thompson, G. H. 31, 32, *191*
Thorndike, E. L. 35, 143, *202*
Thurstone, L. L. 30, 35–43, 46, 54, 55, 58, 59, 62, 81, 104, *203*
Titchener, E. B. 31, 32, *203*
Todd, J. 82, *202*
Tolhurst, D. J. 48, *203*
Tolman, E. C. 108–109, *203*
Towsend, J. T. 118, *203*
Trabasso, T. 135, *191*
Trope, Y. 152, *194*
Tukey, J. W. 25, *203*
Tulving, E. 113, 130–131, 133–136, *202, 203*
Tversky, A. 7, 67, 126, 137, 150–166, 168–170, 177, 179, 186, *192, 196, 203*
Tweney, R. D. 20, 22, 23, *201*

U

Ullman, S. 84, *203*

V

Venn, J. 7, *203*

W

Wald, A. 45, *203*
Wallach, H. 84, *203*
Wascow, N. E. 80, *195*
Wason, P. C. 147, 156, *203*
Watkins, M. J. 134, *203*
Watson, J. B. 107–108, 110, 141, *203*
Waugh, N. C. 117, *203*
Weber, B. J. 60, *194*
Weber, E. H. 30, 35, 49, *203*
Weiner, B. 177–178, *193, 204*
Weller, A. 146, *204*
Wellek, A. N. 68, *204*
Wertheimer, M. 85, 140, 145, *204*
Wheeler, K. 82, *194*
Whiting, H. F. 18, *204*
Wickelgren, W. A. 115–119, 122, 135, *200, 204*
Wilkening, F. 94, 96, *204*
Willis, T. 107, *204*
Wilson, K. V. 23, *204*
Wong, P. T. P. 177, *204*
Woodworth, R. S. 31, 32, *204*
Wright, J. H. 60, *194*
Wundt, W. 18, 138–140, 145, *204*

Y

Yellott, J. J. 57, *204*
Yerkes, R. M. 144, *204*

Subject Index

A

All-or-none learning, 125
Ambiguous figures, 90
Analysis of variance, 2, 17–28, 80, 93–103, 175–179
Articulatory loop, 124
Associationism, 60, 107–109, 138
Associative strength, 131–132
Auditory processing, 54–57

B

Base rates, 89, 150–174
Bayes' theorem
    and causal reasoning, 178
    and Gregory's hypothesis, 90–91, 104
    and problem solving, 147–174
    defined, 7, 25, 148
Behaviorism, 107, 141, 145
Biometrika, 12
Binocular fusion, 64
Binocular rivalry, 64
Blind spot, 87
Brain activity, 34–36

C

Cab problem, 153, 157–174, 186

Causal reasoning, 174–179
Causal vs. incidental base rates, 152, 159–162
Central tendency, measures of, 33
Children's ratings, 102
Chi-square test, 5
Cognitive algebra, 84, 91–105
Cognitive maps, 108–109
Cognitive revolution, xi–xiii, 113, 183
Comparative judgment, law of, 37
Conditioning, 107, 109
Confidence ratings, 114, 115–123, 125
Consciousness, 107, 112, 124, 128, 140
Consensus, 176
Conservatism, 147–150
Consistency, 176
Constancy
    brightness, 81–82
    object, 83
    size, 69, 76, 84
Content independence, 155, 178
Context independence principle, 67, 94, 156, 178
Correlation, 76–81, 103, 122
Counting models, 54, 120
Covariance, 176
Criterion, decision, 9, 12–17, 42–53, 114, 119–123, 135, 169–173
Critical ratio, 18, 182
Cue learning, 68–69, 75
Cue utilization, 78

SUBJECT INDEX **211**

D

d', 44, 46–49, 59, 115–118, 120, 171
Decision-making, 108
Decision rule
  in Fisher, 10
  in Neyman and Pearson, 13
  in Stevens, 40–41
  in Thurstone, 37
Decision time, 57–58, 128–129
Detection
  analogy with statistical hypothesis testing, 42
  object, 29
Determining tendency, 140
Determinism, 27
Direct perception, 82–87
Direct scaling, 68
Discriminal processes, Thurstone's, 36–38
Discrimination, 29, 51
Distance cues, 63, 64
Distinctiveness, 176
Distributed and massed learning, 108
Distribution
  chi-square, 57
  double exponential, 55
  normal, 9, 31, 36, 43, 55, 57
  Poisson, 55, 57
  sampling, 9, 15
Distribution computer, 50–52
Duplicity principle, 69

E

Educational psychology, 27
Engram, 110
Epistemic versus ontic probabilism, xii–xiii
Euclidean geometry, 174
Evolution, xii
Expectation, 109

F

Factor analysis, 175
False alarms, 14, 44, 46, 114
Fechner's Law, 33
Forgetting, 116–118
Frequency theory, 7, 17

G

Generation-recognition model, 133–136
Gestalt psychology, 17, 61, 79, 138, 140–147, 174

H

Habits, 107
Height plus width rule, 93–103
Hybrid theory of statistical inference, 21–28, 91, 182–183
Hypothesis testing
  in cab problem, 168–173
  in causal reasoning, 178
  in Gregory, 86–91
  in Neyman and Pearson, 12–17
  in signal detection theory, 42–60

I

Imageless thought, 139–141
Images, xi
In-between-object principle, 70, 72
Indeterminism, xii, 32, 80
Indifference, principle of, 7
Inference, *see also* Unconscious inference
  in Brunswik, 68–81
  inductive, 8, 10, 20
  in Tolman, 109
  Statistical
    Bayes' theorem, 6–8
    history, 3–6
    hybrid model, 5, 21–28
    in Fisher, 8–12
    in Neyman and Pearson, 12–17
    mechanized, 180
Inference revolution
  and Brunswik, 80–81
  and deductive theory of perception, 92–103
  and Gregory, 86–91
  and memory, 106–123
  and problem-solving, 138–147
  and psychophysics, 29–41
  defined, xiii, 17–28, 182–187
Information integration theory, 92–103
Inhibition, Pavlovian, 107–108

212 SUBJECT INDEX

Insight, 143
Insurance, 165
Internal scalable magnitudes, 38
Introspection, 75, 95, 139–141
Intuitionism, 63
Intuitive statistician, xiii, 29, 60–62, 65, 74–82, 103, 146, 183–187
Invariants in perception, 83–86
IQ (intelligence quotient), 78
Isomorphic assumption
  concept isomorphism, 163–165
  structural isomorphism, 165–167

K

Korsakoff's psychosis, 117
Kuhnian revolution, 19–20

L

Language, 107
Latency, retrieval, 118–123, 128–129
Learning
  classical theory, 106–109
  in Tanner's model, 51–53
  stochastic models, 126
Learning curve, 125–126
Likelihood
  and representativeness, 153–155
  defined, 7, 148, 151
  in Gregory, 88
  in Neyman and Pearson, 12
Likelihood ratio, 44–45
Local signs, 64

M

Magnitude estimation, 38, 48
Matching area, 70–74
Matching shape, 70–74
Measurement problem, 25
Memory
  and inference, 106–112
  and signal detection theory, 114–123
  auditory, 51
  auditory-verbal-linguistic, 125, 127
  Bartlett's theory, 111–112
  distributed, 121–123

  episodic vs. semantic, 135
  iconic, 124
  in classical learning theory, 107
  in Tanner's model, 48–53
  long-term, 113, 116, 125–127, 130–136
  Semon's theory, 110–111
  short-term, 3, 113, 116, 124–127
  working, 124
Metaphors, *see also* Intuitive statistician
  betting machine, 88–91
  computer/mind, 2
  inference/mind, 61, 87
  memory, 1, 106
  resonance, 119
  search, 127–132
  statistical tools/mind, 2, 3
Metathetic continua, 38–39
Moon illusion, 85
Motion parallax, 85
Müller-Lyer illusion, 64, 85
Multidimensional psychophysics, 66–74
Multiple regression, 61, 65, 75–81, 89, 97, 103

N

Nativism, 63, 84
Nazism, 145–146
Neural timing theory, 54
Null hypothesis
  Arbuthnot's test, 4
  in base rate problem, 151
  in causal reasoning, 175–179
  in Fisher, 9–12
  in Gregory, 89–91
  in hybrid theory, 21–28, 183
  in Neyman and Pearson, 14–15
  in N.H. Anderson, 92–103

O

Objectivity, 27
Optimal observer, 44, 52, 104

P

Parapsychology, 20

SUBJECT INDEX   213

Perception
  Brunswik's view, 65–81
  deductive view, 62, 91–105
  inductive view, 62, 86–91, 104
  naive realistic view, 62, 81–86, 104
Perceptual compromises, 66–74
Personal constructs, xi
Phantom limb, 63
Phase sequences, 86
Phi phenomenon, 85
Poles of intention, 71
Power function, psychophysical, 33–34, 38
Power of test, 15, 23, 26–27, 48–49
Probabilistic functionalism, 66, 76–81, 92,
    174
Probabilistic revolution, xi–xiii
Probability
  direct, 8, 12
  inverse, 8, 10–11
  posterior, 7, 148, 151, 164
  prior, 7, 17, 89, 148, 164
  theory
    and rationality, 137
    history, 6, 174
    in Fechner, 32–34
    in measuring thresholds, 31–32
    in physics, 74
    in Stevens, 39
    search theory, 128
Probability matching, 173
Probable error, 10, 18, 182
Problem solving, 3, 141–174
Prothetic continua, 38–39
Psychoanalysis, 76
Psychophysics, 29–60, 122

Q

Quality control, 13–14

R

Random sampling, 15, 80, 166
Rationality, 137, 179–181
Recall, 113, 133–136
Receiver operating characteristic (ROC),
    46–49, 57, 168–173

Recognition, 110–123
Relative centrations, law of, 96
Reminiscence, 108
Repetition, effects of, 107, 125
Replication, 26
Representative design, 17, 79
Representativeness, 152–155
Resonance, 119–121, 129–132
Restructuring, 142–145
Retrieval, 130–136
Reward and punishment, 107
Riemannian geometry, 174

S

Scaling, 38
Schema, 112
Search, 111, 113, 127–132, 157
Serial order, 123
Signal detection theory
  and cab problem, 168–173
  and memory, 114–123, 132
  and Neyman and Pearson, 2, 42–45, 184
  and psychophysics, 42–49
  and Thurstone, 40
Significance levels
  in Fisher, 10
  in Neyman and Pearson, 15
  interpretation, 24
Significance tests
  earliest, 3–5
  in Fechner, 33
  in Fisher, 8
  in Gregory, 89
Similarity, 135
Single cell recording, 48
Size
  of effect, 26–27
  of sample, 15
Sleep loss, 117
Speed-accuracy tradeoff, 121
Subjective judgment
  and rationality, 179–181
  in Neyman and Pearson, 16
  in signal detection theory, 45, 59
Symmetric hypothesis testing, 14–15, 90–91
Synergistic ecphory, 110, 130

214 SUBJECT INDEX

T

T-test, 20–26, 102
Teleological explanation, 177
Theory construction, 26
Threshold
 absolute, 29–32, 35–46
 differential, 29–32, 35, 46
 energy, 60
 in signal detection theory, 59–60
 observer, 60
Thinking, 137–187
Timing models, 48
Tools, statistical, 3, 58, 62, 104, 187
Tracking, 87
True-false tasks, 136
Type I error, 13–17, 42, 59
Type II error, 13–17, 42, 59

U

Unambiguous answer assumption, 162,
 167–174
Unconscious inference, 61–65, 74, 75, 81,
 86, 88, 92, 103

V

Validity
 ecological, 77–81, 85
 functional, 77–81, 85
Variability
 in Thurstone, 36–38
 of brain activity, 34–36
 of errors, 26
 of judgments, 33
 of signal distribution, 48, 132
Vector analysis, 121–123
Vicarious functioning, 75
Vienna circle, 67–68, 74

W

Weber's Law, 29, 33, 35
Würzburg school, 138–147, 181

Z

Zeitgeist, 40
Zöllner illusion, 64

CPSIA information can be obtained
at www.ICGtesting.com
Printed in the USA
BVHW04*0401020918
525864BV00006B/112/P